Adobe® Analytics with SiteCatalyst®

CLASSROOM IN A BOOK®
The official training workbook from Adobe Systems

Vidya Subramanian with foreword by David A. Schweidel

Adobe® Analytics with SiteCatalyst® Classroom in a Book®

Adobe Press books are published by Peachpit, a division of Pearson Education located in San Francisco, California. For the latest on Adobe Press books, go to www.adobepress.com. To report errors, please send a note to errata@peachpit.com. For information on getting permission for reprints and excerpts, contact permissions@peachpit.com.

Acquisitions Editor: Victor Gavenda
Project Editor: Rebecca Gulick
Development Editor: Margaret S. Anderson / Stellarvisions
Copy Editor: Gretchen Dykstra
Proofreader: Patricia Pane
Production Coordinator and Compositor: David Van Ness
Technical Reviewer: Joe Christopher
Indexer: Valerie Haynes Perry
Cover Designer: Eddie Yuen
Interior Designer: Mimi Heft
Printed and bound in the United States of America

ISBN-13:   978-0-321-92693-7
ISBN-10:   0-321-92693-5

9 8 7 6 5 4 3 2 1

To my parents and in-laws,
the best mentors I could wish for.

To my kids, Rhea and Rishi,
the best blessings I could ask for.

And to my husband, Ravi—
marrying you was the best decision
I ever made without analytical data.

About the author

Vidya Subramanian (www.linkedin.com/in/vidyas/) is the Senior Analytics Insights Manager at Intuit, where she is currently evangelizing and standardizing analytics practices for the Small Business Group–Marketing. She previously designed and implemented SiteCatalyst and end-to-end analytics at Genworth Financial, a Fortune 500 company.

She is a coauthor of *McGraw-Hill's PMP Certification Mathematics with CD-ROM*, published by McGraw Hill, and author of *Data Driven Scrum Framework*, published in the Intellectual Property Library (IP.com).

She holds a master's degree in information systems from Virginia Tech and a master's degree in computer software applications from Mumbai, India. She is a Certified Project Management Professional, Certified ScrumMaster, Certified Usability Analyst (CUA), and an Adobe Certified Expert in SiteCatalyst.

When she's not reading or checking fun projects off her to-do list, she enjoys family trips to museums, zoos, and parks with her two kids, Rhea (4) and Rishi (2), and her husband, Ravi.

Acknowledgments

A lot of thought leaders and coworkers have shaped my thinking and eased my learning. With this book, I am hoping to give back to the analytics community by sharing my knowledge about analytics in general and Adobe SiteCatalyst in particular. I hope you find it useful.

Joe Christopher, director of analytics at Blast Analytics & Marketing, graciously agreed to be the book's technical editor. The depth of Joe's knowledge is one of the best-kept secrets in the analytics community, but I'm sure it won't be that way for long. His work ethic and professionalism are just two of the things that make him a great role model.

I'm grateful to Victor Gavenda, executive editor at Adobe Press, who challenged me to write the first draft in less than a month—even I had no idea I could do it! Rebecca Gulick, senior editor at Peachpit Press, offered continuous support throughout the process. Developmental editor Margaret Anderson was instrumental in getting this book together and orchestrating an impossible schedule. Copy editor Gretchen Dykstra gave the initial draft an "extreme makeover." Margaret's thoughtful suggestions and Gretchen's magic have made this a better book. Much credit is also due to the other members of the publishing team: David Van Ness, Patricia Pane, and Valerie Haynes Perry.

Thanks to David Schweidel, associate professor of marketing at the Goizueta Business School, Emory University, for giving context to the book in the foreword.

My special appreciation goes to the book's early reviewers and critics: Brent Dykes, Dylan Lewis, and Stewart Alaniz. Tom Wilkins, the CEO of Evolytics, thank you for spending your weekend poring over the book—you clearly have a passion for excellence. And I want to extend a huge thank you to Ken Wach, James Niehaus, Rachael Gerson, Brandon Bunker, Rahul Todkar, and Kayden Kelly for believing in the book's value for readers. Nora Denzel and Adam Greco, thank you for your continued support.

Intuit is definitely one of the best places to work, and I'm grateful for the opportunity to work with some of the best people in the industry. Ken Wach, Steve Lin, and Nancy Lee have always taken time out of their busy schedules to mentor me.

I appreciate of Seth Greenberg, Heather Kirkby, Ivy Wu, Dylan Lewis, Ganesh Kundaicar, Brian Weaver, Scott Annett, Lisa Friedman, Shelby Ferrari, Keith Cheung, Anand Mistry, and Mabel Sio for always adding to my learning. Srikanth Devidi, Anji Koppolu, Chris Dowsett, Harish Mohan—our analytics team at Intuit is definitely one of the best in its search for excellence and its innovation.

Here, I'd like to mention that the thoughts in this book are limited to my personal opinion and interpretation of analytics and not a reflection of how analytics is done at Intuit.

Melissa Ehreshman and Adam Foldenauer from Genworth Financial, thanks for letting me run the analytics implementation at Genworth Financial. It certainly opened a whole new world of excitement and learning.

I wish everyone in the world could be gifted with a wonderful mentor like my sister Subha, who's been instrumental in both of my books. I'm also thankful to my sisters Sumathi and Kavitha, and my sisters-in-law, Bhanu and Vidya, for encouraging me to write this book. I am truly fortunate to have a wonderful family! Special thanks to Navin Argulkar for watching my kids so that I could write.

Thank you to both of my kids, whose lullaby has been me typing away on my keyboard while I cranked out this book. Now that I'm done, we can get back to me singing—not sure how happy they'll be about that!

My husband, Ravi, has been very supportive of all my dreams, even when I broke our cardinal rule of not working during family time. I'm not sure this book would have come through without him—I am truly lucky in love.

Finally, the contents of this book are influenced by a lot of people whose names I may have not explicitly acknowledged above. While I've tried my best to keep the book free of errors, I take full responsibility for any of them. Please send me your thoughts and feedback.

Happy analyzing!

—Vidya Subramanian

ADVANCE PRAISE

In today's world of digital marketing, business success rests on an organization's ability to understand—with real data—their customers' behavior. Vidya Subramanian's book is a fantastic tool for any web leader, new or experienced, to help them implement and leverage accurate and actionable web tracking. This is your one-stop source for all you need to know about Adobe SiteCatalyst so that you can optimize your end-to-end funnels and accelerate growth.

—Ken Wach, Vice President Marketing, Intuit, Inc.

If your business is running Adobe SiteCatalyst, you need this book. Whether you are an analyst, a marketer, or a technical engineer, Vidya Subramanian's *Classroom in a Book* is a wonderful companion to anyone tasked with using SiteCatalyst to drive business decisions. This book brings it all together in a compact and straightforward approach. Vidya provides in-depth insights on a number of key web analytics topics from both a strategic and tactical perspective. She also does a great job of breaking down complex topics by explaining what they are, why they're important, and how to leverage SiteCatalyst to measure and manage performance. This book truly is a crash course in how to manage a real-world business using SiteCatalyst.

—James Niehaus, Director of Optimization and Web Analytics, Symantec

Most organizations struggle with the definition and tracking of their business goals, which dooms their analytics efforts from the beginning. Vidya is clearly an experienced marketer and analyst who shares her pragmatic approach to analytics setup and analysis that is aligned to the customer life cycle. If you aren't sure how to set up KPIs, don't know what questions you should be asking or exactly how to answer them with SiteCatalyst, this book is for you. The well-constructed lessons and valuable tips are sure to help you achieve a positive return on your analytics investment.

—Kayden Kelly, CEO, Blast Analytics & Marketing

Adobe Analytics with SiteCatalyst Classroom in a Book differentiates itself from every other resource because it provides more than insights, tips, and tricks about the tool—in this book, Vidya puts forth an evolutionary analytical framework that aligns analysis recommendations with the marketing funnel. This unique framework enables organizations to think conceptually about conversion in alignment with SiteCatalyst capabilities. It is an actionable, must-read for web analysts and anyone else interested in improving their business online.

—Tom Wilkins, CEO & Founder, Evolytics

In a world where analytics is critical to successful digital marketing, breaking web analytics into simple, easy-to-understand steps is highly beneficial, and Vidya has just done that. I have known her as part of my marketing analytics team and as a point person on web analytics at Intuit. She has a remarkable ability to understand broad vision, and at the same time is willing and eager to get into the details so necessary for successful execution. In this book, Vidya has distilled her SiteCatalyst knowledge into a practical, step-by-step guide to connect your business goals to a web analytics roadmap in order to achieve business growth.

—Rahul Todkar, Head of Channel Marketing Analytics, Intuit Small Business Group

Adobe Analytics with SiteCatalyst Classroom in a Book is a well-written and excellent tutorial on digital analytics with Adobe SiteCatalyst. This book provides a thorough foundation on how you can use SiteCatalyst to answer business questions. This book is the fastest way to get started with SiteCatalyst.

—Brandon Bunker, Sr. Manager of Analytics at Sony Electronics

Adobe Analytics with SiteCatalyst Classroom in a Book reads like a friendly teacher who wants to open up her knowledge to new students, rather than being unnecessarily complicated in an effort to separate the "hardcore" analysts from the beginners. The structured lessons are a perfect fit for busy professionals and those looking to learn the program quickly yet thoroughly, and the consistent presentation format of information helps easily guide readers through the text. Chapter lessons are cumulative, but more experienced SiteCatalyst users will easily be able to skip to relevant sections, or even use earlier chapters as a good review.

Providing readers with opportunities to think critically about the information presented inspires new and current analysts to "hurry up and try" these newfound skills on their own client accounts. It is obvious that the author wants readers to immerse themselves (at their own pace) in the datasets that SiteCatalyst offers, and her easily digestible presentation of otherwise highly technical subject matter is refreshing and will be appreciated by her target audience. Her book will be a valuable reference tool for newcomers and old hats alike.

—Rachael Gerson, Head of Analytics, SEER Interactive

FOREWORD

Adobe Analytics with SiteCatalyst Classroom in a Book offers a comprehensive yet accessible walk through the essentials of analyzing and interpreting the wealth of data generated by web visitors. Vidya Subramanian guides readers through the key stages of the purchase process, from customer acquisition and engagement through conversion and retention. At each stage, she provides examples of the metrics that organizations can use to assess their performance along different dimensions and inform decisions to help achieve their goals.

Online data is essential for a wide range of sectors, from retail stores and service providers to nonprofits and universities. How are customers acquired? What attracts them to a website? What are the key drivers of conversion? Which customers are most valuable? Subramanian clearly demonstrates how SiteCatalyst users can answer these questions and others by extracting the appropriate data. Her step-by-step instructions for generating reports within SiteCatalyst make it simple to derive actionable insights. By calling out the link between key performance indicators, the associated metrics, and the appropriate SiteCatalyst report, even those not currently using SiteCatalyst are treated to a web analytics primer and can see exactly what can be learned by mining the data readily available to them.

While it's convenient to silo different data sources and interpret them in isolation, taking an integrated view across platforms is the best way to understand customers. Subramanian goes beyond the standard take on web analytics to make critical links between activities that organizations can observe on their websites and other sources of information, such as CRM systems and customer surveys.

—David A. Schweidel
 Associate Professor of Marketing
 Co-Director of Emory Marketing Analytics Center (EmoryMAC)
 Goizueta Business School, Emory University

CONTENTS

ABOUT CLASSROOM IN A BOOK

Adobe Analytics with SiteCatalyst Classroom in a Book is part of the official training series for Adobe digital marketing software developed with the support of Adobe product experts. The lessons are designed so you can learn at your own pace. If you're new to SiteCatalyst, you'll learn the fundamental concepts and features you'll need to use the program. Classroom in a Book also teaches many advanced features, including tips and techniques for using the latest version of this application.

Additional Resources

Adobe Analytics with SiteCatalyst Classroom in a Book is not meant to replace documentation that comes with the program or to be a comprehensive reference for every feature. Only the commands and options used in the lessons are explained in this book. For comprehensive information about program features and tutorials, please refer to these resources:

Adobe Analytics Community

http://helpx.adobe.com/marketing-cloud/analytics.html

The Adobe Analytics Community page offers help and support for Adobe Analytics. Find tips, tricks, and solutions to common issues. Follow community professionals and join vibrant discussions around Analytics.

For in-product help, click the Help link at the right of the top navigation bar.

Adobe Training Services

http://training.adobe.com/training.html?promoid=JOPCS

Courses offered through Adobe Training Services are available in multiple formats to suit your needs—at one of our regional training centers, online as virtual learning, or on-site at your company.

@AdobeMktgCare on Twitter

http://twitter.com/AdobeMktgCare

Ask the Adobe experts on Analytics and other solutions for help, advice and tips.

Certification

http://training.adobe.com/certification/exams.html#p=1

Becoming an Adobe Certified Expert gives you advanced skills recognized and respected by employers. By proving your expertise with Adobe solutions, you demonstrate your commitment to advancing your skills and taking on greater challenges.

Digital Marketing Best Practices Guides

http://www.adobe.com/solutions/digital-marketing/
guides.edu.html?promoid=KAWSF

Find leading analyst reports and Adobe thought leadership essays.

GETTING STARTED

If you've picked up this book, chances are you're an analyst, a marketer, or someone who's interested in digital analytics. That's great! *Adobe Analytics with SiteCatalyst Classroom in a Book* shows you how to use Adobe SiteCatalyst to establish and measure key performance indicators (KPIs) for your website, walks you through each phase of the marketing funnel, and explains how to run pertinent reports to better understand your site performance. For each report, you can get a quick overview of the insights, the key technical nuances you need to keep in mind to interpret the data, and the SiteCatalyst implementation changes you'll need to instrument.

Here's an overview of the chapters in the book:

Chapter 1, "Preliminary Work," walks you through some basic concepts of the digital world. You might be familiar with most of these ideas, but this will set the stage for the analytics to be discussed and ease your transition into the book. The chapter provides a quick look at how to set the analytics goals for your website and determine your analytical focus. There is also a brief review of marketing channels, most of which you may be using in your current channel portfolio.

Chapter 2, "Establish Business Strategies and KPIs," introduces the concepts of KPIs and appropriate metrics. You'll gain a deep understanding of segments and how to set thresholds, then take a quick trip through SiteCatalyst to set targets, alerts, and calendar events.

Chapter 3, "Awareness Analytics," provides details on reports you can run to review the effectiveness of awareness data. You'll learn the channel types and how these can be set up to inform your channel spend and optimization needs. You'll learn how to determine which marketing channels are driving visitors and which sites are referring them. You'll also gain an understanding of the differences between cross-channel and multichannel attribution and how you can leverage SiteCatalyst to better understand them.

Chapter 4, "Acquisition Analytics," talks about reports you can run to better understand the acquisition phase of the marketing funnel. You'll learn how to get insight into the success of your acquisition efforts by determining the total number of visits and visitors to your site, and do a dive deep into your visitors' geographical and demographic information.

Chapter 5, "Engagement Analytics," details the engagement phase of the marketing funnel. Here your focus will be on tracking lost revenue and learning which content visitors find engaging. You'll learn how the bounce rate and exit rate can help you identify parts of the site where you're losing visitors. You'll also find out what parts of the site visitors are engaging in and trace their preferred navigation paths.

Chapter 6, "Persuasion Analytics," takes you into the persuasion phase of the marketing funnel. Here you'll understand what pages influence the conversion of a visitor and learn how to tell whether testimonials or product comparisons are influencing visitors to convert. You'll also find out how technology, including mobile technology, can influence visitors to your website.

Chapter 7, "Conversion Analytics," reminds you of the analytics pertaining to conversion and how you can determine whether you're effectively driving both microconversions and macroconversions. The chapter will focus on purchase and cart data to help you understand how to optimize conversion, and give you more tools to determine where you're losing customers. You'll also learn how you can gauge the success of cross-selling and upselling your customers.

Chapter 8, "Retention Analytics," shifts gears to the recency, frequency, and monetary aspects of retention analytics. Here you'll find out how to build customer loyalty.

Chapter 9, "External Data Analytics," provides a holistic view of your analytics by providing an overview of how SiteCatalyst data can be connected to other vendor systems using Genesis Integration or connected to the data stored in disparate databases.

Chapter 10, "Dashboards," gives you an understanding of how to approach a problem and design the analytics solution for it. More importantly, it shows you how to present your findings in a dashboard to different audiences based on their role and level.

Appendix, "Implementation Details," follows up on how you can instrument a successful implementation when you're starting out. Even if you have a solution in place, the exercises presented will help ensure that you've crossed all these off your list. **Joe Christopher** has shared his thoughts on the top ten plug-ins that are used commonly in implementations.

Review of the SiteCatalyst user interface

This quick introduction is intended for those who are just getting started. If you're already familiar with the SiteCatalyst interface, feel free to skip this section.

Top navigation—Adobe Marketing Cloud

Adobe Marketing Cloud is a newly branded suite of analytics products designed specifically to help you answer the wide range of analytics questions that you may have. Each product is listed below with a summary of its capabilities.

Adobe Marketing Cloud > SiteCatalyst > SiteCatalyst Reporting

SiteCatalyst Reporting gives you detailed insights into the health of your website. The reports cover a broad spectrum of data points across the marketing funnel and beyond. SiteCatalyst offers the ability to integrate data from third-party tools, and provides click stream data to customers to import into their internal data warehouse. This gives you the option of building your business intelligence based on SiteCatalyst data collection.

Adobe Marketing Cloud > SiteCatalyst > DataWarehouse

DataWarehouse enables users to focus their analysis on a nonstandard report that is unavailable in SiteCatalyst. DataWarehouse lets you run reports on raw click stream data compared to the processed data in SiteCatalyst. This gives power users data with higher granularity. DataWarehouse reports are available for global and normal report suites, but not for rollup suites. Many of the advanced segmentation capabilities of DataWarehouse have been moved into SiteCatalyst 15 to allow for real-time segmentation.

Adobe Marketing Cloud > SiteCatalyst > SiteCatalyst Widget

The SiteCatalyst Widget enables you to embed SiteCatalyst data in any web page. It can be added to iGoogle, the Google toolbar, Windows Live, and the Yahoo desktop. The widget can be manually embedded by adding a short line of HTML to the source code.

The widget allows you to choose from saved bookmarks and dashboards available in your user account. You can add or remove reports from the widget by making changes to the reports in your SiteCatalyst account.

Adobe Marketing Cloud > SiteCatalyst > Report Builder

Report Builder is an add-in for Microsoft Excel that lets you build more robust dashboards to exploit Excel's rich formula and macro capabilities. Data from SiteCatalyst can be configured to display in any Excel worksheet or cell. Report Builder uses a keyboard-centric design to structure data blocks. It is designed for power users and uses SiteCatalyst reporting.

Adobe does not currently offer a version of Report Builder for Mac OS. However, you can use your Intel-based Mac to install Windows (using Boot Camp or a virtual machine), and then install Excel and Report Builder in Windows to use Report Builder on your Mac.

Adobe Marketing Cloud > SearchCenter+

SearchCenter+ is a search engine optimization tool that lets you manage bids, keywords, and text ads across multiple search engines in a single interface. It allows you to report on paid search campaign performance. It integrates with SiteCatalyst to provide data on return on investment, impressions, return on ad spend, and advanced analytics.

Adobe Marketing Cloud > Discover

Discover provides a comprehensive perspective on visitor engagement and participation across visit sessions. It enables you to perform advanced analysis on customer transaction data in real time. You can view multiple reports simultaneously and apply segments across multiple dimensions. You can also build custom data tables using any combination of dimensions, metrics, and segments. New calendar settings let you apply date ranges, preset dates, rolling date ranges, and custom presets.

Adobe Marketing Cloud > Test&Target

Test&Target enables you to target different test experiences to your audience to determine which will be the most successful. A test is a campaign that compares two or more experiences against the success metrics you specify, so you can choose the experience that is most likely to compel visitors to complete your website goal.

There are three popular types of campaign tests:

- A/B/n testing, or split testing, attempts to do a real-time test on visitors to your site by rendering one of the versions of the page to 50 percent of the visitors and the other version to the other 50 percent during the same time period. Note that this percentage is adjusted if you have 'n' versions of the page. A/B/n tests work best when you have completely different layouts or large interaction between elements.

- Multivariate testing pertains to testing subtle differences in a page. Multivariate testing acknowledges the fact that one size does not fit all. Each visitor to your site has a unique personality and your site needs to cater to that. With segmentation and web metrics, you have the advantage of analyzing visitor behavior and creating personalized rules that optimize for the website goals. A multivariate test helps you optimize the elements or the assets displayed on the page for a predetermined layout.

- A landing page test allows you to optimize the landing page contents based on the channel or other visitor attributes. This lets you personalize the contents of the landing page based on visitor needs. A landing page test compares different versions of the page to help you see which version produces more successful results.

Adobe Marketing Cloud > Genesis

Genesis is a visual tool that allows you to integrate tools from other vendors into SiteCatalyst. Any external vendors who have partnered with Adobe will be featured in this list. The integration requires additional variables as discussed in Chapter 9 of this book.

Adobe Marketing Cloud > Insight

Adobe Insight provides powerful visualization capabilities on large sets of data to draw insights. Adobe Insight can combine SiteCatalyst data with data from other sources to give a more comprehensive understanding of insights that are not myopically restricted to the web. It also gives you the capability of creating unlimited real-time segments and correlating data with n-dimensional analysis.

Adobe Marketing Cloud > Search&Promote

Adobe Search&Promote enables marketers to display relevant content to visitors based on the spectrum of data, including geographical location, referrer site, or the search keyword used in the current visit. This data can also be correlated to the campaigns and channels that visitors responded to in past visits to uncover the intent of their visit. Search&Promote automates merchandising and promotions activity via KPI-based triggers or metrics.

Adobe Marketing Cloud > Survey

Survey essentially provides the qualitative aspect of analytics. It integrates seamlessly with SiteCatalyst to provide behavioral- and sentiment-based insights. It gives you the ability to design and create surveys with an easy-to-use interface.

Adobe Marketing Cloud > Recommendations

Recommendations provide capabilities to provide the right engaging content based on visitors' behavioral data. Marketers gain the opportunity to cross-sell and upsell by algorithmically comparing the visits from visitors displaying similar demographic and behavioral characteristics. Product choices can be based on inventory levels or visitor choices. You can also test and evaluate the accuracy of recommendations based on historical data.

Adobe Marketing Cloud > Scene7

Adobe Scene7 is a cloud-based solution for hosting and publishing digital assets to replicate them optimally across devices. Digital assets need to be optimized for each device. Adobe Scene7 determines the device from which it is receiving traffic and provides optimized digital assets for that device in real time. This provides a rich and consistent visitor experience across devices.

Adobe Marketing Cloud > Social

Adobe Social provides a publishing platform for social content, social ads, interpreting social conversation to derive the sentiments and respond in real time to any social media content. You can draw insights from popular terms word clouds and determine social impact by trending mentions, potential audience, page views, and daily unique visitors. It also provides terms, trends, and authors influencing the social space. Also, the social intelligence report provides a sentiment analysis that determines the overall attitude of your audience words, your brand, and company.

Adobe Marketing Cloud > AudienceResearch

AudienceResearch is an indispensable tool for advertisers and media planners to understand the potential audience across the web, digital edition magazines, and mobile apps. This helps to plan the digital advertising aspect to improve return on investment.

The data is independently validated and accredited by the Media Rating Council and the Interactive Advertising Bureau. The tool provides audience and engagement data encompassing websites, mobile applications, and digital magazines. This data can be further segmented by publisher data, geographical data, and technology preferences of your potential audience.

Top navigation—Favorites

The key aspects of favorites are discussed in the chapters ahead. So in an effort to keep repetition to a minimum, the chapters are referenced here. Dashboards are covered in Chapter 10, while calculated metrics, targets, alerts, calendar events are discussed in Chapter 2, "Establish Business Strategies and KPIs."

Scheduled Reports allows you to see a list of reports that you, as user, have scheduled. At any point, you could edit the scheduling changes and/or delete the scheduled report. Archived reports lists the reports that have been archived.

Top navigation—Admin

The functionality in the Admin section is restricted to users who are designated as an administrator in SiteCatalyst.

Admin > Admin Console > Admin Console Home

The Admin Console Home provides an easy way to navigate to popular aspects of the Admin Console.

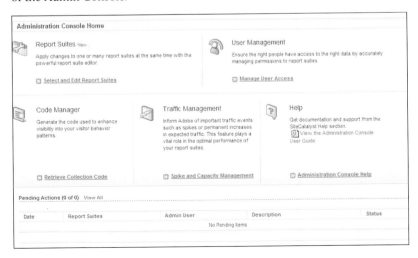

Admin > Admin Console > Report Suites

This section lists the report suites. One of the lesser-known and used function-alities is the report suite groups. Based on filter criteria, you can group together report suites. For example, you can group all the production report suites as a group or a set of report suites that are saved for a particular business group.

Admin > Admin Console > Tag Manager

Tag Manager is a solution designed for creating a tag container for SiteCatalyst tags. The tag manager is designed to abstract the tags from the web page and add them all in a single tag container for easier tag management and reduce the risk of errors.

Admin > Admin Console > Code Manager

The Code Manager lets you generate, edit, and save the code that you need to insert in your web pages for data collection. The code is based on a number of parameters—the report suite (assuming static report suite variable assignment), the character encoding, the currency used for transaction, and the number of periods in the domain name.

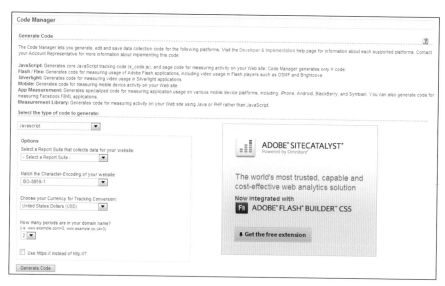

Admin > Admin Console > Company Home

The Company Home allows you to set up company-wide settings related to security, policy, and reports. The Security Manager allows you to set security policy across passwords, email delivery, and IP restrictions.

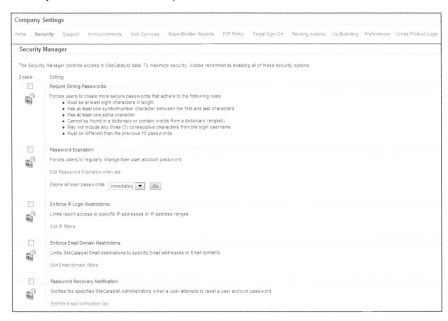

Admin > Admin Console > User Management

The User Management console allows you to add, edit, delete, or view users, groups, and report suites allocation to users and groups. You can also manage publishing lists. You can also email all users of SiteCatalyst or admins using the email users functionality.

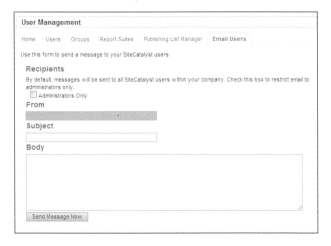

Admin > Admin Console > Traffic Management

The Traffic Management console allows you to look at the trends of traffic your site has been receiving. Any sudden traffic spikes can be flagged for further investigation. If there is a consistent surge in traffic, you can request a permanent traffic change.

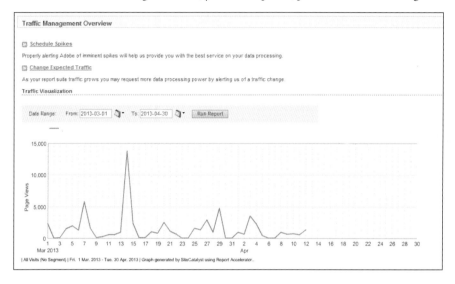

Admin > Admin Console > Billing

The Billing center provides information on the primary and secondary server calls.

Admin > Admin Console > Logs

Logs provide three kinds of information for you to audit the usage of SiteCatalyst and its data. First, you could review the event logs for alerts, API calls, and so on. The usage and access logs provide information on the reports and actions of different users logging in to your systems. Finally, the report suite change logs describe any changes to report suites.

Top navigation—Community

The Community aspects provide a forum for SiteCatalyst users across the globe to share their insights and issues through a common forum. This enables you to share best practices from the analytics industry. The community forum is normally for questions on current features and issues you are facing.

Adobe also provides an intracompany forum to resolve issues internal to your implementation.

The customer portal gives you a ready look at the health of your Adobe suite of products. You can view any incidents that were opened and resolved or a scheduled maintenance. High-priority open incidents can also be viewed. Clicking on the icon gives you details on the incident report.

The link allows you to link to other web analytics professionals and connect to the blogs from industry leaders and thought leaders in the analytics arena.

The Ideas Exchange is a forum for users to share feature requests that are voted on by the community. The popularity of a feature request in turn drives the priority list of features for Adobe to add to any of its products.

Top navigation—Notices

The Notices section gives your SiteCatalyst Administrator the ability to share company-wide notices.

Top navigation—Help

In the Help section, the "what's new" section gives an overview of the release notes from the latest code release across the Adobe suite of products.

The Help home links you to the thoughtful blogs from Adobe thought leaders on analytics.

The Knowledge Base boasts more than two thousand frequently asked questions (FAQs). Answers to most questions or issues can be answered by searching this portal.

Training videos is a collection of video libraries that provide an audiovisual overview of the different aspects of Adobe's suite of products.

ClientCare is Adobe's premium customer support services. You can submit a question to the support team via LiveChat. You can also see a history of incidents opened by you and its status.

Before you get started

Before you start using SiteCatalyst, ensure that you have a thorough understanding of the following aspects of your SiteCatalyst implementation. Your SiteCatalyst admin should be able to guide you through the following:

1 **Credentials, groups, and publishing lists**

    Get your credentials set up. Your admin should be able to create or validate your username and password. Identify the name of the company as provided by Adobe. Also ensure that you're part of the appropriate groups and distribution lists to receive scheduled reports pertinent to your role in the organization.

2   Report suite names

Especially if you're part of a large organization, familiarize yourself with the report suites where the data for your website is being sent. If your organization is writing data to multiple report suites (multisuite tagging), learn about the ecosystem of pages writing data to each of the report suites.

3   Report suite settings

All report suites allow you to choose the calendar, time zone, and internal URL filters. These settings add context to interpreting the reports and data.

4   VISTA rules applied to the report suite

Visitor identification, segmentation, and transformation architecture (VISTA) rules allow a company to transform its data before it is used for reporting, based on the identification of a visitor or a segment. Your SiteCatalyst administrator should have a list of the variables that were transformed and the rules on which those are based.

5   Custom traffic variables

Having a handy list of all traffic variables and the pages on which they are set helps you understand what custom traffic reports you can run. It also helps you interpret that data.

6   Custom conversion variables and their allocations

Custom conversions and their allocations will help you understand if the variables expire within a visit, after a visit, or are retained at the visitor level. This will help you correlate conversion data.

7   Success events, names, and types, and serialization information

Success events are vital to understanding the success of macro- and microconversions. Knowing the correct event numbers will help you set up the right marketing funnel steps.

8   Calculated metrics and their formulas

Having a list of calculated metrics and the formulas used will help you determine the right metrics for the business question you are evaluating.

Now let's get started!

1 PRELIMINARY WORK

Lesson overview

This book will delve into how to get the most out of Adobe Analytics using SiteCatalyst. Before you can analyze your website, there are some fundamental definitions you'll need to know. If you're part of a large organization, you'll need to align these definitions with the goals of senior management, who must drive primary business and analytics strategies.

The goals of this section are to:

- Understand the type of site you're analyzing and its macro and micro goals.

- Determine the kind of analytical focus your website needs.

- Determine the channels your business is invested in.

 This lesson will take 15 minutes to complete.

If you have already been using Adobe SiteCatalyst, you will have seen the detail and range of information it provides. But how do you know which reports will be most helpful to your business? What insights can you glean from the data to guide your marketing and organizational planning?

Understand your website goals

Adobe SiteCatalyst is a robust analytics tool that can help you determine if your website, campaigns, and mobile apps are adding value to the strategic vision of your business. Implementing SiteCatalyst is fairly easy, if you understand what analytics you're looking for. This book helps you navigate through the wealth of information you can derive from SiteCatalyst, and distill that information to guide your decision-making process.

The approach to analytics varies by the type of site you're trying to evaluate and analyze. The goal of the site, the channels through which you market it, and the metrics you use determine the focus area for analytics. Before you get started, do the following:

1 Review your website to understand its structure and goals.

2 Determine your business sales cycle for the products sold on your website.

3 Ensure you and all teams across the organization are aligned with senior management's goals for the website.

4 Determine the macro and micro goals of your site.

It's not uncommon for websites to have multiple goals. The primary goal will be the main action that you want to measure on your site (macroconversion) and the secondary, tertiary, and other goals can be ancillary actions (microconversions). Microconversions are baby steps toward a macroconversion. Examples of a macroconversion could be buying products on the site, while examples of microconversions could include recommending products to others, contacting the sales team, or subscribing to an RSS feed.

Table 1.1 is intended to get you started on determining the macro- and microconversions for your website type.

Table 1.1 Macroconversions and microconversions based on website type

TYPE OF WEBSITE	WEBSITE DESCRIPTION	MACROCONVERSION	MICROCONVERSION
Affiliate agency	Acts as a broker between publishers and advertisers	Increase the number of customers signing up for an affiliate partnership	Offer testimonials
Blog	Offers chronological posts about a specific or general topic	Increase engagement through posts, comments, and time spent on the site	Subscribe to an RSS feed Generate more inbound links
Branded site selling its proprietary products	Provides product information with the goal of influencing the visitor's decision-making process	Promote purchases by providing information on different products with biased influence	Provide feedback Take a customer survey Recommend products on social sites Subscribe to email newsletters Chat with a customer representative Call a customer representative
Educational	Offers a forum for education on a particular area of interest	Increase the number of signups	Take advantage of online learning through content, videos, and apps Gather feedback on site
Search engine	Provides a platform for users to search for web pages using keywords	Increase the number of searches	Increase the number of sites crawled
Social networking	Provides a forum for people to connect	Increase the number of account signups	Increase engagement through posts and comments

Determine your analytics focus

The goal of this exercise is to determine the aspects of analytics you should focus on based on the kind of site you have. But before we dive in, let's take a few moments to go over some fundamental concepts and terms, in case you're new to the world of web analytics.

Essentially, you'll use analytics to determine the effectiveness of marketing strategies. Not all of them will be relevant to your business, but it's good practice to know about each of them. At a broad level, we think of analytics in terms of outbound and inbound marketing strategies.

Marketing strategies

Outbound marketing refers to the mass distribution of marketing content with little personalization. Examples include TV segments, print, and radio. Here, the messaging and content is not tailored and targeted to individuals, but rather to the masses. Outbound marketing helps to reach a wider target audience. However, it comes at a higher cost and offers limited flexibility in personalizing marketing efforts. Perhaps the harder aspect for marketers is the inability to gauge the success of the campaign early on and the difficulty in measuring immediate feedback.

Inbound marketing is a set of strategies that allow personalization of messages and content at the individual level. Over the past decade, marketing efforts have transitioned heavily to this kind of marketing. Inbound marketing overcomes the disadvantages of outbound marketing with a lower cost, personalization of marketing efforts, and near real-time feedback.

The marketing funnel section that follows presents the sales cycle pattern that most visitors experience in a website.

The marketing funnel

To understand what influences a buyer's decisions, it's important to know the sales cycle. The marketing funnel depicted below visualizes the stages of this journey. This model has evolved (and is still evolving) over time. The advent of social media has made it easier to advocate products and services to a broader audience, making customer experience on the website a focal point of marketing.

Awareness

Acquisition

Engagement

Persuasion

Conversion

Advocacy

Retention

The Marketing Funnel

Awareness

The focus of channel analytics and reports is to gauge the success of marketing channels in reaching out to your target audience—the user segment you care most about. Key aspects to be analyzed are:

- The brand value of the company
- The preferred online channel for prospect
- The influence of offline marketing channel(s)
- Behavior patterns driven on the site by the channel
- The quality of the traffic from a specific channel

Acquisition

Acquisition metrics help to determine the type of visitors coming to the site. You can use acquisition metrics to interpret those visitors' attributes and intent. Key aspects to be analyzed are:

- The most common landing pages (where visitors enter the site)
- The geolocations of visitors
- The traffic sources referring most traffic to the website
- The landing pages with the highest bounce rate

Engagement

Engagement focuses on the learning and orienting process through which visitors become more interested in the site content. Key aspects to be analyzed are:

- The content that visitors are most interested in
- Visitors' preference to learn about the product offerings through text, interactive apps, or videos
- How user experience is affected by technology choice; for example, some sites don't render well in certain browsers or devices, which impacts the user experience.

Persuasion

Given the sheer number of product choices, most visitors compare and review products and features before making the journey down the conversion funnel. To persuade them, we need to know what motivates and influences them.

To help you distinguish between the engagement and persuasion stages of the funnel, consider how you might approach buying a camera. You might start by learning about cameras and researching products and features on Nikon's or Canon's website and putting together a comprehensive list of the features you're interested in. The persuasion stage begins when you compare and contrast products from both Nikon and Canon to decide which camera to buy.

Key aspects to be analyzed are:

- The influence of testimonials
- The influence of social media advocacy
- The influence of content persuading the visitor to start the conversion funnel
- Visitors' preference to compare and contrast products or features offered on the site

Conversion

Conversion metrics are restricted to the steps that visitors take to achieve the goal of the site. The conversion *requirements* for each site are different. Key questions to be asked are:

- What are visitors buying?
- Are visitors signing up for the newsletter?
- How many leads are being generated?
- How many ecommerce transactions are being generated?
- How many customers are calling customer representatives?
- How many customers are providing comments and feedback?
- How many visitors are subscribing to RSS feeds?

Advocacy

Advocacy metrics are driven by feedback and recommendations (positive/negative) of a product or service received from users. Key questions to be asked are:

- How many customers have a negative experience? How many have a positive experience?
- Who are the influencers and followers?
- In the industry space, what are thought leaders recommending?
- Is there a need for reputation management?
- Are there any incorrect statements or inaccuracies that need to be addressed?

Note: Advocacy is largely determined by social media. Social media metrics are discussed in Chapter 3, "Awareness Analytics," but advocacy is not treated as a separate chapter in this book.

Retention

Retention helps to measure visitor loyalty. The rate of retention depends on your sales cycle. For example, people normally shop for clothes every season of the year, while they may shop for a car once in seven or eight years on an average. Key questions to be asked are:

- When was the visitor's last purchase?
- How often are visitors coming back to the site?
- How much are they buying?

Determine marketing channels

▶ **Tip:** If you're new to tracking channel traffic, see the Appendix, "Implementation Details."

The focus of channel analytics and reports is to evaluate the success of marketing channels in reaching out to your target audience. Finding the best marketing channel for a given situation is a challenge. Answering the following questions will help you find the right channel for your website:

- Which online channel did your prospects come from?
- What marketing channel(s) did they prefer and in which sequence?
- Were they influenced by any offline marketing channels?
- What behavior patterns did the channel drive on the site?
- What's the quality of the traffic from that channel?

External online campaigns

External online campaigns are run outside the ecosystem of your website and domain. Following are descriptions of the various kinds of external campaigns as well as some goals and key analytics.

Subscription marketing

Subscription marketing requires you to seek the explicit permission and intent of subscribers before you target them with any such campaign. Following are descriptions of the types of subscription marketing.

Email marketing

Email marketing refers to commercial email messages sent to subscribers to promote a product or service and drive them to your site. Be aware that the CAN-SPAM Act (U.S. Congress) applies to all bulk emails, commercial emails, service email advertisements, and email promotions of a product, service, or website content. Key goals of an email marketing campaign are:

- Increasing email subscriptions and decreasing unsubscribes
- Decreasing bounces
- Increasing visits and click-through rate (CTR)
- Increasing conversions and return on investment (ROI)
- Decreasing cost per acquisition (CPA)

Mobile marketing (SMS, MMS)

Short message service (SMS), as the name suggests, includes sending short text advertisements to prospects. These messages can include special offers and discounts. In some cases, a callback number or URL provides additional information. Multimedia message service (MMS) is similar to SMS except that the advertisement has multimedia content (videos, images, and so on) in it. Key goals of a mobile marketing campaign are:

• Increasing SMS/MMS subscriptions

• Decreasing unsubscribes

• Increasing visits from SMS advertisement

Search engine marketing

Any traffic to a website originating from a search engine falls under the purview of search engine marketing. The source of the traffic could be organic or paid search.

Organic search

Organic search refers to the nonpaid search results displayed to users when they search for keywords or phrases. Most search engines distinguish between paid and organic search results by displaying paid ads in a separate section and with different background colors. The search result snippet below highlights the organic search result in the red box.

Key aspects to be analyzed for organic search are:

- Increase in impressions
- Ranking on the search engine results page (SERP) for branded and non-branded keywords
- Keywords that drive engagement versus conversion
- Landing page optimization based on keywords used

Paid search

Paid search refers to the sponsored ads listed by the search engines that are contextually related to a user's search. The search result snippet below highlights the paid search result in the red box.

Key aspects to be analyzed for paid search are:

- Number of impressions
- Increase in visits and CTR
- Increase in conversions and ROI
- Decrease in CPA
- Analysis for branded and non-branded keywords and type of match

Social media

Social media is an important aspect of the modern analytics strategy. Some of the more popular social platforms are blogs, Twitter, Facebook, and LinkedIn. These differ in their marketing strategies and in the type of the information they provide.

Data from your social media campaigns should help you determine:

- How social media is influencing your traffic and conversions
- Which social platform is influencing visitors most

Display advertising

Display advertising is Internet-based advertising that includes text or banners ads that contain images. Some of the different types of display ads are local listings, contextual networks, and display ads. Key aspects to be analyzed for display advertising are:

- Number of impressions and view-through rate
- Number of clicks and CTR
- Visits, conversion, revenue, units, and orders
- ROI, cost per click, and cost per customer

Affiliate marketing

Affiliates act as catalysts to channel traffic to partner sites. Key aspects to be analyzed for affiliate marketing are:

- Number of impressions
- Number of clicks and CTR
- Visits, conversion, revenue, units, and orders
- ROI, cost per click, and cost per customer
- Returns or cancellation from affiliate customers

Mobile ads

Mobile ads are the emerging industry space to create more brand awareness. The key aspect to be analyzed is engagement and conversion from mobile ads.

Internal online campaigns

Internal online campaigns include online banners, ads, and links promoting products from within the website.

Internal banners and links

Internal banners and links drive visitors' attention to the site's micro and macro goals by adding a creative banner or links for them to click on.

Internal search

Along with organic and paid search, it's good practice to include internal search analysis to evaluate keyword performance. Internal search helps visitors find things quickly. The insight from that data allows you to fix navigation. Also, it helps you understand the jargon that prospective customers use, so you can incorporate the same messaging in your keywords and advertising.

Cross-selling

Cross-selling presents additional products that visitors may be interested in buying. Increasingly, this is driven algorithmically by matching them with similar personas. For example, if you browse a product on Amazon, you are shown suggestions of other items that others bought along with that item.

Offline campaigns

Offline campaigns are run using traditional media such as:

- Public relations
- Brand recognition efforts
- Phone
- Interactive voice response (IVR)
- TV and radio ads
- Print ads (newspapers and magazines)
- Print marketing (direct mail)
- Partners
- Retail

You may also use certain codes or coupons and ask users to redeem those on your website in order to track the effectiveness of your offline campaigns. Alternatively, you could use vanity URLs or URLs that are easy for visitors to remember and redirect them to your website.

Now that we understand our goals and strategy, let's get started!

Review questions

1 What is the difference between macro and micro goals?

2 What metrics can be used for advocacy metrics in SiteCatalyst?

Review answers

1 Macro goals are the primary goals of your site. All other supporting goals are your micro goals.

2 Advocacy metrics need to be imported into SiteCatalyst. SiteCatalyst currently does not provide advocacy metrics out of the box.

2 ESTABLISH BUSINESS STRATEGY AND KPIS

Lesson overview

In this lesson, you'll learn how to think about key performance indicators (KPIs) and how to create a list of KPIs that apply to your business. Ideally, you want to align your entire organization to a shared vision and establish measuring practices to evaluate whether your team achieves the set goals. You'll also learn how to incorporate this information into Adobe SiteCatalyst.

The goals of this section are to:

- Understand your business objectives for the reporting period.

- Determine the KPIs, measures, metrics, and segments.

- Understand the different types of metrics available in SiteCatalyst.

- Include targets, segments, and alerts information in SiteCatalyst.

 This lesson will take 45 minutes to complete.

This chapter is at the beginning of the book for a reason: no matter what industry you're in, the first step is to set your business objectives and key performance indicators, then do the hard work of aligning your organization behind them. Once you do that, you can measure your performance against them.

Business objectives

Business objectives are efforts that support the corporate strategy. They have all the characteristics of a SMART (specific, measurable, attainable, relevant, and time-bound) goal. Ensuring that each of these attributes is incorporated into your business objectives will increase your odds of making your business successful.

Business objectives can include directives like these:

- Increase revenue generated through web sales of Product A by 15 percent in the current year.
- Decrease the cost per acquisition of Product A by 5 percent in the current year.
- Increase sales leads by 8 percent in the current year.
- Increase account sign-ups by 5 percent in the current year.
- Increase customer satisfaction by 5 percent in the current year.

Key performance indicators

Let's look at a simplified example of how to structure your thinking to create appropriate KPIs for your website. You can use this example to build on and develop KPIs that apply to your business.

Key performance indicators are aggregative measures that have a target. So if your business objective is to increase revenue by 15 percent, the indicators of whether you'll make that goal could be to:

- Increase quality traffic to your website so there's a corresponding increase in conversion.
- Optimize the visit-to-conversion ratio.

Well, that's not a complete KPI yet since it can't be measured. This is exactly what our first task will be: to understand how to determine the numeric value we need to add to the KPI. Then it will indicate whether we're heading in the right direction to meet the business goal. To do this, we'll set what SiteCatalyst calls **success events**.

Task: Quantify your goal

Our first step is to find the numeric value that should be assigned to the goal. Running just the Key Metrics report will help you make an informed decision. Below we will run some reports in sequence to help you rationalize the numbers.

● **Tip:** If you have a website with conversion funnels that are order-based, then run the Purchase Conversion Funnel report. If not, then run the Custom Event Funnel.

Purchase Conversion Funnel

This option assumes that you have a conversion that tracks orders and revenue.

1 Navigate to Site Metrics > Purchases > Purchase Conversion Funnel.

2 Click Selected Events and choose the success events.

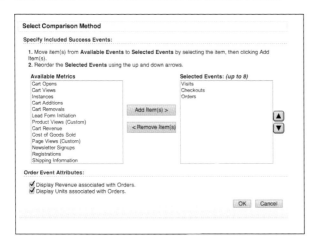

3 Choose the calendar date range as a comparison of the previous two years or any time period you're framing your KPI for.

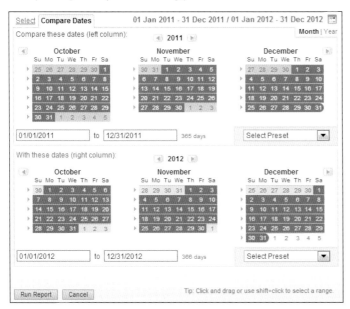

4 Now the purchases funnel looks like this:

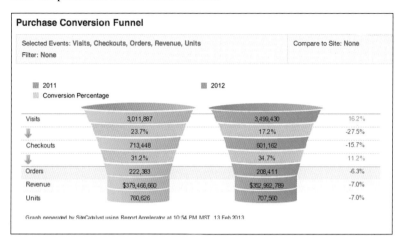

5 Compare the two funnels that indicate growth and decline in traffic and conversion.

6 Now compare trends of all these metrics across months for both years. This final step will help you figure any seasonal trends or one-time trends that you need to factor into your growth rate calculations. To do that, you'd need to run five reports for each year separately by week.

- Site Metrics > Visits

- Site Metrics > Shopping Cart > Checkouts

- Site Metrics > Purchases > Orders

- Site Metrics > Purchases > Units

- Site Metrics > Purchases > Revenue

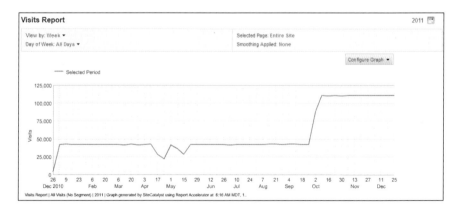

This should help you project the expected growth for the next reporting period, which means you have a numeric measure for your KPI!

Custom Events Funnel option

If your website has a nonmonetary conversion, then you may need to run the Custom Event > Custom Events Funnel. Confirm the event names with your SiteCatalyst admin.

1 Navigate to Custom Events > Custom Events Funnel.

2 Click Selected Events and choose the success events.

3 Choose the calendar date range separately for the previous two years or any time period you're framing your KPI for.

4 Navigate to Custom Events > Custom Events Funnel.

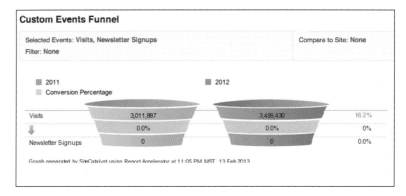

5 Compare the two funnels that indicate growth and decline in traffic and conversion.

6 Now compare trends of the success event across months for both years. This will help you figure any seasonal trends or one-time trends that you need to factor into your growth-rate calculations.

To run the report, navigate to Site Metrics > Custom Events > Custom Events (Number to Number) > Specific Event Number (the event you are comparing). Remember that in the custom events report, you cannot compare two dates, so you may have to run the report twice to compare periods of time.

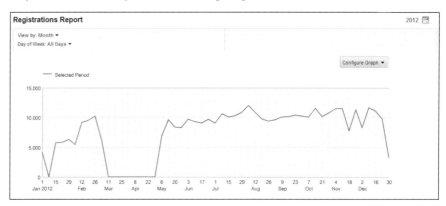

This should help you project the expected growth for the next reporting period, which means you have a numeric measure for your KPI.

Repeat steps 1–6 in the Custom Event Funnel report for other macro or micro goals as well.

You now have a fair idea of the visit-to-conversion ratio. This will help you quantify the KPI.

Examples of KPIs

Here are two examples of KPIs that are quantified. The first goal and KPI would only apply to a retail site:

Business goal

Increase revenue generated through web sales by 15 percent in the current year.

Suggested KPIs

- Increase orders in the current financial year by 10 percent.
- Increase units sold by 8 percent.
- Increase visits to website by 54 percent.

How to arrive at the KPIs

Assume that to increase revenue by 15 percent, there must be a 10 percent increase in orders for tricycles and an 8 percent increase in orders for bikes. Base this on the value of your orders and the amount of revenue generated by each order. Remember to factor in cancellations and returns of orders as well.

Assume that for a 10 percent increase in orders, there must be a proportional percentage increase in acquisition. Bake in your company's visit-to-conversion rate here.

This second example could be relevant to any online experience:

Business goal

Promote the best customer experience.

Suggested KPIs

- Customer satisfaction scores should be greater than 90 percent.
- Comments in customer surveys should reflect 75 percent positive sentiment.
- The net promoter score should be greater than 70 percent.

How to arrive at the KPIs

If you're tracking customer satisfaction in an event or a custom conversion variable, you can trend the satisfaction scores to envision the goal for the following year.

KPIs cannot be evaluated based on a single dimension, metric, or report. Insights are derived by slicing, dicing, and statistically analyzing the data. Measures refer to those dimensions of the data. For example, a KPI might include increased traffic to the site, but a spike or dip would need additional measures such as segmenting traffic by referring domains, referrers, traffic from search engine, traffic from campaigns, bots, and geosegmentation, to name a few.

Metrics

Metrics are measures that help you aggregate data to determine how you're doing.

▶ **Tip:** Determine which metric is right for you based on what you're selling. For example, if you're selling a high-priced item like a television set, chances are that a customer will buy only one every few years, so you may want to keep the metric visitor-based. But, if you're selling an item that a customer buys multiple times a week or a month, then you may want to track visits. Align the metrics to your sales cycle and your business.

Let's look at the different types of metrics in SiteCatalyst.

Standard metrics

Standard metrics include awareness, acquisition, engagement, conversion, and success event metrics. These metrics give a single traffic credit based on the current image request. However, the pages, channel, and server variables are attributed based on linear allocation for conversion events. Remember that the custom traffic variables (s.props in SiteCatalyst) do not get any credits by default. You can enable conversion credit with allocation and participation metrics. For custom conversion variables (eVars in SiteCatalyst), the credit is based on the custom conversion allocation. Standard metrics also support decimals in measurement.

Awareness metrics

Awareness metrics determine the success of channel performance.

* **Click-throughs** indicate the number of times a campaign link was clicked after the ad impression was served. Impressions can be tracked only if the data is imported into SiteCatalyst.

* **Entries** refer to the number of times the specified landing page was viewed from a particular marketing campaign.

Acquisition metrics

Acquisition metrics are based on the initial page of the visit. The numbers for daily, weekly, monthly, quarterly, and yearly unique visitors may vary based on the calendar configuration in the admin section. The default is the Gregorian calendar.

* **Daily / Weekly / Monthly / Quarterly / Yearly unique visitors** are determined by recording only the first visit by each visitor during each day throughout the reporting period. For example, if a visitor comes to the site on five days during a week and multiple times in a day, he will be counted as five daily unique visitors in that reporting week.

* **Visits** are counted as new if 30 minutes have elapsed without activity from that visitor.

- **Bounces** refer to the number of visits in which the visitor came to the site but exited without interacting with any aspects of the page. Often, bounce rate is also referred to as the "stickiness" or the "lack of stickiness" on your site. What distinguishes a bounce from single access is the fact that bounces contain only a single call to the Adobe data servers. For example, if a visitor clicks on any links, reloads a page, or clicks on any tabs that trigger a call to the Adobe data server, her visit is no longer classified as a bounce in Version 14. However, in Version 15, reloads and link clicks are now additional hits, and hence, any visitor session that has a visit to a single page which has been reloaded would be classified as a single access visit and not a bounce.

Tip: All bounces are included in the single access visits. not all single access visits are included in the bounces.

- **Bounce rate** compares the percentage of the number of bounces to the total number of visits.

- **Single access** refers to the number of visits in which the visitor came to the site and interacted with links or video on the site, but did not navigate to another page. Single access is determined by the number of visits in which the session has only one unique page-name value.

Engagement metrics

Engagement metrics help you to understand the user experience on your site.

- **Page views** refer to the total number of times each page was viewed.

- **Exits** refer to the number of times a page was the last page viewed in a visit.

- **Average time spent** refers to the average time spent on a page or a sequence of pages, or the duration of the total visit.

- **Searches** refer to the number of page views in which the referrer contained an Adobe-recognized search engine, and the keyword that was searched was passed in the URL as a querystring parameter.

- **Average page depth**, with respect to pages where a specific value has been assigned, refers to the average number of pages visited before reaching that page. This metric is available on all variables where pathing is enabled. Pathing refers to the sequence of pages (or custom traffic variables) visited by the visitor.

- **Instances** refer to the number of times a value is assigned to a variable in the reporting period. For example, if a visitor uses internal search, the instances metric will reflect the number of times a search was done. This of course assumes that this data is being stored on a custom conversion variable. If a visitor uses the search multiple times in a visit, the instances will keep incrementing. Since instances reflect the number of times a variable was set, the number of instances could potentially be greater than the number of visits, if the variable is set multiple times in a single visit.

- **Visits** refer to the number of new sessions on the website. A new visit is initialized after 30 minutes of inactivity, after 12 hours of continuous activity, or after 2,500 pages were viewed. Continuous activity within SiteCatalyst refers to the continuous image requests being sent to the Adobe server.

- **Path views** refer to the number of times a visitor navigated a site in a specific sequence of paths.

- **Product views** refer to the number of times the product view event is set (the number of times the visitor looks at a product).

- **Reloads** refer to the number of times a page is refreshed, as indicated by two sequential page views that have the same page name.

- **Total time spent** cumulates the total time spent on the page, site, or visit.

Conversion metrics

Conversion metrics are used to track standard success events as well as custom success events.

- **Visits (report-specific)** refer to the total number of visits in which that value was set. This is typically a subset of the total visits.

- **Cart open** refers to the total number of times the first item was added to the cart.

- **Cart additions** refer to the total number of times any item was added to the cart.

- **Cart removals** refer to the total number of times any item was removed from the cart.

- **Cart views** refer to the total number of times the cart was viewed.

- **Checkouts** refer to the total number of times the user clicked the checkout button. The checkout success event can be incremented in any step of the funnel, such as the addition of personal information or billing information.

- **Orders** refer to the number of orders placed. An order can contain multiple units.

- **Units** refer to the quantity purchased in the order.

- **Revenue** refers to the total currency of all orders placed. The currency can be configured at the report suite level for sites that do not track revenue in US dollars.

Success event metrics

A success event can be numeric (such as visits), percent (such as click-through rate), currency (such as revenue), or time (such as average time spent on page). Any success event can be used to aggregate custom data; for example:

- Number of forms submitted

- Number of leads generated

- Number of posts and comments

Participation metrics

Participation metrics for success events (including defaults) can be enabled by ClientCare at Adobe. This assigns participation metrics for the pages, campaigns, or other custom variables assigned in any visit in which that success event occurred.

For example, assume the following scenario:

1 On Monday, a visitor comes to the site through a display ad but does not convert (complete the goal of the site).

2 On Wednesday, the same visitor returns using paid search but does not convert.

3 On Saturday, the visitor returns and places a $500 order.

Revenue *participation* would report $500 for all three campaigns, as each of them *participated* in the conversion. If participation is not enabled, the allocation is based on the attribution.

When the success event is recorded for the participation metrics, the metrics:

- Attribute the success events in full to all values stored in that custom conversion variable (eVar) based on its expiry period.

- Equally and fully credit all the props in that visit.

- Fully allocate success to pages, channels, and server variables.

- Fully allocate success to all custom traffic variables.

Video metrics

- **Video views** indicate the number of times a video was viewed, either partially or fully.

- **Video time views** indicate the amount of time for which the video was viewed.

- **Video segment views** indicate the number of times the video segments were viewed.

- **Video completes** refer to the number of times the video was played for the full duration of its length.

Calculated metrics

Calculated metrics allow SiteCatalyst administrators to customize how the metrics that measure the health of their website are defined and shared. This involves using the standard metrics expressed in algebraic expressions, and measuring the outcome as a percent, number, currency, or time. The calculated Metric report appears as a standalone report under Favorites. Calculated metrics cannot combine traffic metric with conversion metric unless visitors and visits have been enabled on the report suite. Then you can use daily unique visitors and visits with conversion metrics in the formula.

For example, if "conversion visitors" is enabled, a calculated metric formula can be set as Orders / Monthly unique visitors. Note that an order is a conversion metric while monthly unique visitors is specific to traffic reports only.

Examples of calculated metrics include:

Page-based metrics

- Page views per visit

- Bounce rate

Cost-based metrics

- Cost per acquisition (CPA)

- Cost per lead/order (CPL)

- Cost per click (CPC)

Revenue-based metrics

- Revenue per search

- Return on ad spend

- Return on investment

This can extend to all standard success events plus all the values imported to SiteCatalyst Attribute Importing and Naming Tool (SAINT) classification. (To learn more about SAINT classification, see "Data classification tasks" in the Appendix.)

Mobile metrics

Mobile views from Version 14 included the page loaded on the mobile device plus any page events that occurred on the page. Version 15 now replaces mobile views with page views which includes page loads on a mobile device but exclude page event hits.

Lifetime metrics

The idea behind lifetime metrics is to keep a cumulative total of values stored in the variable from the start of the implementation. However, the *lifetime* name is confusing, as you might reasonably think that the values were aggregated from the first day of the company or product initiation instead of the first day of the implementation. These metrics are under evaluation in Version 15 at the time of this writing, and it is not clear whether this metric will still be available.

Segments

Segments let you further break down the data to better understand the reasons for spikes and dips. In Version 14, segments were available in the data warehouse reports. As of Version 15, real-time segmentation is available from within SiteCatalyst.

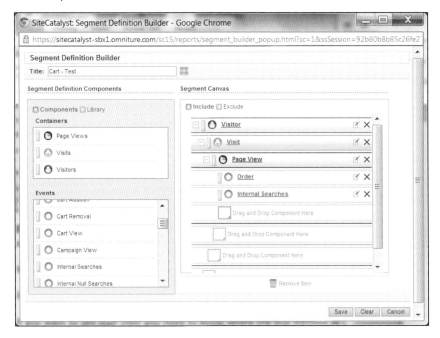

The Segment canvas allows you the flexibility of filtering the data you want to work with.

● **Note:** The Include and Exclude Tabs are independent of each other, but the Include filters run before the Exclude filters. So the segment definition first determines what data needs to be included, then what data needs to be excluded. You can also nest containers. The nested segment rule applies only to the data after its parent rule has been applied.

There are four types of containers that allow you to decide which data you want to include or exclude. These containers have a specific hierarchy, from highest to lowest: Visitors, Visits, Page, and Events.

- The **Visitors** container lets you include and exclude data at the visitor level. This container can nest other containers like visits, page views, and events. A visitor container cannot nest another visitor container.

  For example, if you have a common site for prospects to buy and customers to sign in, you want to ensure that your conversion rate excludes customers who sign in. In this case, you could create a segment that excludes visitors who sign in or excludes visitors where a certain custom traffic or conversion variable identifies them as customers.

- The **Visits** container lets you include or exclude entire sessions or visits. This container can nest other containers like page views and events. A Visits container cannot nest a visitor container or another visit container.

  For example, if you want to exclude visits in which the visitor is clearly looking for customer support details or looking at the investor/media pages, you could use the Visits container.

- The **Page View** container lets you specify at the page level. A page container cannot nest visitors, visits, or another page view container.

  An example of when you would use this in the include filter is to check the influence of a page on conversions. If you're trying to understand how many conversions were influenced by a page view, you could segment visits that included that page view.

- The **Events** container lets you specify filters at the row level. This container cannot nest any other containers. An example of when to use multiple events is to include visits where an internal search event occurred and an order was created.

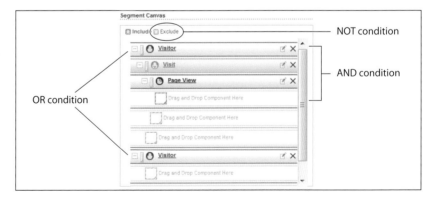

However, the order in which the data is processed determines how the segment needs to be defined:

1   The segment applies the include filter first. The data set now includes data that matches the include filter. If there are multiple containers within the include filter, an "OR" condition is applied.

2   The segment then applies the exclude filters on the data set that already filtered the include criteria. Here, the "NOT" condition is applied.

3   The segment results now include only data that encompasses data matching the include criteria and excludes data from the exclude criteria.

When nesting segment containers, you're trying to discard data and work with data sets that satisfy the filter criteria in the order you have specified:

1   Apply the filter from the outermost container.

2   Apply the first nested rule to the data filtered by the outermost container.

3   Apply the second nested rule to the data filtered by the first nested rule.

4   Repeat until all nested container rules have been calculated. The remaining data is then included in the resulting report.

Segments help you optimize your insights by giving you smaller and pertinent data sets to work with.

Establish thresholds

When we decide on a KPI target, we can't be very precise, since we're trying to predict the future. So we build in an allowable margin of fluctuation. You can make a ballpark estimate of the fluctuations after leafing through the reports available in SiteCatalyst and getting an understanding of your business. If you want to be thorough, you can define upper and lower limits for the threshold of acceptable criteria.

When any metric fluctuates more than the threshold we set, that needs to bubble up for action. This can be set as alerts or with a gauge in dashboard. Alerts are discussed in the next section.

Enter all relevant data in SiteCatalyst

The following tasks will walk you through setting targets, alerts, and thresholds in SiteCatalyst.

Task: Set targets for key performance indicators

Setting targets for key performance indicators gives you the ability to track how the website is performing against a goal. Now we're specifically looking into what KPIs need to be set based on the goals, channels, and metrics applicable to your business.

Here are the steps to add a KPI:

1   Navigate to Favorites > Targets > Manage Targets.

2   Click to add new target and name the target. As a suggestion, you can name the target as Channel_All_Visits when you choose the scope as all channels and the metric as visits. However, when you are listing a target for a specific channel, you could name the target as email_visits. Similarly, you can create a target for all the channels your business portfolio includes for multiple metrics.

3 For the scope, choose either the entire site or a specific variable—you have an exhaustive list of all default variables of SiteCatalyst, custom conversion, and traffic variables.

4 Choose from any metric or events or calculated metric.

5 Choose the start and end dates.

6 Choose granularity. Options are based on the date range you choose:

- For a date range of a day or less than a week, granularity is restricted to daily.

- For a date range of more than a week, granularity is restricted to daily and weekly.

- For a date range of more than a month, granularity is restricted to daily, weekly, and monthly.

- For a date range of more than three months, granularity is restricted to daily, weekly, monthly, and quarterly.

- For a date range of more than a year, granularity is restricted to daily, weekly, monthly, quarterly, and yearly.

Task: Set alerts

Setting alerts will automatically turn your attention to the crucial metrics that you need to assess to inform your future marketing actions. In any report, you're interested in monitoring, navigate to More Actions > Add Alert. Once saved, these alerts can be accessed under the Favorites folder.

Task: Set Calendar Events

Setting Calendar Events may seem like a trivial task, but it's one of the most over-looked items in the Adobe feature set. It helps marketers and analysts explain the fluctuations in data. This is particularly helpful for large businesses where different teams are not colocated.

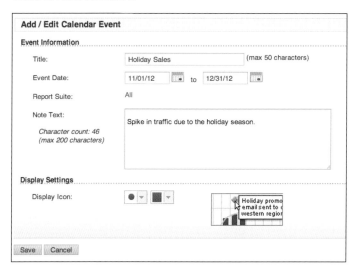

Here are the steps to create a Calendar Event:

1 Navigate to Favorites > Calendar Events.

2 Set the title of the Calendar Event per your company's naming convention.

3 Set the duration of the event.

4 Choose the Report Suite where the event is applicable. You can choose either a specific Report Suite or all Report Suites.

5 In the Note Text section, enter an explanation of how the Calendar Event impacts different metrics.

6 Select Display Settings Icon and Color.

   Although there are four icons and 12 colors—48 potential unique combinations—available to denote events, it can very quickly get confusing to click on multiple icons in a single day to grasp all the events.

SiteCatalyst offers four display icons (circle, diamond, triangle, and square) in 12 colors. It is recommended that you adopt a standard for your organization like the one proposed below:

- Red circle—Indicates issues that cause high fluctuation in data
- Green triangle—Indicates campaign durations
- Black square—Indicates competitor effects
- Yellow diamond—Indicates spikes or dips with no obvious cause

7 Click Save to see the Calendar Events Manager listing with the new event added.

8 Click the Share checkbox to see the event duplicated in the Shared Calendar Events manager.

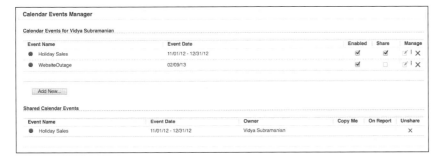

Be aware that notes are not report-specific or metric-specific, so they appear in any report that has the date on the report. Also, if you're doing multi-suite tagging, you may need to replicate the Calendar Event, if you decide to keep the Calendar Event report suite-specific.

Conclusion

In conclusion this chapter helps you understand and create targets, create alerts and establish thresholds.

Next, we'll review each stage of the marketing funnel and see which reports in SiteCatalyst can help you optimize your marketing efforts. These will in turn help you measure against your Key Performance Indicators, which inform you whether or not you are on track to meet your business goal.

Review Questions

1 How many targets would you need to set?

2 How do I set alerts on my target reports?

3 Can I share the calendar with a specific group?

Review Answers

1 Since SiteCatalyst gives you an option to create at metric granularity, you could potentially create a lot of targets. For example, you could create one target per dimension (all custom traffic variables, conversion variables, standard variables, SAINT classification columns) for each metric. You could also create targets for the metrics that correspond to your micro and macro goals.

2 Alerts cannot be set on target reports. Because the alert feature is not currently available in SiteCatalyst, you cannot be notified if or when you hit your target.

3 Calendar events can be private or shared with any user with access to that report suite. It cannot be shared with a specific group or publishing list.

3

AWARENESS ANALYTICS

Lesson overview

In this lesson, you'll learn to analyze awareness data. This will be particularly helpful if you're a channel marketer or a channel analyst who's optimizing channel performance or focusing on cross-channel and multichannel attribution.

The goals of this section are:

- Understanding how to evaluate digital channels to acquire high-quality customers

- Understanding the difference between cross-channel and multichannel attribution

- Determining which Adobe SiteCatalyst reports to run based on your analysis needs

- Identifying issues that impact the data and implementation details that affect the data quality

 This lesson will take 45 minutes to complete.

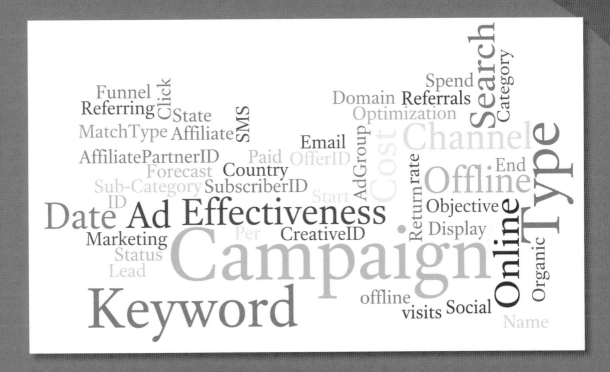

Every day brings new digital marketing channels, offline channels, and technologies. Directing the right message to the right audience at the right time is essential. The awareness stage of the marketing funnel is about optimizing channels to woo prospects to your business.

Assumptions

In Chapter 1, "Preliminary Work," we reviewed many digital channels and offline channels you may be currently using to make your prospective customers aware of your business and the products or services you offer. But how do you evaluate which channel works best for your business? Awareness analytics is the measurement related to your business brand awareness. Channels are a medium for you to make more prospects aware of your business and increase the eyeballs on your site.

Before you run reports in SiteCatalyst, you may need to do some setup. Let's take a quick detour to look at the SiteCatalyst setup assumptions these reports are based on.

To better understand channel analytics, you'll need to aggregate them on several attributes.

SAINT classification

Note: If you're unfamiliar with SAINT classifications, refer to the Appendix.

SiteCatalyst Attribute Importing and Naming Tool (SAINT) classification is a tool that lets you classify variables based on additional attributes. **Table 3.1** introduces some suggested attributes that you can use to aggregate channel data.

Table 3.1 SAINT classification attributes

FOCUS	MEASURES
Campaign ID	(Default key)
Channel name	Email campaign
	SMS
	Organic search
	Paid search
	Social
	Display ad
	Affiliate
	Offline campaign
Channel type	Online
	Offline

(continues on next page)

Table 3.1 SAINT classification attributes (continued)

FOCUS	MEASURES
Campaign country	Name of the country where the campaign is running
Campaign state	Name of the state where the campaign is running
Referring domain	Name of the referring domain
Category	Match type/access type
Subcategory	Additional data
Campaign start date	
Campaign end date	
Campaign status	Active Inactive
Campaign cost	Monetary value
Marketing objective	Drive email subscriptions Drive signups Create awareness of brand Drive conversion
Subscriber ID	Subscriber ID for emails and SMS
Creative ID	Creative ID for emails and display ads
Affiliate Partner ID	Affiliate Partner ID
Ad group	Ad group for paid search
Keyword	Keyword used
Keyword type	Branded and non-branded keywords
Keyword match type	Match type (broad, exact, phrase, negative)
Offer ID	Any discount given (used in SMS campaigns and paper campaigns)

Setting events

If your conversion funnel has multiple steps, it is assumed for simplicity that those are mapped to events 1, 2, and 3 as indicated in **Table 3.2**. When you're doing a deep dive, you may need to reference the event mapping specified by the admin in your SiteCatalyst instance. For example, you could set up each event as a conversion step funnel to see the drop-off on your conversion funnel as well.

Table 3.2 Assumed success events

EVENT NUMBER	STEP IN THE FUNNEL
1	Step 1 in the funnel
2	Step 2 in the funnel
3	Step 3 in the funnel
4	< For subsequent steps in the funnel>
5	Registration
6	Sign up for newsletter

Task: Define KPIs

Let's revisit how to set KPIs for goals. With the focus on awareness analytics in this session, your business goal might be to increase revenue by 25 percent for the financial year. Your KPIs will need to correlate to this goal in terms of awareness metrics. Think backward: to increase conversion by 25 percent, how much would you need to increase traffic to your site from each channel? What conversion rate would you need to factor in? To increase revenue by 25 percent, you'd need to increase traffic at least proportionately. We'll assume for now that the quality of the traffic acquired is the same. (We'll talk more about traffic quality in future lessons.) Examples of KPIs for channels could be:

- **Online to offline channel ratio**

    Online to offline visits ratio = Total number of visits from online channels ÷ Total number of visits from offline channels

    With this ratio, you may be able to determine the ratio of the contribution of both online and offline channels. Trend the online channel visits and notice the spikes from an influence of an offline channel campaign to make a compelling argument of the effectiveness of the offline campaign. Measuring the effectiveness of online channels is definitely easier than measuring that of offline channels. But offline channels can be measured with an approximate scale using vanity URLs and special microsites.

- **Cost per lead or cost per acquisition**

  Cost per lead = Spend on specific channel (like paid search) ÷
  $\qquad$ Total number of leads

  Cost per acquisition = Revenue from a specific channel like PPC ÷
  $\qquad$ Spend on specific channel (like paid search)

  Your target cost per lead (CPL) or cost per acquisition (CPA) will be based on the budget allocated to paid search. With this ratio, if your actual CPL is greater than your target CPL, there might be issues in that campaign, ad group, or keyword that need your attention. If your actual CPL is less than your target CPL, then your campaign, ad group, or keyword is performing on par with your goals (or better).

- **Click-through rate**

  Click-through rate = Total number of clicks ÷ Total number of impressions

  Click-through rate (CTR) is an excellent indicator of how well your paid ads are performing. The logic is pretty straightforward: if you have a high CTR, your ad copy is resonating with visitors who search, while a lower CTR suggests problems with your ad copy, your landing page, or even the way your account is structured. Ensure that you base this decision on a higher sample size to make the right decisions. If your CTR is high and your conversion rate is low, the ad copy messaging may not be reinforced on your landing page.

- **Return on ad spend**

  Return on ad spend = Total revenue from paid search channel like paid search ÷
  $\qquad$ Total spend on paid search channel like paid search

  With return on ad spend (ROAS), you can determine the overall profitability of your ad spend. Compare the revenue to the spend to determine whether you have a positive or a negative return.

Real-world example

Your company sells flowers online. One of your major marketing spends is on television commercials. By placing an offer code that is unique to television, you can tie conversions back to this offline channel with at least some precision. You're also planning an SMS campaign with another offer code. Your awareness KPI is the online to offline ratio to determine each channel's effectiveness in driving visits to your website:

- Ratio of online to offline visits and conversion. This could be further segmented by channel name (TV, SMS, and other online acquisition channels).

- Visits by region. If you targeted a specific geographical location for the TV ad, what is the impact on your online channels trended over time?

- New visits from SMS subscribers. How do the conversions compare?

Table 3.3 suggests an approach to understanding which SiteCatalyst reports can help you understand factors that affect the KPI. Deepen your analysis by looking at the data with multiple metrics, then sharpen your insights by segmenting the data. Segments can include any custom traffic variable, any custom conversion variable, and any SAINT classification.

Table 3.3 Awareness/channel marketing reports and metrics

FOCUS	MEASURES	SITECATALYST REPORT	METRICS
Channel type effectiveness	Online vs. offline campaign effectiveness Halo effect of campaigns	Campaigns > Campaign status	Visits Visitors Units Orders Downloads Cart additions Cart removals Revenue Cost per acquisition
Channel effectiveness	Compare channel performance	Campaigns > Channel name	
Channel forecast	Compare channel performance to target	Admin > Target > (Create a target for each metric)	
Channel funnel optimization	Channel funnel optimization	Campaigns > Campaign conversion funnel	Event 1 indicating step 1 of the funnel Event 2 indicating step 2 of the funnel Event 3 indicating step 3 of the funnel Orders Revenue
Referrals	Key referring sites	Traffic sources > Referring domains	
		Traffic sources > Original referring domains	
		Traffic sources > Referrers	Instances
		Traffic sources > Referrer types	

Task: Analyze marketing efforts effectiveness

The primary goal of channel analytics is to measure the effectiveness of the channels that create awareness. In the previous section, we looked at several attributes that channels can be aggregated by to determine their effectiveness on multiple scales.

Report: Online vs. offline campaigns

Navigate to Campaigns > Tracking code > Channel Type. This report focuses on analyzing the success of online campaigns versus offline campaigns.

Navigate to Campaigns > Tracking code > Campaign Status. Filter by inactive status. This report focuses on analyzing the halo effect of inactive campaigns.

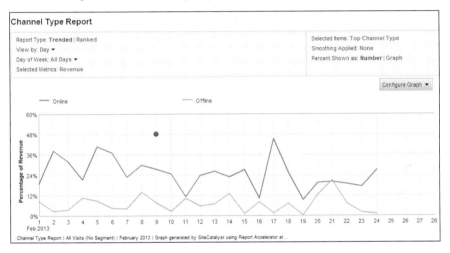

Key insights

Reports analyzing online versus offline campaigns can help answer questions such as:

- **How effective are your offline campaigns in driving online sales?** You can determine whether your offline campaigns effectively drive sales online by trending the online campaigns and looking for spikes in traffic on the days when you're running an offline promotion. When you run a TV ad, does it create a buzz to drive more visitors to your site? Compare that with the buzz created by a print ad. Is there a difference?

- **What's the halo effect from campaigns that are no longer active?** This will also help you determine the point at which the campaign starts having diminishing returns after it is inactive. For example, if you're running a PR campaign, there may be some spillover visits from visitors who read the article after the campaign was officially closed.

- **How does the ROI compare in online and offline campaigns?** It's important to know the ROI of every channel, but comparing online and offline ROIs isn't exactly comparing apples to apples. A visitor might have heard about your brand in a TV ad or a press release, but used online search to arrive at your site. Also, with print media, you may be using a vanity URL, but many of your visitors might not use it. Use this data directionally, but don't use the numbers as the only guiding star to make your spend decisions.

Interpretation of report data

In interpreting the data with respect to online versus offline campaigns, keep the following in mind:

- Organic search does not have campaign tracking and hence will not be part of the reports of online and offline campaigns.

- If you have client-side redirects, the campaign data will be lost unless the URL parameters are programmatically appended to the page the visitor is redirected to.

Code implementation and console settings

The assumption here is that you're tracking offline campaigns by navigating them to a campaign-specific microsite or appending necessary URL parameter tracking.

The `s.campaign` parameter must be updated once with every session.

SAINT classification needs to be up to date for all online and offline campaigns based on the assumptions described earlier in this chapter.

Report: Channel performance

Navigate to Campaigns > Tracking Code > Channel Name. This report focuses on analyzing the effectiveness of all the channels, including ad metrics, click-throughs, bounces, orders, units, and revenue.

Navigate to Marketing Channels > Channel Overview Report. This report focuses on analyzing the attribution of channels in the first and last clicks.

Channel Type by Channel Name	Visits		Orders		Units		Revenue ▼	
1. Online	1,312		218		900		$11,464	
1. Paid Search	472	12.1%	61	6.7%	244	6.8%	$3,072	6.6%
2. Email	254	6.5%	47	5.2%	201	5.6%	$2,355	5.1%
3. Social	144	3.7%	24	2.7%	104	2.9%	$1,489	3.2%
4. Display Advertising	215	5.5%	22	2.4%	107	3.0%	$1,403	3.0%
5. Mobile	154	4.0%	25	2.8%	98	2.7%	$1,351	2.9%
6. Partners	183	4.7%	21	2.3%	73	2.0%	$916	2.0%
7. Affiliates	148	3.8%	18	2.0%	73	2.0%	$878	1.9%

Key insights

Reports comparing channel performance can help answer questions such as:

- **Which channel is most effective in driving traffic and revenue?** Since you set up the SAINT classification, you can break down the online channel by channel name to determine which channel drives the most traffic and conversions.

- **Which channel is delivering qualified traffic?** Relate the quality of traffic by comparing the bounce rate across channels. This is a great indicator to measure channel performance.

- **Which channel and campaign have the most impact in terms of ROI? How should you plan your ad spend?** With the different spend across different campaigns, you can gauge the ROI of different channels to better allocate your spend.

- **Which channel leads visitors toward engagement or persuasion rather than conversion?** Some channels are used more often to drive visitors who are looking to learn and orient. They, for example, may have a higher tendency to use unbranded search keywords in organic search. Once they're very specific in wanting to convert, their tendency to use a branded keyword would be higher in search or they might directly visit your site. You can use this information to optimize your landing page performance.

Interpretation of report data

In interpreting the data comparing channel performance, keep in mind that the analysis here will be as accurate as the data in the SAINT classification.

Code implementation and console settings

The assumption here is that you're tracking offline campaigns by directing visitors to a campaign-specific microsite or URL appending necessary tracking.

SAINT classification needs to be up to date for all online and offline campaigns based on the assumptions described earlier in this chapter.

Report: Referring domains

Navigate to Traffic Sources > Referring Domains. This report focuses on analyzing the referring domains that your visitors are coming from.

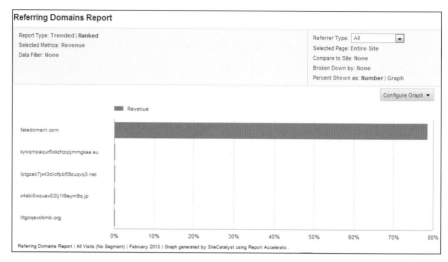

Key insights

Reports comparing referring domains can help answer questions such as:

- **Which domain is referring most of the traffic that has a high conversion rate?** This analysis can help you determine whether you can optimize links from these domains.

- **For traffic from a particular domain, which product are visitors most inclined toward?** You can optimize your landing page content based on the product that most appeals to visitors. For example, if the referring domain is from a women-centered site, it might be safe to assume that the bulk of the visitors referred by this site may be women. So your landing page can be optimized to target this segment.

- **For traffic from a particular domain, are visitors more inclined toward learning or converting? For traffic from a particular domain, are visitors more inclined toward engaging in the text content or the video/rich media content?** Again, this points to landing page optimization, where you can optimize for learning and orienting or conversion. Also, what type of content do visitors prefer? Those from a site geared toward teens might prefer videos to text content.

Interpretation of report data

In interpreting the data analyzing referring domains, keep in mind that as long as the referrer information is passed in the HTTP header, SiteCatalyst will automatically read that data. However, if the visitor is redirected at the landing page to another page, you'll lose the referrer information (assuming the redirected page is not tagged with SiteCatalyst or it is not explicitly forwarding the referrer). Also, no referrer is passed if the true referring domain is using the HTTPS protocol (SSL).

Code implementation and console settings

No code implementations are necessary. The s.referrer is auto-populated. It can, however, be overwritten for pages that are redirecting.

Report: Referrers and referrer types

Navigate to Traffic Sources > Referrers. This report focuses on analyzing the referring pages to your site. A referring site is a site that has a link to your site. For example, if your report suite is tracking data for myexamplesite.com and if a link in abc.com sends the visitor to your site, then abc.com will be listed as referrer to your site. However, if you indicated that xyz.com is also your internal site in the `s.linkInternalFilters` variable, it will not be included as a referrer.

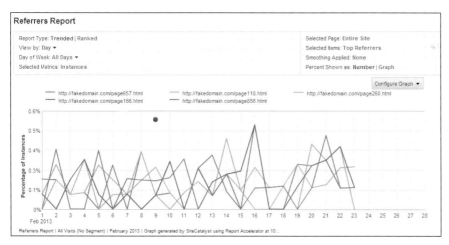

Key insights

Reports of referrers and referrer types can help answer questions such as:

- **Who are the top referrers to your site?** You can determine which referrer is contributing the most to your bottom line. Work to get more links to your site from their site. Rather than evaluating referrers by visit and visitor counts, evaluate them based on their contribution to your macro and micro goals.

- **What are the demographics of your visitors?** You can determine the demographics of your visitors based on the referring site description.

Interpretation of report data

In interpreting the data about referrers, keep the following in mind:

- Referrer information is carried forward only to the next page. So if your landing page has a redirect, the referrer information is lost.

- You'll see http://www.google.com listed as a referrer to your site when users have clicked I'm Feeling Lucky and reached your site. However, this happens only when your site is the first search result for the keyword phrase searched by the user. The same is true if the user is coming from, say, the iGoogle homepage.

- If your site is loaded from within an iframe, the referrer will match the address loaded in the parent window or frame. For example, if you go to www.mysite.com, and there's an iframe that loads www.yoursite.com with SiteCatalyst code, the referrer on the image request in the iframe would be www.mysite.com.

Code implementation and console settings

Referrer data depends on the accuracy of internal URL filters and `s.linkInternalFilters` settings.

Task: Analyze email marketing campaigns

The first type of external online campaign we'll examine is one that is commonly used by many types of organizations: email marketing.

Email performance indicates the effectiveness of email campaigns by:

- Comparing the overall email campaigns on different metrics

- Comparing the campaigns to forecast

- Determining how effective the email creative was—whether it drives more conversion or engagement

- Determining how many visits it takes to convince a prospect using a nurture campaign

- Optimizing the funnel for traffic

Table 3.4 presents a suggested approach to using SiteCatalyst reports to help you understand email analytics.

Table 3.4 Email marketing reports and metrics

FOCUS	MEASURES	SITECATALYST REPORT	METRICS
Email campaign effectiveness	Awareness	Campaigns > Campaign name = "Email"	Clicks (Additional metrics listed in Chapter 9 if you enable Adobe Genesis Integration) Visits Visitors Bounces Average time on site Orders Units Revenue
Forecast	Email campaign forecast	Admin > Target > Email target for all metrics	Any metric
Email creative	Email creative effectiveness	Campaigns > Creative ID	
Email subscriber	Nurture campaign / Drip campaign effectiveness	Campaigns > Subscriber ID	Visit number
Funnel	Email channel funnel optimization	Campaigns > Campaign conversion funnel Select filter with "channel name" as email	Event 1 indicating step 1 of the funnel Event 2 indicating step 2 of the funnel Event 3 indicating step 3 of the funnel Orders Revenue

Report: Email channel performance

Navigate to Campaigns > Tracking Code > Channel Name. Click on email. This report focuses on analyzing the effectiveness of the email channel.

Channel Name Summary: Email		Feb 2013	
Success Metric		**Total**	**% of All**
1.	Revenue	$2,355	5.1%
2.	Orders	47	5.2%
3.	Units	201	5.6%
4.	Carts	112	4.5%
5.	Cart Views	107	4.4%
6.	Cart Additions	93	3.9%
7.	Cart Removals	9	3.1%
8.	Checkouts	73	4.0%
9.	Internal Searches	44	4.2%
10.	Internal Null Searches	21	4.9%
11.	Product Views (Custom)	160	4.1%
12.	Page Views (Custom)	912	4.2%
13.	Newsletter Signups	65	3.8%
14.	Emails Sent	0	0.0%
15.	Emails Opened	0	0.0%
16.	Emails Bounced	0	0.0%
17.	Emails Unsubscribed	0	0.0%

Key insights

Comparing email channel performance can help answer questions such as:

- **How much traffic is the email channel generating compared to the subscribers emailed?** You can determine the success of your email campaign based on your subscriber base. This also reflects on the quality of your subscriber base. You could have campaigns targeted to visitors opting in to your email campaign.

- **What is the bounce rate of the traffic from email campaigns?** If the email creative was targeted to a specific audience, this will help you determine whether or not the landing page was of interest to them.

- **Are visitors engaging in the key pages that you want them to?** Once you get a visitor to your site, you need to determine whether he is engaged in your key pages. You can run campaign reports for email traffic and further segment that traffic by visits in which at least one key page was visited.

- **Which email campaign has the most ROI?** The return on investment incorporates the revenue and the cost of the campaign to determine the ROI on the campaign.

- **Can you integrate offline data like subscribers, bounces, and emails opened and read?** Using the Genesis Integration described in Chapter 9, "External Data Analytics," you can analyze this to get a holistic look at your email channel.

Interpretation of report data

In interpreting the data comparing email channel performance, keep the following in mind:

- Email bounces are different from bounces in web analytics. Email bounces refer to emails that were not delivered to the recipients due to email server issues. Most vendors classify bounces as hard bounces and soft bounces. Some vendors also classify technical bounces and general bounces. Knowing the types of bounces will help you determine whether the subscriber should be excluded from future email lists.

- The metrics **email opened** and **read** are normally skewed, since most email clients like Outlook and Gmail don't load images explicitly. So the pixel call is not fired.

- The metric **clicks** will accurately reflect the number of clicks received, but if the same visitor clicks on the link multiple times, the visitor will be counted as many times as he clicked on the link.

Code implementation and console settings

An email campaign is uniquely identified in a URL parameter (reserved for tracking campaigns) and that information is stored in `s.campaign` on the landing page of the visit.

If there is a redirect on the landing page, the campaign tracking information should be forwarded to the redirected page.

SAINT classification needs to be up to date for all online and offline campaigns based on the assumptions described earlier in this chapter.

Task: Analyze mobile (SMS/MMS) marketing

Another powerful type of external online campaign is mobile messaging. SMS and MMS are more often used by retailers and restaurants that are trying to reach customers with offers and discounts. Then again there are companies that use SMS to create brand awareness or ask a quick survey question. They are more targeted to getting the visitor to complete a specific goal in a specific timeframe. This channel is not designed like the other channels to increase engagement. For example, retailers may send immediate offers that customers can enjoy. Bear in mind that the SMS channel is similar to email in that subscribers must opt in to be messaged with an offer.

The main aspects for analysis are:

- Comparing the overall reach of the campaign
- Segmenting the subscribers by offers and click-through

Table 3.5 presents a suggested approach to using SiteCatalyst reports to help you understand SMS and MMS analytics.

Table 3.5 SMS/MMS marketing reports and metrics

FOCUS	MEASURES	SITECATALYST REPORT	METRICS
SMS campaign effectiveness	Awareness	Campaigns > Campaign name = SMS	Visits
			Visitors
			Bounces
			Orders
			Units
			Revenue
Forecast	SMS campaign forecast	Admin > Target > SMS target for all metrics	Any metric
Funnel	Email channel funnel optimization	Campaigns > Campaign conversion funnel Select filter with "channel name" as SMS	Orders Revenue

Report: SMS channel performance

Navigate to Campaigns > Tracking Code > Channel Name. Click on SMS. This report focuses on analyzing the effectiveness of the SMS and MMS channels.

Key insights

Comparing SMS channel performance can help answer questions such as:

- **How much of a revenue spike do you receive with SMS offers?** SMS offers can be used to help bridge the gap between your revenue goal and the revenue currently realized. These campaigns can be targeted to increasing the volume of visitors, but having to compromise on the price per unit. You will, however, make up the lost revenue in quantity.

- **What's the conversion rate of the traffic from SMS campaigns?** Compare the number of SMS offers sent to the orders you may be getting from these explicit campaigns. You can also determine whether or not the SMS model is well suited to your business. For example, few visitors will look for an offer on a BMW in an SMS channel, right?

- **Are you able to integrate offline data like subscribers and number of unsubscribes?** Note that the SMS channel is similar to the email channel in that subscribers must opt in, and they can choose to opt out. These are the data points you can use to evaluate the success of your specific SMS campaign and of SMS as a channel.

Interpretation of report data

In interpreting the data comparing SMS channel performance, keep in mind that SMS offers will cause an immediate and short spike in traffic.

Code implementation and console settings

These settings apply to SMS campaign reports:

- An SMS campaign is uniquely identified in a URL parameter (reserved for tracking campaigns) and that information is stored in `s.campaign` on the landing page of the visit.

- If there is a redirect on the landing page, the campaign tracking information should be forwarded to the redirected page.

- SAINT classification needs to be up to date for SMS campaigns.

Task: Analyze search engine marketing (organic search optimization)

SiteCatalyst tracks search engine optimization (SEO) data differently from other channels. It takes the total traffic from all search engines and excludes the paid search traffic. To ensure that SEO data is correct, ensure that the paid search detection rule is in place. The main aspects for analysis are:

- Determining SEO effectiveness
- Optimizing keywords
- Optimizing search ranking in search engines

Table 3.6 presents a suggested approach to using SiteCatalyst reports to help you understand organic search analytics.

Table 3.6 Organic search reports and metrics

FOCUS	MEASURES	SITECATALYST REPORT	METRICS
Keyword optimization	Optimize keywords across search engines	Traffic sources > Search keywords–natural	Visits Visitors Bounces Orders Units Revenue
Search engine	Optimize keywords by a search engine	Traffic sources > Search engines–natural	Visits Visitors Bounces Orders Units Revenue
Forecast	SEO traffic forecast	Admin > Target > Choose search keywords or search engine	Any metric
Keyword page rank Optimization	Keywords optimization for page rank	Traffic sources > All search page ranking	

Report: Organic search keyword performance

Navigate to Traffic Sources > Search Keywords–Natural. This report focuses on analyzing the effectiveness of organic search keywords, including metrics such as bounces, orders, units, and revenue.

Key insights

Analyzing organic keyword performance can help answer questions such as:

- **What is the ROI of organic search? How do conversions in your organic keywords compare to those in paid search or internal search?** You can use this report to understand which keywords are being used in organic searches, paid searches, and internal searches. Break this down by Traffic Sources > All Search Page Ranking to see the impact of search rankings.

- **What types of keywords are best at driving engagement versus conversion?** Different keywords indicate the visitor's level of awareness about your product. A visitor may tend to choose broad and generic search terms when he's learning and orienting as opposed to an exact and specific search phrase when he is ready to convert.

- **Which keywords drive high and low bounce rates? Which landing pages are optimized for which keywords?** Analyze the landing pages by keywords and bounce rate to get an idea of which landing pages are most effective.

- **How are the different types of keywords performing?** Compare branded and non-branded search terms to evaluate brand awareness. Also, if you compare this data with paid search keywords and internal search keywords, you can optimize your landing pages for more SEO-related keywords.

Interpretation of report data

In interpreting the data about organic search word performance, keep the following in mind:

- On October 18, 2011, Google released an update to its search policies that encrypts search keywords for all users who are logged in to a Google account. This change hampers data collection of keywords by any analytics tool. When a keyword is unavailable and the referrer is a search engine, SiteCatalyst attributes it to "keyword unavailable." Recent versions of Chrome and Firefox also default to secure search and thus block the keyword even when visitors are not logged in to a Google account (http://marketingland.com/chrome-to-gain-encryption-31085). Firefox 14, launched in summer 2012, defaults to Google SSL Search. Google+ users increased the number of logged-in Google users attributing to this. The Safari browser in iOS6 defaults to Google

SSL search as well and, at the time of this writing, shows up as direct traffic (http://searchengineland.com/ios-6-change-google-traffic-from-safari-135002).

- Organic traffic is not tracked using campaign-tracking variables and hence is not part of the campaigns report.

- Search engine and search keyword values cannot persist longer than the visit in which they occurred. Navigate to Admin > Admin Console > Report Suites. On a specific report suite, Edit Settings > Conversion > Finding Methods allows you to set cookie expiration based on custom events and other conversion events, but in this case, the search engine or keyword value can expire only if the event happens in the same visit as the search or keyword value, otherwise the expiry will default to a visit.

Code implementation and console settings

When you review reports on organic keyword performance, a few things to note are:

- Organic traffic in SiteCatalyst is calculated as the traffic from search engines minus the traffic from paid search (this is deduced from the rules set in paid search detection in the admin section). It is also impacted by the settings in the finding methods in the admin section.

- Keywords cannot be classified unless they are assigned to a custom conversion variable.

Report: Organic search engine effectiveness

Navigate to Traffic Sources > Search Engines–Natural. This report focuses on analyzing the effectiveness of organic search keywords, including metrics such as bounces, orders, units, and revenue.

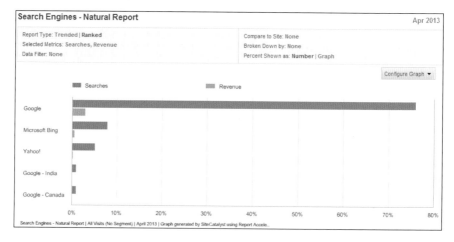

Key insights

Understanding organic search engine effectiveness can help answer questions such as:

- **How do tier-one search engines perform against tier-two search engines?** The tier-one search engines—Google, Yahoo!, and Bing—constitute most of your search traffic. You could make a conscious decision to focus your efforts on these search engines rather than the tier-two search engines, which include all search engines other than these three.

- **Which search engine is optimizing landing pages for keywords?** You could run the search engine reports and further break them down by entry page to gauge performance. Comparing visits, the bounces and the conversion would give you a strong indicator of the pages crawled tagged by each search engine.

Interpretation of report data

In interpreting the data in reports of organic search engine effectiveness, keep in mind that Google lists the search engine for each country separately (Google Canada, Google Australia). So if you're looking for traffic and conversions from Google as a whole, you may need to add all that up.

Code implementation and console settings

If you have no data in the natural search engines report, then you haven't set up paid search detection. Until paid search detection is set up, SiteCatalyst can't distinguish between paid clicks and natural clicks.

Task: Analyze paid search engine marketing

SiteCatalyst tracks Pay Per Click (PPC) data to determine the quality of your paid search campaigns.

SiteCatalyst tracks paid search by the paid search detection rule in place. The main aspects for analysis are:

- Determining paid search effectiveness
- Optimizing keywords
- Determining how paid search traffic guides engagement and conversion

Table 3.7 presents a suggested approach to using SiteCatalyst reports to help you understand paid search analytics.

Table 3.7 Paid search reports and metrics

FOCUS	MEASURES	SITECATALYST REPORT	METRICS
Campaign effectiveness	Compare campaign performance	Campaigns > Campaign name	Impressions
			Clicks
			Click-through rate
			Visits
			Visitors
			Bounces
			Orders
			Units
			Revenue
			Cost per lead
			Cost per acquisition
Forecast	Paid search traffic forecast	Admin > Target > Choose paid search	Any metric
Funnel	Email channel funnel optimization	Campaigns > Campaign conversion funnel	Event 1 indicating step 1 of the funnel
		Select filter with channel name as paid search	Event 2 indicating step 2 of the funnel
			Event 3 indicating step 3 of the funnel
			Orders
			Revenue

Report: Paid search performance

Navigate to Campaigns > Tracking Code > Channel Name. This report focuses on analyzing the effectiveness of all the channels, including metrics such as click-throughs, bounces, orders, units, and revenue.

Key insights

Analyzing paid search performance can help answer questions such as:

- **How do conversions in your paid keywords compare to conversions in organic search or internal search?** Compare the conversion from your paid search to determine the effectiveness of the keywords you're bidding on.

- **What types of keywords are best at driving engagement versus conversion?** Compare the keywords that are driving conversions with the ones that don't by segmenting this report by paid search traffic. These can help you determine your spend.

- **Which keywords drive high and low bounce rates? What are the primary driving factors to visitors using your paid search?** If the bulk of your visitors use paid search to find your site and then log in to their account, you're effectively paying for existing customers and not acquiring new ones.

- **Which ad group or campaigns perform best? How do the different types of keywords perform?** Compare branded and non-branded keywords and their conversion rates. Also compare how broad match, exact match, phrase match, and negative match correlate to the conversion. You can optimize your campaigns better.

- **What is the ROI of paid search, cost per click (CPC), cost per acquisition (CPA), and return on ad spend (ROAS)?** These calculated metrics are also some of the key performance indicators for how your search portfolio is doing.

- **What quality score or average position are most of your top keywords in?** You'll need to import this data into SiteCatalyst using SAINT classification to evaluate it.

Code implementation and console settings

Paid search data depends on the accuracy of the `s.campaign` information and the paid search detection set up.

Report: Paid search engine effectiveness

Navigate to Traffic Sources > Search Engines–Paid. This report elaborates on the search engines used by your visitors for paid search.

Key insight

Understanding paid search engine effectiveness can help answer questions such as:

- **Which search engines should you spend more with?** You can understand the search engine with the higher number of impressions, click-through rate, and the number of conversions it translates to. That can help you effectively allocate funds across different search engines.

Code implementation and console settings

In interpreting the data in reports of paid search engine effectiveness, keep in mind that paid search detection rules need to be set up.

Report: Paid keywords performance

Navigate to Traffic Sources > Search Keywords–Paid. This report focuses on analyzing the effectiveness of all the channels, including metrics such as click-throughs, bounces, orders, units, and revenue.

Key insights

Analyzing paid keyword performance can help answer questions such as:

- **Are you bidding on the right keywords?** Compare the conversions on each keyword by match type to determine whether you have the right portfolio of keywords.

- **What types of keywords are performing better at driving engagement versus conversion?** Based on your business, they might be certain branded and generic terms that are better at driving visitors toward conversion.

- **Is your landing page optimized for paid search?** Add the CTR, bounce rate, the time on site metrics to determine whether the landing age is optimized for the experience that a visitor is expecting when he uses specific keywords.

- **How are the different ad groups and campaigns performing?** Aggregate the data by search engine, ad groups, campaigns, keyword, and match type using SAINT classification to determine the performance of all the keywords.

- **What is paid search ROI?** Based on the KPI, add the metrics that best pertain to your business: the cost per acquisition (CPA), the cost per sales (CPS), or the return on ad spend (ROAS) will help you determine whether you're bidding on the right terms.

Code implementation and console settings

The assumption here is that you are tracking paid search campaigns by a campaign-specific code appended to the URL.

SAINT classification needs to be up to date for all keywords based on the assumptions described earlier in this chapter.

Task: Analyze social media campaigns

When you're tracking social media metrics, a unique type of external online marketing, the primary indicator may not be ROI. Prospects are heavily influenced by social media. They read reviews or discuss products with their friends, but rarely use a campaign link from a social networking site. This translates to lower conversions from social media. However, there's no debating that social media adds high value.

The main aspects for analysis are:

- Determining social media effectiveness
- Determining which social site contributes to campaign effectiveness

Table 3.8 presents a suggested approach to using SiteCatalyst reports to help you understand social media analytics.

Table 3.8 Social media reports and metrics

FOCUS	MEASURES	SITECATALYST REPORT	METRICS
Campaign effectiveness	Compare campaign performance	Campaigns > Campaign name	Visits
			Visitors
			Bounces
			Orders
			Units
			Revenue
Forecast	Social media forecast	Admin > Target > Choose social media	Any metric
Funnel	Social media channel funnel optimization	Campaigns > Campaign conversion funnel	Event 1 indicating step 1 of the funnel
		Select filter with channel name as social media	Event 2 indicating step 2 of the funnel
			Event 3 indicating step 3 of the funnel
			Orders
			Revenue

Report: Social channel performance

Navigate to Campaigns > Tracking Code > Channel Name. Click on social.

Key insights

Reports comparing social channel performance can help answer questions such as:

- **How is your customer base trying to reach you, and what is your visibility?** You can use several metrics to determine the number of fans, followers, and subscribers you have. This data is not traditionally available in SiteCatalyst, but you can import the data into SiteCatalyst or use Genesis Integration (described in Chapter 9) to view that data.

- **Is the content on your site engaging enough to be shared socially?** By tracking clicks of the social buttons on your site, you can determine how many times content on your site is being tweeted or shared on Facebook and other social networking sites. The interactions with the social buttons can be tracked in SiteCatalyst using the custom traffic and conversion variables.

- **When you run social media campaigns, what is the traffic and conversion impact on your site?** By tracking the correlation between the social media campaigns and the traffic conversion patterns, you can determine the effect of your brand evangelists. Also, you can correlate the impact of negative sentiments in social media to the loss of revenue.

Interpretation of report data

The campaigns report can only provide insights on visits in which a social media campaign had a link to your site and had campaign tracking enabled. Also, some metrics are proprietary to social media sites and are not shared with SiteCatalyst. SiteCatalyst maintains a list of referring domains it classifies as social networking sites and only visits from those sites fall in the social media bucket.

Code implementation and console settings

The campaign link needs a URL parameter that identifies it uniquely.

Task: Analyze online display advertising

Display advertising is a popular external online campaign choice to make prospects aware of your products and your company. Analytics assess the importance of banner ads and contextual advertising to determine the impact of display advertising on conversion.

The main aspects for analysis are:

- Determining display advertising effectiveness
- Comparing performance to target
- Analyzing funnel optimization

Table 3.9 presents a suggested approach to using SiteCatalyst reports to help you understand display advertising analytics.

Table 3.9 Display advertising reports and metrics

FOCUS	MEASURES	SITECATALYST REPORT	METRICS
Campaign effectiveness	Compare campaign performance	Campaigns > Campaign name	Visits
			Visitors
			Bounces
			Orders
			Units
			Revenue
			Cost per lead
			Cost per acquisition
Forecast	Display forecast	Admin > Target > Choose display	Any metric
Funnel	Display channel funnel optimization	Campaigns > Campaign conversion funnel	Event 1 indicating step 1 of the funnel
		Select filter with channel name as display	Event 2 indicating step 2 of the funnel
			Event 3 indicating step 3 of the funnel
			Orders
			Revenue

Report: Display channel performance

Navigate to Campaigns > Tracking Code > Channel Name. Filter by display. This report focuses on analyzing the effectiveness of all the channels, including metrics such as click-throughs, bounces, orders, units, and revenue.

Key insights

Reports comparing display channel performance can help answer questions such as:

- **Which display campaign is driving the most traffic and conversions?** Compare the calculated metrics you created for paid search like ROAS, CPC, and CPA. But don't do a complete apples-to-apples comparison between paid search and display. Stanford and Yahoo! partnered to study of the impact of display advertising on user search behavior using a field experiment. Their results indicated that users exposed to a display ad submit 5 percent to 25 percent more relevant search queries compared to users who were not (http://ilpubs.stanford.edu:8090/993/2/displayadinfluenceTR.pdf).

- **How effective are display ads?** There has been a lot of discussion of the effectiveness of display ads in terms of comparing the traditional click-through rate. The view-through rate measures the number of times an ad impression is served to a visitor who subsequently visited the site. SiteCatalyst does not have the view-through rate as a default metric. That data must be imported into SiteCatalyst using SAINT classification for each display ad.

Code implementation and console settings

The URL parameter for the link used in the display ads needs a unique value. That value must be set in the `s.campaignID` variable on the landing page that the visitor arrives on. SAINT classification can be used to add additional attributes.

Task: Analyze affiliate marketing

The final type of external online campaign we'll consider leverages your relationships with affiliates online. Analyzing affiliate traffic helps determine which affiliates are sending you quality traffic. In this context, the term *affiliates* refers to sites that promote your site and products either free of charge or for a fee.

The main aspects for analysis are:

- Determining display advertising effectiveness
- Comparing performance to target
- Analyzing funnel optimization

Table 3.10 presents a suggested approach to using SiteCatalyst reports to help you understand affiliate analytics.

Table 3.10 Affiliates reports and metrics

FOCUS	MEASURES	SITECATALYST REPORT	METRICS
Campaign effectiveness	Compare campaign performance	Campaigns > Campaign name	Visits
			Visitors
			Bounces
			Orders
			Units
			Revenue
			Cost per lead
			Cost per acquisition
Forecast	Affiliates forecast	Admin > Target > Choose affiliates	Any metric
Funnel	Affiliates channel funnel optimization	Campaigns > Campaign conversion funnel	Event 1 indicating step 1 of the funnel
		Select filter with channel name as affiliates	Event 2 indicating step 2 of the funnel
			Event 3 indicating step 3 of the funnel
			Orders
			Revenue

Report: Affiliate channel performance

Navigate to Campaigns > Tracking Code > Channel Name. Click on affiliate. This report focuses on analyzing the effectiveness of all the channels, including metrics such as click-throughs, bounces, orders, units, and revenue.

Key insight

Reports comparing affiliate channel performance can help answer questions such as:

- **Which affiliate sites drive the most traffic but not conversions?** A truly great affiliate partner sends quality visitors who fit the demographics of your target audience. There have been several instances of affiliate fraud where the affiliate site sends a large number of visitors, but the visitors don't fit the profile of visitors that your business requires.

- **How are performance of affiliates trending?** You can compare the performance of multiple affiliates to see which affiliate drives better visits and conversions. The trends willl also display consistencies or artificial spikes in the traffic and conversions affiliates bring.

- **Which affiliates do better with different types of promotions?** If you are targeting a broad spectrum of visitor demographics, each affiliate might be specializing in bringing visitors with a specific demographic set. Segment your campaigns by the visitor persona to get a better understanding of that.

Code implementation and console settings

The assumption here is that you are tracking offline campaigns by navigating them to a campaign-specific microsite or URL appending necessary tracking. SAINT classification needs to be up to date for all online and offline campaigns based on the assumptions described earlier in this chapter.

Task: Analyze internal online campaigns

The campaigns we've discussed up to this point have all been external. Internal campaigns consist of cross-selling banners on your own site or sites. The performance indicators below assume that eVar1 is tracking internal campaign names. The great advantage of internal banners, of course, is that there is no cost to place them on your site. Of course, you might be giving up ad space you could sell to others, and thus be losing revenue.

Table 3.11 presents a suggested approach to using SiteCatalyst reports to help you understand internal campaign analytics.

Table 3.11 Internal campaigns reports and metrics

FOCUS	MEASURES	SITECATALYST REPORT	METRICS
Campaign effectiveness	Compare campaign performance	Custom conversion > Variable reserved for internal campaigns	Instances Orders Units Revenue
Forecast	Internal campaign forecast	Admin > Target > Choose custom conversion variable	Any metric
Funnel	Internal campaign channel funnel optimization	Custom conversion > Variable reserved for internal campaigns	Event 1 indicating step 1 of the funnel Event 2 indicating step 2 of the funnel Event 3 indicating step 3 of the funnel Orders Revenue

Report: Internal banner and links performance

Navigate to Custom Conversion > 1–10 > eVar1 (assuming custom conversion variable 1 is being used for internal campaigns). This report focuses on analyzing the effectiveness of internal banners and links, including metrics such as instances, bounces, orders, units, and revenue.

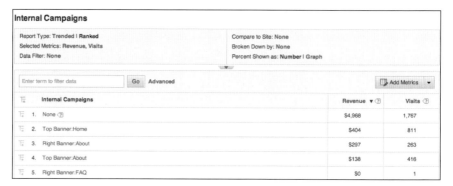

Key insights

Analyzing the performance of internal banners and links can help you answer questions such as:

- **Which internal banner influences more conversions**? Determine which internal creative is influencing the visitor more by comparing the performance metrics across the internal links and banners. Bear in mind that the results may be skewed by the placement of the banners and links.

- **Which internal banner drives more clicks?** An interesting story or offer in an internal banner may drive the traffic to the banner. So to get a deep analysis, you could look at the pathing report to see if the navigation on your site was altered with the internal banner.

Code implementation and console settings

When comparing internal banner and links performance, be sure to enable participation metrics on links to see which of them contribute to your conversion more.

Task: Understand multichannel and cross-channel visits and attribution

Now that we've looked at each channel independently, let's compare performance across all of the channels. Multichannel and cross-channel are used interchangeably, but there is a subtle difference between them.

The term *multichannel* indicates that you're treating every visitor the same, giving each of them the same messaging and putting the onus on them to decide which channel works best for them. You're casting a wide net to a broad range of prospects in an effort to increase acquisition of visitors. The quality of the visitors is not the focus in multichannel campaigns. For example, if a visitor uses paid search to visit your site and then uses organic search in the visit in which he converts, that's an example of a multichannel campaign.

On the other hand, a *cross-channel* campaign typically involves segmenting traffic from one channel or visitors from a single demographic in an effort to pitch them a message that is tailored specifically to them. If you target all the customers who abandoned their shopping cart with an email campaign offering a heavy discount to lure them back to the site and complete their conversion, that's a cross-channel campaign.

Now comes the attribution part. Attribution indicates which channel gets credit for the conversion—is it the channel that first brought the visitor to the site or the channel that was used in the visit in which the visitor converted? Other attribution models used in the industry, such as linear models, give equal credit to all the channels used by a visitor before he converts. Then there's a time decay model that applies decreasing weight to the channels used over time.

However, SiteCatalyst has only two models. We'll focus on those for the time being. First-touch attribution credits the entire success of the conversion to the first channel through which a visitor arrives at your site, assuming he has not deleted his cookies. Last touch attribution credits the entire success of the conversion to the last channel used by the visitor to convert on your site. Let's look at some of the reports that SiteCatalyst offers and how we can use them.

Report: Marketing channel overview

Navigate to Marketing Channels > Channel Overview. This report gives you an overview of all the channels you've configured and the instances in which they contributed to first touch or last touch for any of the conversion variables.

Navigate to Marketing Channels > First Touch Channel. This report gives you an overview of all the channels that the visitor used on his first visit to your site.

Navigate to Marketing Channels > First Touch Channel Detail. This report provides additional detail of the visit source based on the channels that the visitor used on his first visit to your site.

Navigate to Marketing Channels > Last Touch Channel. This report gives you an overview of all the channels that the visitor used to convert on your site.

Navigate to Marketing Channels > Last Touch Channel Detail. This report provides additional detail of the visit source based on the channels that the visitor used on his visit to convert on your site.

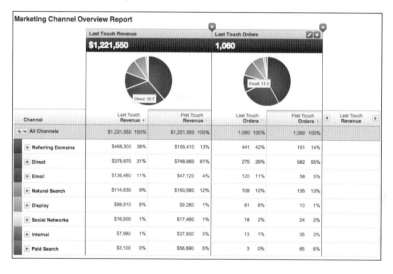

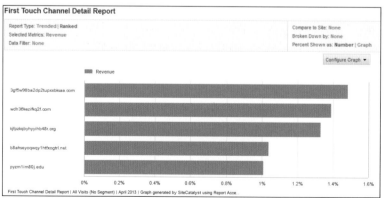

Key insights

Reports analyzing marketing channel data can help answer questions such as:

- **Which channels were commonly used?** If you run the first-touch channel report and break down the channel by the last-touch channel report, you can evaluate which channel was the first and which was the last. The visitor could have used the same channel in the first and last visit, so don't interpret this data completely as the visit in which he first arrived at your site and converted.

- **Which "opening" channels are visitors using?** The report gives you an overview of the performance of all the channels across first-touch visits, impressions, cart variables, orders, and revenue metrics, and so on, plus a host of user-defined calculated metrics. This will help you determine which channels are more designed for the first-touch experience that visitors are using the channel for.

- **Which "closing" channels are visitors using?** The last-touch report gives you an idea of how many times the channel was specifically used with the intent to convert. You can further look at the revenue that the channel contributed as a closing channel.

- **Which channels are neither the "opening" nor "closing" channels?** The channels that are not performing well as first- or last-touch visits can be evaluated against the campaigns report to see how many times they are used for learning and orienting or engaging with the content.

Interpretation of report data

In interpreting the data in reports of marketing channel overview, keep in mind that the marketing *channel* processing rules need to be set up correctly:

- The marketing channel processing rules run after any VISTA rules run and hence can access any data that already has the VISTA rule applied. This rule is applied to the data in real time and is permanent.

- Changes to the marketing channel processing rules cannot be applied to historical data since these rules are run in real time.

- Changes to the marketing channel processing rules apply to last-touch data, but may not impact first-touch data until visitor engagement expires. So first touch does not always follow the processing rules. However, last touch will always follow the current processing rules.

- Manually expiring the visitor engagement will delete all first- and last-touch channels across all visitors, so be sure you really want to do this.

Code implementation and console settings

These settings apply to marketing channel reports:

- First, navigate to Edit Settings > Marketing Channels > Marketing Channel Manager and enable and add all the channels that are pertinent to your business. You can even decide the color that represents that channel.

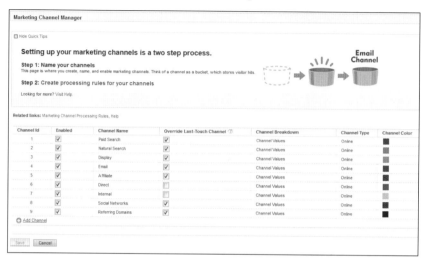

- Next, navigate to Edit Settings > Marketing Channels > Marketing Channel Processing Rules and add the rules to identify the channels. Here is where the naming convention of the marketing channels comes in handy. Name all your paid search campaigns with a prefix of "ps_" and use a prefix of "em_" for emails. Setting up these processing rules becomes easy. Remember that the rules run in the order they are created here, so be sure that this processing order is correct.

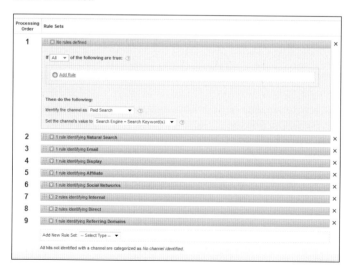

- Finally, and optionally, navigate to Edit Settings > Marketing Channels > Marketing Channel Costs to add any cost or budget information. These values will be reflected in the overview report when you choose the cost or the budget metric.

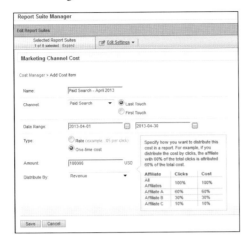

Campaigns report and marketing channels

The campaigns report and the marketing channels report are designed to give insight into how your campaigns are performing, so you might be confused as to why SiteCatalyst has these two reports.

Both are based on your campaign variables, but they differ in allocation, expiration, and classification of channels. For allocation, channel variables that the campaign reports use can take only one type of allocation—first touch, last touch, or linear. So you're forced to make a choice here. For marketing channels, you can compare first touch and last touch. However, linear allocation is not an option here. In the campaign reports, the expiry can be set to a number of events or custom days, so you have more flexibility. Marketing channels have a rolling 30-day expiration, regardless of whether or not a channel was touched. The campaign tracking rules are dependent only on the paid search detection rules. The other channels must be classified based on a SAINT classification. However, the marketing channels are determined by the marketing channel processing rules. The order in which the rules are defined can impact the data.

Conclusion

Awareness reports help you validate some key information about your visitors:

- **How effective are your marketing campaigns at driving visits and conversion?** This helps you understand the success of each channel you're invested in and the portfolio of your campaign spend.

- **Which channel attributes drive the most revenue?** This helps you to understand whether you're bidding on the right set of keywords, affiliates, and so on.

- **Who are the top referrers to your sites?** This will give you insight into the demographics of your visitor traffic from specific referrers.

Next, we'll review the acquisition reports and track the KPIs, the reports, and metrics. Sharpen your pencils!

Review questions

1 Can you write your internal channels to `s.campaignID`?

2 What is the difference between the view-through rate and the click-through rate?

Review answers

1 You can, but it's not advisable. It is recommended that you write internal banners and ads to a separate, custom conversion variable and enable participation metrics so that each banner ad can be credited with influencing the conversion.

2 View-through rate measures the ratio of the number of times a visitor visited your site after an ad impression to the total number of impressions. Click-through rate measures the ratio of clicks to the number of ad impressions. Both of these metrics are not measured in SiteCatalyst and need to be imported into SiteCatalyst, since both these metrics rely on impressions data.

4 ACQUISITION ANALYTICS

Lesson overview

In this lesson, you'll learn to analyze acquisition data. This will be particularly helpful if you're an analyst who's optimizing landing pages or a marketer who's trying to determine which geographical location to focus your marketing efforts on.

The goals of this section are:

- Understanding what to measure to evaluate your success in acquiring customers

- Determining which Adobe SiteCatalyst reports to run based on your analysis needs

- Identifying issues that impact the data and the implementation details that affect the data quality

 This lesson will take 30 minutes to complete.

A visitor's first impression of your site is critical. Landing pages that virtually read the visitor's mind and anticipate the intent of his visit are almost expected. The acquisition stage of the marketing funnel is about optimizing landing pages to meet the visitor's needs based on demographic and geographic location.

Task: Define KPIs

First, let us revisit how we set goals and key performance indicators (KPIs). With the focus on acquisition analytics in this session, your business goal may be to increase revenue by 25% for the financial year. Your KPIs will need to correlate to this goal in terms of acquisition metrics. Think backwards—to increase conversion by 25%, how much do you need to increase the traffic to your site by. So when we talk about traffic, you, of course, think in terms of visits, visitors and their traffic sources, and geolocation. Examples of KPIs for acquisition could be:

- **Average visits per visitor**

  Average visits per visitor = Total number of visits ÷ Total number of visitors

  Assume your business is like Amazon's, which means you want to optimize this KPI since a visitor will keep coming back to your site and converting.

- **Unique visitor ratio**

  Unique visitor ratio = Unique visitor ÷ Total number of visitors

  If your website conversion goal is to get visitors to sign up for a newsletter, then your business is very visitor centric. In that case, multiple visits may not be important to you. You would need to optimize for the visitor in this KPI.

- **New to return visitor ratio**

  New visitor ratio = Total number of new visitors ÷ Total number of visitors

  Return visitor ratio = Total number of return visitors ÷ Total number of visitors

  Find out which visitors are the first-time visitors versus those who have been to your site before. If your site has a lot of return customers, you could personalize the content based on the preferences you noted about them earlier.

- **Average visits from geolocation**

  Average visits from geolocation = Total number of visits from <North America> ÷ Total number of visits

  If you are running a campaign in a specific geolocation, you may look at the ratio of visits your site received before the campaign and after the campaign. Trending this over time will help you evaluate the geolocation of your audience.

Table 4.1 presents a suggested approach to understand which report(s) in SiteCatalyst can help you understand that. Deepen your analysis by looking at the data with multiple metrics and sharpen your insights by segmenting the data. Segments can include any custom traffic variable, any custom conversion variable, and any SiteCatalyst Attribute Importing and Naming Tool (SAINT) classification.

Here are a few suggestions that you can use to segment the conversion; the list is not meant to be exhaustive.

- By geosegmentation
- By channel
- By campaign
- By new or repeat cisitor
- By first-time or return customer
- By referrer
- By mobile devices
- By nonmobile devices

Table 4.1 Acquisition reports and metrics

FOCUS	MEASURES	SITECATALYST REPORT	METRICS
Site Visits	Total visits to the site	Site metrics > Visits	Visits
Visitor	Visitor trends	Site metrics > Visitors > Unique visitors	Unique visitors
		Site metrics > Visitors > Hourly unique visitors	Hourly unique visitors
		Site metrics > Visitors > Daily unique visitors	Daily unique Visitors
		Site metrics > Visitors > Weekly unique visitors	Weekly unique visitors
		Site metrics > Visitors > Quarterly unique visitors	Quarterly unique visitors
		Site metrics > Visitors > Yearly unique visitors	Yearly unique visitors
Visitor Geolocation	Geotargets	Visitor profile > Geosegmentation > Countries	Visits Unique visitors
		Visitor profile > Geosegmentation > Regions	Visits Unique visitors
		Visitor profile > Geosegmentation > Cities	Visits Unique visitors
		Visitor profile > Geosegmentation > US states	Visits Unique visitors
		Visitor profile > Geosegmentation > US designated marketing area (DMA)	Visits Unique visitors
Converted Visitor Geoprofile	Visitor demographics	Visitor profile > Visitor state	Visits Unique visitors
		Visitor profile > Visitor zip/postal code	Visits Unique visitors

Real-world example

You work in marketing at an online news organization that has paywall logic in place to only let people read a few articles for free until they have to pay. The content is highly specific to a region of the United States. Your business goal is to increase free trials and ultimately paid subscriptions. You have several acquisition KPIs that tie into your business goal:

- Average visits per visitor. This could be further segmented by type: anonymous, trial, subscribers. For each user group, how does their visit frequency trend over time?

- Visits by region segmented by type. Trended over time, are you meeting your growth goals by region?

- New visits by traffic source. What traffic sources are bringing in your new readers?

Task: Understand visits

Understanding visits helps you determine whether you have continued interest in your business. Visits can be defined as the number of sessions or the number of times a visitor sees one or more pages of your website.

Report: Analyze total visits

Navigate to Site Metrics > Visits. This report focuses on analyzing the trend of visits to the site over time.

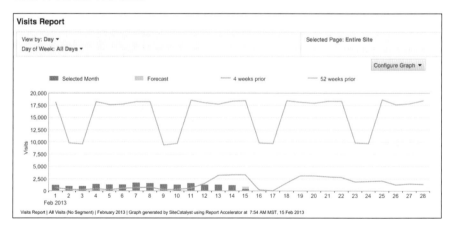

Key insights

Analyzing the *total visits* to your site can help answer questions such as:

- **Is there continued market interest in your site?** The key to a sustainable business is to maintain a steady flow of visits to your site. You can compare recent visits to previous periods to gauge fluctuations.

  Change the view of data from day to week, month, quarter, or year to see trends in larger sets of data. Compare this data with the data available in any competitor analytics tools to see how you stack up to your competitors in the market space.

- **Are your marketing campaigns successful?** The total visits also indicate the success of your marketing efforts, both online and offline. Further segmenting this data by other campaign attributes gives you deeper insights into visits by campaign.

- **What is your business's seasonality?** Seasonality varies from business to business. For example, retail businesses see a spike in November and December, and a marked slowdown in January. Websites that have lead-generation forms for work-related products may see high traffic on weekdays rather than weekends.

  These insights will help you optimize your campaigns on the days, weeks, months, or even quarters when traffic is at its peak or lull on your site.

▶ **Tip:** If you see too much fluctuation in your data, apply a moving average or linear algorithm that smoothes short-term fluctuations and shows longer-term trends with greater clarity.

- **Where are your visits originating from?** Based on your segments, you can determine which geographical location and referring domain your visits are from.

- **What percentage of visits are you losing?** Determine the bounce rate and single-access metrics to understand the attrition of your visits. If the bounce rate is too high, segment the data further to analyze which landing page, channel traffic, or geographical location has the highest attrition.

Interpretation of report data

In interpreting the data with respect to total site visits, keep the following in mind:

- A new visit is initialized after 30 minutes of inactivity, 12 hours of continuous activity, or 2,500 pages viewed. Inactivity is defined as no pixel calls to SiteCatalyst.

- SiteCatalyst records the visit on the day the visit started. So if a visit goes past midnight, the day the visit started is credited for the visit.

- Visits from multiple browsers on the same machine by the same person are credited as two separate visits.

- Visits from multiple tabs of the same browser on the same machine are credited as a single visit.

- Visits from multiple devices by the same person are counted as separate visits.

- In browsers that don't maintain persistent cookies, if the visitor exits the site or closes the browser and revisits the site after 30 minutes, then a new visit is counted unless the same IP or browser is used.

- Visits are tracked based on the cookie stored in the visitor's browser or by a combination of user-agent string and IP address.

- If your site has power users or bots that contribute to a lot of visits, this data may look skewed.

Note: In Version 14, a visitor who has disabled JavaScript or cookies is not included in the visit count. However, in Version 15, a combination of user-agent string and IP address is used to count them.

Code implementation and console settings

Variable s_account identifies the report suite to write the SiteCatalyst data to. A main point to remember is that any page that sends data to this report suite will be automatically included in your site reports. For example, assume you configured this report suite to report data for your production site. If pages on the production server were not tagged due to an oversight, and your staging website erroneously has pages writing to this report suite, then this data could impact the data quality.

One way to check for this data quality is to monitor the Site Content > Pages Report to see which pages from your ecosystem are missing. Another way would be to use a traffic variable or the s.server variable to track the website/hostname that sent the hit.

Task: Understand unique visitors trends

Understanding visitor trends helps you to understand patterns in visitor behavior. The seven reports described here have similar basic definitions, but each gives you different insights. The first, the unique visitor report, serves as a general overview. The period that defines uniqueness can then be set to hourly, daily, monthly, quarterly, or yearly.

Report: Analyze unique visitors

Navigate to Site Metrics > Visitors > Unique Visitor Report. This report identifies unique visitors to the site during the timeframe you specify in the calendar.

Note: Other reports can define unique visitors more specifically as those that are unique within a specific time period (for example, daily unique visitors). Many of the insights, data interpretation guidance, and technical settings discussed here apply to those reports as well.

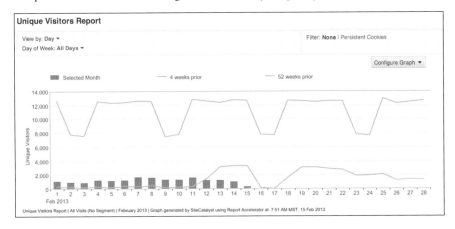

Key insights

Analyzing reports of unique visitors to your site—including the more specific reports for unique hourly through unique yearly visitors—can help answer questions such as:

Note: A "unique visitor" refers to a single person (as identified by a cookie or a combination of user-agent string and IP address) visiting your site.

- **What are the unique visitor trends?** Comparing the number of visits and visitors can help you determine whether power users are artificially inflating the visit count. You can compare the visits to the visitor count. Change the view of data from day to week, month, quarter, or year to find trends in larger sets of data.

- **What are visitors' preferred times to visit the site?** You can figure out visitors' preferences for visiting the site in terms of the hour of the day, day of the week, month, and so on.

- **How much of the visit data is being underreported?** Filter the data by *persistent cookies* (Version 14 only). This will segment the unique visitors by tracking method. It distinguishes between visitors who had persistent cookies and the ones who were tracked using the combination of user-agent string and IP address. How visitors were tracked may not seem significant (as long as they were tracked!), but this highlights how many visitors are not included in the visit count. If you can gauge the average ratio of visitors to visits, you can better track visits with higher accuracy. In Version 15, all visits are included irrespective of the cookie settings.

- **What's the best window of opportunity to release code or bug fixes in production?** The day of the week and the hour of the day with the least amount of traffic can help you determine the best time to release code, to minimize site unavailability to visitors.

- **What's the best time to run advertising campaigns?** First, determine the day of the week and the hour of the day with highest traffic. Then, depending on the media, you can time the campaign to coincide with your advertising efforts. Correlating visitor data with the geographical data can help you tailor your advertising campaigns to specific geographical locations.

Interpretation of report data

In interpreting the data with respect to unique visitors to your site, keep the following in mind:

- SiteCatalyst records the visit on the day the visit started. So if a visit goes past midnight, the day the visit started is credited for the unique visitor as well.

- Visits from multiple browsers on the same machine by the same visitor are credited as two separate visitors.

- Visits from multiple tabs of the same browser on the same machine are credited as a single visitor.

- In browsers that don't maintain persistent cookies, if the visitor exits the site or closes the browser and revisits the site after 30 minutes, then the visitor ID is the same.

- Visits are tracked based on the cookie stored in the visitor's browser or a combination of user-agent string and IP address.

- The date and time of the visit correspond to the time zone selected on the report suite setting, not the visitor's time zone.

The considerations above apply to most of the unique visitor reports described below, as well.

Code implementation and console settings

The settings below apply to all of the unique visitor reports described below, regardless of the time period chosen. However, some time periods involve additional complexities, as noted under those reports.

- Adobe SiteCatalyst uses a persistent cookie (s_vi) to identify visitors to your site. This cookie contains an encrypted visitor ID value that is passed into SiteCatalyst with each image request. There are no variables that need to be set explicitly on your site. As of a recent SiteCatalyst H code release, the fallback visitor ID is called s_fid.

- The report suite time zone setting determines the visit time that is recorded. The time zone cannot be configured to client-side time zone.

- The day unit ranges from midnight to midnight and is not configurable at the report suite level or at the login level.

Report: Analyze hourly unique visitors

Navigate to Site Metrics > Visitors > Hourly Unique Visitor Report. This report focuses on aggregating unique visitors for every clock hour in the timeframe you select in the SiteCatalyst calendar. You may also see this report available as an option to break down other reports. The hourly unique visitor granularity is not available for a reporting period of more than two weeks.

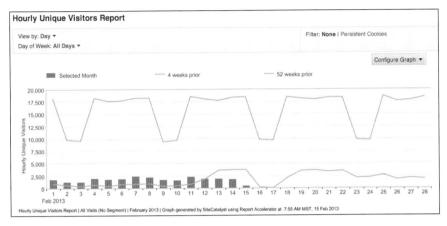

Interpretation of report data

In interpreting the data with respect to *hourly* unique visitors to your site, keep the following in mind:

- An hourly unique visitor resets at the top of the hour, not an hour from the start of the visit.

- If a visitor's session spans hours, the visitor will be counted as unique for each hour that contains data.

- If a visitor returns to the site multiple times in a day, the visitor details are duplicated for every clock hour during which she visits.

- The hourly unique visits total for a day will always be greater than the daily unique visits total for the same period, since the hourly report counts visitors multiple times across hours (once per relevant hour).

The interpretation considerations listed under "Analyze unique visitors" above also apply.

Code implementation and console settings

The code implementation and console settings for hourly unique visitors are the same as those for unique visitors in general.

Report: Analyze daily unique visitors

Navigate to Site Metrics > Visitors > Daily Unique Visitor Report. This report focuses on aggregating daily unique visitors for the timeframe you select in the SiteCatalyst calendar. You may also see this report available as an option to break down other reports.

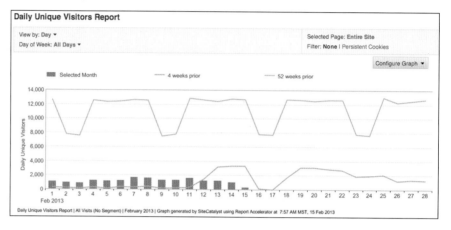

Interpretation of report data

In interpreting the data with respect to *daily* unique visitors to your site, keep the following in mind:

- You may report more daily unique visitors than visits if a large number of visits cross midnight based on the time zone of the report suite.

- The daily unique visitors total for a week will always be greater than the weekly unique visits report for the same period, since the daily report counts visitors multiple times across days.

The interpretation considerations listed under "Analyze unique visitors" above also apply.

Code implementation and console settings

The code implementation and console settings for daily unique visitors are the same as those for unique visitors in general.

Report: Analyze weekly unique visitors

Navigate to Site Metrics > Visitors > Weekly Unique Visitor Report. This report focuses on aggregating weekly unique visitors for the timeframe you select in the SiteCatalyst calendar.

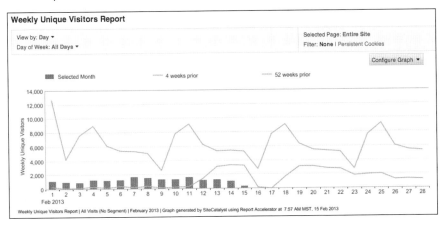

Interpretation of report data

In interpreting the data with respect to *weekly* unique visitors to your site, keep the following in mind:

- You may report more monthly unique visitors than weekly unique visitors (over a one-month period) if a month starts in the middle of the week.

- The weekly unique visitors total for a month will always be greater than the monthly unique visits report for the same period, since the weekly report will count visitors multiple times across weeks.

The interpretation considerations listed under "Analyze unique visitors" above also apply.

Code implementation and console settings

The weekly unique visitor report relies on the calendar settings of the report suite. The default calendar is Gregorian (with weeks starting on Sunday and ending on Saturday). The weekly unique report will be impacted if the default calendar is changed to a modified Gregorian calendar with a different first day of the week or a custom calendar.

All other code implementation details and console settings are the same as those for unique visitors in general.

Report: Analyze monthly unique visitors

Navigate to Site Metrics > Visitors > Monthly Unique Visitor Report. This report focuses on aggregating monthly unique visitors for the timeframe you select in the SiteCatalyst calendar. You may also see this report available as an option to break down other reports.

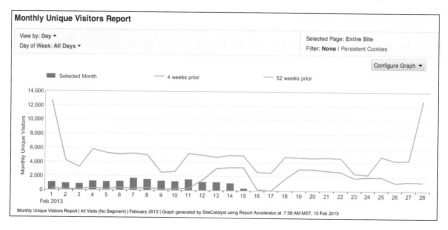

Interpretation of report data

The interpretation considerations listed under "Analyze unique visitors" above apply to monthly unique visitor reports.

Code implementation and console settings

The monthly unique visitor report relies on the calendar settings of the report suite. The default calendar is Gregorian (with months in a 4-5-4 or 4-4-5 week pattern). The monthly unique report will be impacted if the default calendar is changed to a modified Gregorian calendar with a different first day of the week or a custom calendar.

All other code implementation details and console settings are the same as those for unique visitors in general.

Report: Analyze quarterly unique visitors

Navigate to Site Metrics > Visitors > Quarterly Unique Visitor Report. This report focuses aggregating quarterly unique visitors for the timeframe you select in the SiteCatalyst calendar.

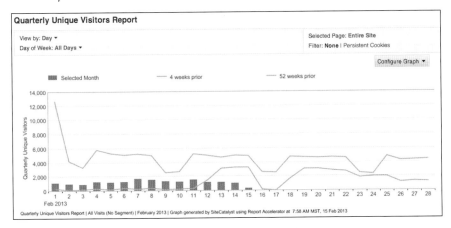

Interpretation of report data

In interpreting the data with respect to *quarterly* unique visitors to your site, remember that a quarter is defined as 13 weeks in SiteCatalyst.

The interpretation considerations listed under "Analyze unique visitors" above also apply.

Code implementation and console settings

The quarterly unique visitor report relies on the calendar settings of the report suite. The default calendar is Gregorian (with 13 weeks for each quarter). The quarterly unique report will be impacted if the default calendar is changed to a modified Gregorian calendar with a different first day of the week or a custom calendar.

All other code implementation details and console settings are the same as those for unique visitors in general.

Report: Analyze yearly unique visitors

Navigate to Site Metrics > Visitors > Yearly Unique Visitor Report. This report focuses on aggregating yearly unique visitors for the timeframe you select in the SiteCatalyst calendar. A year is defined as 52 weeks in SiteCatalyst. If the reporting period is a calendar year, you can see how many visitors have come to your site that year (with none counted twice).

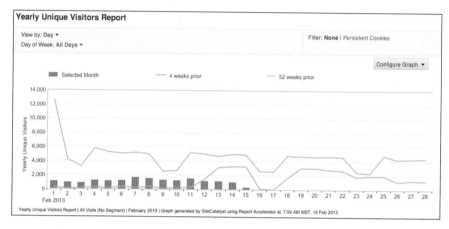

Interpretation of report data

The interpretation considerations listed under "Analyze unique visitors" above apply to yearly unique visitor reports.

Code implementation and console settings

The yearly unique visitor report relies on the calendar settings of the report suite. The default calendar is Gregorian (with 52 weeks for each year). The yearly unique report will be impacted if the default calendar is changed to a modified Gregorian calendar or a custom calendar.

All other code implementation details and console settings are the same as those for unique visitors in general.

Task: Understand where to focus your marketing efforts

Now you have an understanding of how many visitors come to the site and how many visits that adds up to. But, how about where those visitors come from? That would be interesting to know so you can target marketing efforts in specific geographical locations where you want to expand your business.

Internet service providers (ISPs) in each market area supply the American Registry for Internet Numbers (ARIN) with the IP addresses they use. Adobe partners with

Digital Envoy to provide a geographical tracking tool based on IP addresses. Digital Envoy uses that data to map the IP address of each visitor with the geographic city, state, zip code, and designated marketing area (DMA). Audited independently by Keynote Systems, Inc., Digital Envoy data offers over 99 percent accuracy at the country level, 97 percent accuracy at the region level, and 90 percent accuracy at the city level.

Report: Analyze country, region, city, state, or DMA of visit origin

We'll discuss this suite of reports on geographical locations together, since they're very similar, but each uses a specific granularity of geographical area.

Navigate to Visitor Profile > Geosegmentation > Countries Report. This report focuses on identifying which *country* the visit originated in.

Navigate to Visitor Profile > Geosegmentation > Regions Report. This report focuses on identifying which *region*, or area within a country, the visit originated in. The region drills down on the country you selected in the Visitor Profile > Geosegmentation > Country Report.

Note: Region is the same level of granularity as the US states. For countries without states, the region is more pertinent.

Navigate to Visitor Profile > Geosegmentation > Cities Report. This report focuses on identifying which *city* the visit originated in. The city drills down on the region/states you selected in the Visitor Profile > Geosegmentation > Regions/US States Report.

Navigate to Visitor Profile > Geosegmentation > US States Report. This report focuses on identifying which *US state* the visit originated in.

Navigate to Visitor Profile > Geosegmentation > US DMA Report. This report focuses on identifying which US Designated Marketing Area (DMA) the visit originated in.

Countries Report

Report Type: Trended | Ranked | **Map**
Selected Metrics: **Daily Unique Visitors**
Data Filter: None

Percent Shown as: **Number** | Graph

■ 3,132.8 - 3,916
■ 2,349.6 - 3,132.8
■ 1,566.4 - 2,349.6
■ 783.2 - 1,566.4
□ 0 - 783.2

Daily Unique Visitors

Countries Report | All Visits (No Segment) | February 2013 | Graph generated by SiteCatalyst using Report Accelerator at 8:00 AM MST, 15 Feb 2013

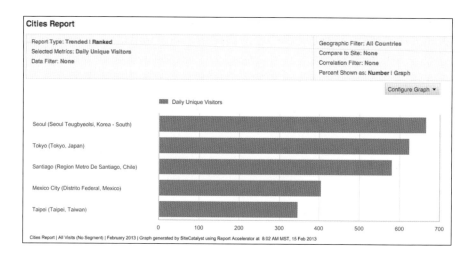

Cities Report

Report Type: Trended | Ranked
Selected Metrics: Daily Unique Visitors
Data Filter: None

Geographic Filter: All Countries
Compare to Site: None
Correlation Filter: None
Percent Shown as: **Number** | Graph

Configure Graph ▼

Daily Unique Visitors

Seoul (Seoul Teugbyeolsi, Korea - South)
Tokyo (Tokyo, Japan)
Santiago (Region Metro De Santiago, Chile)
Mexico City (Distrito Federal, Mexico)
Taipei (Taipei, Taiwan)

0   100   200   300   400   500   600   700

Cities Report | All Visits (No Segment) | February 2013 | Graph generated by SiteCatalyst using Report Accelerator at 8:02 AM MST, 15 Feb 2013

Key insights

Reviewing reports that analyze the area of origin for visitors to your site—whichever type of area you choose—can help answer questions such as:

Note: Geosegmentation reports are traffic reports. If you're looking to break down conversions by geographical data, you'll need to create a VISTA rule that replicates the geographical data in your custom conversion variables.

- **Which geographical area contributes the most daily unique visitors for pages tracked in this report suite?** Each SiteCatalyst report in this suite shows you the geographical area (country/region/city/state/DMA) from which the visit originated. In addition to the standard "Ranked" and "Trended" views, the "Map" view color-codes the area according to their relative contribution to your total traffic based on the intensity of the color. The intensity of the color increases with the number of daily unique visitors.

- **Which geographical area contributes most to the conversion?** Assuming you've written these variables to a custom conversion variable, you can segment the conversions by geographical locations to determine which area has the highest conversion.

Interpretation of report data

In interpreting the data with respect to geosegmentation of visitors to your site, it's important to remember the following:

- Corporate proxy servers mask the IP address of the visitors accessing the site, so all visits originating from the proxy server are treated as a visitor from the same country, thus underreporting that data.

- Mobile IP targeting varies from provider to provider.

- The IP addresses of visitors who use satellite Internet service providers (ISPs) are masked.

- Military and government IPs record the IP of the home location, not the military base where they are stationed.

- AOL users originally showed up as "McLean, Virginia," no matter where the visitor was located. To overcome that, SiteCatalyst now buckets all AOL users into the AOL US segment.

Code implementation and console settings

No specific implementation detail is required to track geosegmentation data. It's automatically tracked using each visitor's IP address.

Consider using a visitor identification, segmentation, and transformation architecture (VISTA) rule to automatically replicate the geographical data in five custom conversion variables. This will help you segment the conversions by geographical locations.

Report: Analyze preferred time zones

Navigate to Visitor Profile > Time Zones Report. The browser's time zone is based on the visitor's operating system time zone. SiteCatalyst uses that information to determine the visitor's time zone.

To optimize your channel spend based on geotargeting, determine which time zone visits are high at what time of day. You can tailor your content to the specific time zones that generate most of your traffic.

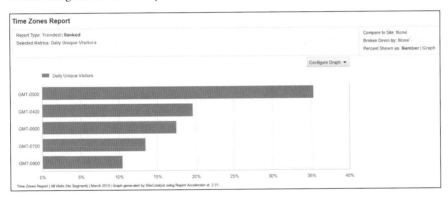

Key insights

Analyzing your visitors' preferred time zones can help answer questions such as:

- **At what time should you run a geotargeted campaign?** For example, you might have visitors in geographical areas that include the Pacific time zone and the Eastern time zone.

- **When are visitors most likely to convert into customers?** This report indicates which time zones your visitors are coming from. All time zones are present in Greenwich Mean Time (GMT), which is the international time standard. If you evaluate the conversions, you can also identify the times when your visitors are more likely to convert.

Code implementation and console settings

No specific implementation detail is required to track time zone data. It's automatically tracked using default information from the browser.

Task: Understand visitor demographics

Visitor demographics let you identify customers at the zip code level. From their zip code you can infer characteristics that are associated demographically with that zip code.

The zip code is the lowest-level granularity of data that is not considered personally identifiable information (PII), as described in the sidebar. Having this clarity about the visitor helps you target your marketing efforts locally.

Personally Identifiable Information (PII)

Personally Identifiable Information is defined as any information or a combination of information that can be used to identify a person. All analytics information is based on anonymous aggregation and Adobe SiteCatalyst does not endorse storage of PII. The following fields are considered PII by the U.S. Office of Management and Budget:

- Full name (if not common)
- Email address (if private from an association/club membership, etc.)
- National identification number like Social Security Number
- IP address (only in some cases)
- Vehicle registration plate number

- Driver's license number
- Face, fingerprints, or handwriting
- Credit card numbers
- Digital identity
- Date of birth
- Birthplace
- Genetic information

More generic information common to multiple people is not considered PII as a standalone piece of information. However, these fields are potentially PII, because they can be used in combination with other personal information to identify an individual. Examples are:

- First or last name, if common
- Country, state, or city of residence
- Age, especially if nonspecific
- Gender or race

- Name of the school they attend or workplace
- Grades, salary, or job position
- Criminal record

(http://en.wikipedia.org/wiki/Personally_identifiable_information)

Report: Analyze visitor demographics

Navigate to Visitor Profile > Visitor Zip/Postal Code Report. This report is not auto-populated. It requires a code change on the web page that is part of the order process. You'll need to decide whether you will accept the visitor's billing or shipping zip code (the shipping zip code is recommended to determine the geographical location of your customers). That value is then assigned to the zip information.

Navigate to Visitor Profile > Visitor State Report. This report is not auto-populated. It requires a code change on the web page that requests that the visitor provide her US State. That value is then assigned to the state information.

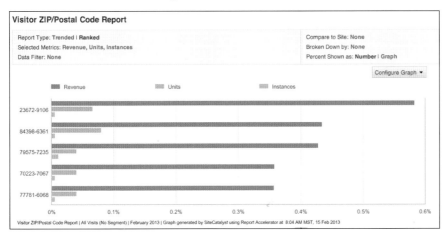

Key insights

Analyzing the demographics of your visitors can help answer questions such as:

- **Which states and zip codes are your customers based in?** You can use this report to determine the success of a localized advertising campaign down to a specific town or city. This data needs to be explicitly solicited from the visitor, most likely in the address section of the order form.

- **Where should you advertise to optimize your advertising spend?** By state and zip code, you can determine the geographical locations with the highest visits, revenue, and interest in a certain product or product family. Using a calculated metric, you can also evaluate the conversion rate. This will give you insights to run personalized advertisement campaigns.

- **Which state and zip code should you expand your business in?** You can also identify where the bulk of your orders are being shipped to in order to evaluate distribution center placement or expansion. Over time you can identify growth patterns.

Interpretation of report data

For reports on the demographics of your visitors, based on zip code, Version 14 does not allow for the `s.zip` variable to be auto-populated from geosegmentation data. Version 15 requires that you request that this variable be enabled.

Code implementation and console settings

Set value in variables `s.state` and `s.zip` explicitly from a user input form (collected from information submitted by visitors).

Task: Understand domains of origin

How your visitors connect to the web determines their domain of origin. If they are connecting from work, this can be more revealing than if they are using a popular consumer-level service. The top-level domain can tell you the source country, within limits. This is only very basic information, but it can be useful.

Report: Analyze domains

Navigate to Visitor Profile > Domains Report. This report provides the list of Internet service providers (ISPs) used by visitors to your site.

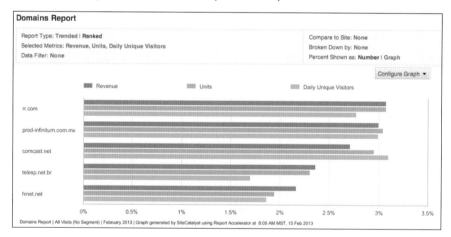

Key insights

Analyzing domains in this way can help answer questions such as:

- **Which ISPs are preferred by your customers, and where should you target promotional campaigns?** You can refine this based on the ISP preferences of your customers.

- **Which businesses/companies are visiting your site?** It's also common for the domain of a business to be listed here, and this data can be used to identify the names of companies that are visiting your site.

Code implementation and console settings

No specific implementation detail is required to track domain data. SiteCatalyst does a lookup to determine the domain associated with each visitor's IP address.

Report: Analyze top-level domains

Navigate to Visitor Profile > Top-Level Domains Report. This report provides an overview of which country visitors come from based on the domain extension of their domain of origin.

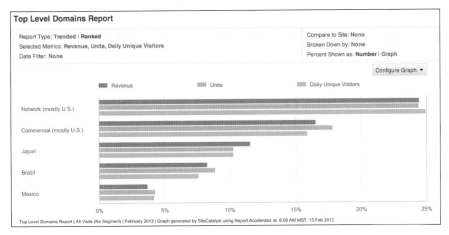

Key insights

Analyzing top-level domains can help answer questions such as:

- **Do you need a separate site for countries with the highest number of visits and conversion rate on your site?** This report identifies key metrics based on the top-level domain contribution. Understanding visitors' engagement and conversion will help you determine whether you need a separate site and experience for traffic from that country.

- **Do you have many visitors from educational or not-for-profit organizations?** This report can identify the .edu and .org domains from which visitors originate.

Code implementation and console settings

No specific implementation detail is required to track top-level domain data. All countries have a unique domain extension, for example, .in for India and .fr for France. The United States has additional extensions that distinguish commercial (.com), network (.net), educational (.edu), government (.gov), and organization (.org) sites.

Conclusion

Acquisition reports help you validate some key information about your visitors:

- **What are the total number of visits and unique visitors to your site?** This helps you understand your brand's value and determine general interest in your products.

- **Which new and repeat unique visitors are coming to your site?** This helps you understand the sustained interest in your brand and your products.

- **What are the geographical locations of the visitors to your site?** This helps you understand whether you need to run geotargeted marketing campaigns specific to the geographical locations where you want to increase traffic or expand operations.

- **What are the demographics of the key visitors coming to your site?** This question may be pertinent if you're collecting specific visitor information.

Next, we'll review the engagement reports to understand how visitors use and navigate your site. Are you ready?

Review questions

1   How can you break down conversion by geosegmentation?

2   Is a first name considered personally identifiable data (PII)?

3   Which unique visitors metric should I use—hourly, daily, weekly, quarterly, or yearly?

Review answers

1   In Version 14, you cannot break down conversion by geodata unless you have a VISTA rule that copies the data into custom conversion variables. However, in Version 15, you can create a visitor container with geosegmentation data. If you apply that segment to any report, you can break the conversion data by any geodata.

2   Yes, if it is unique enough to identify a person. Even if it is a very common name, if there is other data that can be used in conjunction with the first name to identify a person, then it is considered PII.

3   It depends on your conversion rate and, more importantly, your sales cycle.

5 ENGAGEMENT ANALYTICS

Lesson overview

In this lesson, you'll learn to analyze engagement data, which measures how connected visitors feel to your site. This chapter will be particularly helpful if you're an analyst optimizing the site content or performance or running A/B tests to determine which type of content your audience prefers.

Goals of this section are:

- Understanding what you need to measure for engagement analytics

- Determining the Adobe SiteCatalyst reports to run based on your analysis needs

- Determining the issues that impact the data and the implementation details that affect the data quality

 This lesson will take 60 minutes to complete.

Usability and user experience are the uber goal of engaging a customer. Errors and poor content quality erode the user experience. The engagement stage of the marketing funnel is about diving into the visitor's preferences and choices to tailor content—and the way it is served—to his interests.

Task: Define KPIs

Start by setting goals and key performance indicators (KPIs). This time the focus is on engagement analytics; your business goal may be to increase revenue by 25 percent for the financial year. Your KPIs will need to correlate to this goal in terms of engagement metrics. Think backwards—to increase conversion by 25 percent, how much do you need to better visitor engagement and experience on your site? When we think of engagement, it's all about what the visitor does on the site. Examples of KPIs for engagement could be:

- **Average visits with errors**

  Average visits with errors = Total number of visits with a page not found error ÷ Total number of visits

  The page not found errors reflect lost revenue from bad experiences that the visitor had on your site. The fastest way to get management to prioritize fixing of these issues is to report it as a KPI. In Chapter 7, "Conversion Analytics," we'll talk about giving these errors a monetary value as well.

- **Bounce rate**

  Bounce rate = Total number of bounces ÷ Total number of visits

  One of the key areas of improvement is landing page optimization. Most visitors make up their mind as soon as they land on your site. So basically visitors came, saw your site, and left! By focusing on the bounce rate, you can optimize the landing page experience based on the channel or another level of granularity like keywords.

- **Average page views per visit**

  Average page views per visit = Total page views ÷ Total number of visits

  Average page views per visit helps you figure the level of engagement that the visitor has on your site. Unless you're a content-oriented site, you don't want the average page per visit to be too high.

- **Average downloads per visit**

  Average downloads per visit = Total number of downloads ÷ Total number of visits

  If your site is targeting downloads as the conversion factor, you need to optimize the number of downloads per visit.

- **Video views per visit**

  Video views per visit = Total number of video views ÷ Total number of visits

To gauge the influence of videos and the number of visits in which they were viewed, you may want to understand the number of visits in which a video was viewed versus the total number of visits.

Table 5.1 presents a suggested approach to understanding which report(s) in SiteCatalyst can help you understand engagement. Deepen your analysis by looking at the data with multiple metrics and sharpen your insights by segmenting the data. Segments can include any custom traffic variable, any custom conversion variable, and any SiteCatalyst Attribute Importing and Naming Tool (SAINT) classification. The table contains a few suggestions you can use to segment the conversion and is not meant to be exhaustive.

- By geosegmentation
- By channel
- By campaign
- By new or repeat visitor

- By first-time or return customer
- By referrer
- By mobile devices
- By nonmobile devices

Table 5.1 Engagement reports and metrics

FOCUS	MEASURES	SITECATALYST REPORT	METRICS
Page error	Number of page not found errors	Site content > Pages not found	Visits Revenue
Single page visits		Paths > Pages > Entries and exits > Single page visits	Visit is the only metric available. No breakdowns are available in this report.
Content	Engaging content	Site metrics > Page views	
Time spent		Site metrics > Time spent per visit	
		Site content > Pages > Pages	
		Site content > Pages report > Site section	
		Site content > Hierarchy 1	
Increase video engagement	Engaging video content	Video > Video Overview	
		Video > Videos	
		Video > Video Detail	
		Video > Video Events	
		Video > Video Variables	

(continues on next page)

Table 5.1 Engagement reports and metrics (continued)

FOCUS	MEASURES	SITECATALYST REPORT	METRICS
Visitor preferences	Path analysis	Paths > Pages > Next page flow	
		Paths > Pages > Next page	
		Paths > Pages > Previous page flow	
		Paths > Pages > Previous page	
		Paths > Pages > Fallout	
		Paths > Pages > Full paths	
		Paths > Pages > Path finder	
		Paths > Pages > Path length	
		Paths > Pages > Page analysis > Page summary	
		Paths > Pages > Page analysis > Reloads	
		Paths > Pages > Page analysis > Page depth	
		Paths > Pages > Page analysis > Time spent on page	
		Paths > Pages > Page analysis > Clicks to page	
		Paths > Pages > Longest paths	
		Paths > (Any prop you can enable pathing on)	
Preferred pages	Preferred pages	Paths > Pages > Entries and exits > Entry pages	
		Paths > Pages > Entries and exits > Original entry pages	
		Paths > Pages > Entries and exits > Exit pages	
Navigation	Rich navigation	Site content > Links > Custom links	
		Site content > Links > File downloads	
		Site content > Links > Exit links	

Task: Manage visitor experience

Understanding visitor experience helps you optimize the page content and structure. Visitor experience is impacted negatively by errors, so you definitely want to track that. You'll also want to tackle single page visits: in this case, the landing page most likely did not address the visitor's intent and caused the visitor to leave the site.

Report: Understand page not found errors

Navigate to Site Content > Page Not Found. When a page is requested from the server, and the server cannot find the page, it returns a 404 error. The 404 errors may occur when cached pages in search engines no longer exist on the server or when a visitor mistypes the URL, for example.

There will always be pages that you want to delete, but showing a visitor a 404 error creates a negative impression. Odds are the visitor may not come back to your site or, even worse, they may share their bad experience on social media.

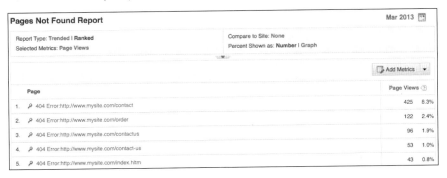

Key insights

Reports on page not found errors can help answer questions such as:

- **Which pages or links that visitors are looking for do not exist?** Finding the URL of pages that are not on the server gives you the option of hosting them on the server again or redirecting the visitor to a new page or your home page.

- **What's the lost revenue from visitors who leave your site after getting an error?** Figuring the traffic to the broken pages helps you quantify the lost revenue. When you talk money, of course, the priority to fix this issue will be high.

- **How many visits are you losing with the broken links?** Figuring the bounce rate from the broken pages helps you quantify lost revenue.

Interpretation of report data

In interpreting the page not found data, keep in mind that pages cached by search engines may have old URLs or may no longer be hosted on your server.

Code implementation and console settings

The following is required for reports on page not found errors:

- Set the `s.pageType='errorPage';`

- If you leave the variable `s.pageName` blank when there's a 404 error, the page name will record the URL of the page that the visitor typed.

- Some sites are heavily driven by query parameters and leaving variable `s.pageName` blank will not capture the full URL with the querystring. In that case, you have to manually set the `pageName` via JavaScript.

Report: Understand single page visits

Navigate to Paths > Pages > Entries and Exits > Single Page Visits. This report will have data similar to the pages report with single access as the metric. Technically, if a visitor session has only one unique page value, it is considered a single page visit.

Not all single page visits are bad news. A visitor who needs your store location, phone number, hours, or address may exit the site as soon as he gets that information—that's good! So consider the single page visit metric with reference to the goal of the web page.

Also, aggressive marketing to search engines can grab unqualified traffic: a visitor might think you're a software developer when you're actually a real estate developer. So he'll leave, but he wasn't your audience.

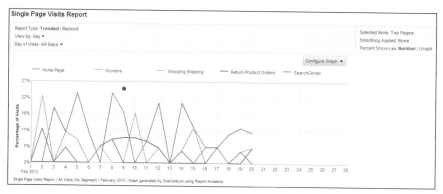

Key insights

Reports on single page visits can help answer questions such as:

- **Which pages are not matching visitor expectations?** By trending the single page visits, you can gauge which landing pages are not meeting visitors' expectations or enticing them to venture further into the site.

- **Is the page taking too long to load or does it have errors?** If the landing page itself has errors, the visitor may not be too motivated to continue engaging with the site. Another possibility could be that the visitor realized immediately that he was at the wrong site.

Interpretation of report data

In interpreting the data with respect to single page visits to your site, keep the following in mind:

- If the only link a visitor clicks is an external link—that is, one outside your site ecosystem—that is a single page visit.

- If you have a landing page with a link to log in and the authenticated pages are captured in a different report suite, the landing page will look misleadingly like a single page visit. Since this report is at the report suite level, you cannot exclude certain URLs from your report.

- Since the visitor goes to only one page, you cannot determine the time spent on the page. This is because time spent on a page is calculated based on when the next page at the site is loaded and there is no next page in a single page visit.

- Assuming that your site design has tabs to display additional content on the same page without refreshing the URL, it's still a single page visit. If a visitor arrives at your site, clicks on those tabs, and then leaves your site, it will be considered a single page visit. From a technical point of view, these tabs may be setup to record values in custom conversion variables (`eVars`) or custom traffic variables (`s.prop`), but they don't generate a new page name (value).

Code implementation and console settings

This data is available by default, and no special code is required for this report.

Task: Understand engaging content

Design your site better by understanding which content your audience is most interested in. Look broadly at site sections and hierarchies to get an idea of which content has high traffic. If you need to dive deeper, you can look at the pages report for information at a page-level granularity.

Report: Analyze total page views

Navigate to Site Metrics > Page Views Report. This report focuses on trying to identify the total page views in the timeframe you select in the SiteCatalyst calendar. This gives you an idea of sustained interest, brand value, and the success of marketing campaigns.

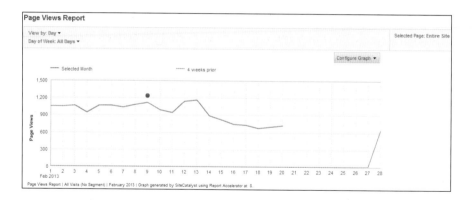

Key insights

Analyzing total page views can help answer questions such as:

- **What are the traffic trends throughout your site?** Analyze the page view trends on the site to gauge traffic to your ecosystem of pages. This displays the number of times your website pages were viewed for the selected calendar period. The report granularity can be aggregated at the website level or at the individual page level.

- **Is the page being viewed multiple times in a visit?** If a page is being visited multiple times in a single visit, then the visitor may be finding the content on the page particularly interesting. You could also cross-check the pathing report to determine whether the visitor is landing on the page repeatedly by mistake while searching for some other page.

Interpretation of report data

In interpreting the data with respect to single page visits to your site, keep the following in mind:

- The page views include reloads and any page that is loaded again when the visitor uses the Back button on the browser. To ensure that your page views are not skewed, check that the number of page reloads is not abnormally high.

- File downloads, exit links, custom links, and media-tracking data are excluded from page views.

- Any traffic from IPs excluded in the IP filters is not included in this report.

- Page views are recorded for all visitors, regardless of whether or not they accept persistent cookies or have JavaScript enabled.

- Total page views are normally higher than total referrer instances, since referral instances do not include hits that match internal URL filters. If a visitor is referred to your site by Google, when the visitor lands on your site, a page view and a referrer instance occurs. However, if the visitor comes to your website ecosystem but is not tracked in the current report suite, the referrer information is lost, but the page view is counted.

- SiteCatalyst 15 provides a page views metric for conversion reports by default, which acts almost exactly like a page view event. This removes the requirement to implement a custom page view event for these visitors. If the custom event does not fire on every single page, page views will be higher than their event-based counterpart. If you have the custom event defined in the `s.linkTrackVars` variable, the page view event will fire in custom links without increasing page views.

Code implementation and console settings

The following are considerations for reports on single page visits:

- If the SiteCatalyst pixel tags are implemented higher on the page, data accuracy is increased to capture partial page loads.

- Page views indicate the number of times the SiteCatalyst pixel call was made in the given date range.

Note: Pixel calls for tracking custom links and downloads are not counted in the page view count.

Report: Analyze time spent per visit

Navigate to Site Metrics > Time Spent Per Visit Report. SiteCatalyst reports the time spent on page metric in minutes and hundredths of a minute (**Table 5.2**). For example, a value of 1.75 is correctly interpreted as 1 minute, 45 seconds:

[.75 minutes] × [60 seconds/minute] = 45 seconds

This report speaks to the amount of time that is spent on the page as an indication of how engaging the content is.

Table 5.2 Values in minutes

ACTUAL HIT INTERVAL	VALUE ASSIGNED IN MINUTES	MEDIAN VALUE
15 seconds	$0 \leq x \leq 0.25$	.125
15–30 seconds	$0.25 < x \leq 0.50$	.375
30–60 seconds	$0.50 < x \leq 1$	.75
1–3 minutes	$1 < x \leq 3$	2
3–5 minutes	$3 < x \leq 5$	4
5–10 minutes	$5 < x \leq 10$	7.5
10–15 minutes	$10 < x \leq 15$	12.5
15–20 minutes	$15 < x \leq 20$	17.5
20–30 minutes	$20 < x \leq 30$	25
>30 minutes	$30 < x$	30

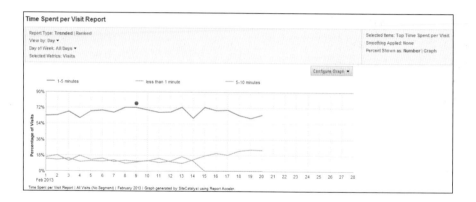

Time Spent per Visit Report

Report Type: Trended | Ranked
View by: Day ▼
Day of Week: All Days ▼
Selected Metrics: Visits

Selected Items: Top Time Spent per Visit
Smoothing Applied: None
Percent Shown as: Number | Graph

Time Spent per Visit Report | All Visits (No Segment) | February 2013 | Graph generated by SiteCatalyst using Report Accelerator.

Key insights

Analyzing time spent per visit can help answer questions such as:

- **What's the best time to deploy code changes?** If you're looking for the best window of opportunity to release code or bug fixes in production, you can get an understanding of which time has the least impact on visitors.

- **What's the best time to schedule email campaigns?** Another good use use of this report is when you want to measure visits by hour relative to a campaign (such as an email campaign) so you can test and adjust delivery schedules.

Note: The concept of unique visitors, and the technical specifics, was introduced in Chapter 4, "Acquisition Analytics." Basically, each visitor is counted only once (or once per defined period).

Interpretation of report data

In interpreting the data on time spent per visit, keep the following in mind:

- Data can be skewed if many visitors walk away from their computers or browse other sites in other tabs or browsers. So the time spent on a page is not a real indication of the time the visitor truly engaged with your site.

- Exit pages are not included in the time spent on page report, since time spent cannot be calculated on those pages because there is no next page.

- Single page visits are excluded from the time spent on page report because they consist of a single page view, so it is not possible to calculate time spent on the page.

- Average time spent data is calculated for each page view in a visit, but is aggregated in the case of reloads. Page reloads do not cause an additional instance to be counted; for example, if a visitor reloads a page every 15 minutes for 45 minutes, this would count as a single instance in the Greater than 30 minutes tally, rather than as three instances in the 10–15 minutes tally.

- To replicate the time spent on a page calculation as a calculated metric, take the average time spent on page metric, and multiply the number of minutes shown there by the total page views minus reloads and exits. Add the calculated metric for a specific page within the pages report.

Code implementation and console settings

No specific implementation detail is required to track the time per visit.

Report: Analyze pages

Navigate to Site Content > Pages Report. The pages report indicates the amount of traffic to a specific page. The pages report can have either the name of the page or the URL depending on the implementation.

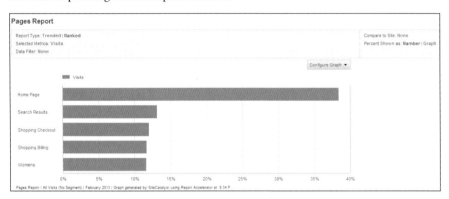

Key insights

Analyzing the pages report can help answer questions such as:

- **Which pages are of interest? Which pages have the highest engagement and the lowest bounce rate?** The pages report defines, at the page level, how many views the page received, the time spent on the page, and the number of bounces and exits. This lets you do an apples-to-apples comparison between pages to determine the visitor's preferences between pages and page content.

- **Which pages have the highest bounce rate?** The bounce rate determines the number of times the visitor saw only that page in a visit and then left your site. This will help you determine your optimization efforts of your landing pages.

- **Is some other website scraping and publishing your content?** In the pages report, if you see URLs that don't match your internal URL filter, you can identify the company that stole your source code and implemented it on its own site.

- **What is the average number of times a specific page was viewed per visit?** With this data, you can determine the popularity of a specific page or the importance of content on the page.

- **When a certain page is part of a visit, how often is it an exit page?** Using the exit metric, you can determine how many times a given page was the last page visited by your visitor. Being an exit page is not necessarily a bad thing—after all, the visitor has to leave your site through some page! If you find out that a product page has a high exit rate, you can determine what content can be switched to make it more engaging, or make offers or cross-sell promotions on that page to delay the exit.

- **When a page is part of a visit, how often is it an entry page?** Using the entries metric, you can determine how many times a given page was the first page visited by your visitor. You can flag an entry page to have more links to other sites or gravitate the visitor toward a specific task or goal.

- **When a page is the entry page, how often does it lead to at least one other page?** If you take into account the visits and subtract the bounces from that, the remainder should give you a clear picture of how often the page leads to at least one other page. You could then use the Paths > Pages > Next Page report to drill down further.

- **How many page views did a page get, not counting reloads, but counting the Back button or additional path views to the page?** If you take into account the page views and subtract the reloads from that, the remainder should give you a clear picture of how many page views occurred on that page.

- **What percentage of the page views were reloads of that page?** Create a calculated metric that divides the reloads metric by the page views. Too many reloads can indicate that a page was not loading fast enough for the visitor or maybe a JavaScript error was causing the page to stop it from loading successfully.

- **What is the ratio per page of how often it is the entry page versus how often it is the exit page?** Create a calculated metric that divides the reloads metric by the page views.

Interpretation of report data

In interpreting the data with respect to traffic to specific pages at your site, keep the following in mind:

- Page names and URLs are case sensitive and limited to 100 character or bytes depending on the character set.

- If you decide to use page names instead of URLs:

  - If two pages have the same name, the data of both pages will be aggregated by page name.

  - If a page name changes, the historic data is still attached to the old page name.

  - If no page name is assigned, it defaults to the URL without the URL parameters.

- If JavaScript is disabled on the page, the page name is not set and hence, the visit is assigned to the URL.

- Page names exceeding the 100-byte limit will be truncated to 100 bytes in the SiteCatalyst interface. For most pathing reports only the first 39 bytes are displayed.

- If you decide to use URLs instead of a defined page name:

  - If the same page has been accessed by the http and the https protocol, it considers them as two separate pages.

  - The querystring parameters (the part after the "?" in the URL) are stripped from the page name.

  - iFrames will display as a separate page view.

- If you switch from a URL to a page name, the historical data will not change. Up to the time the data was collected with a URL, you will see the page names listed as the URL. After the switch, the data will be associated with a page name. For example, if the home page was example.com/home page.html, the old data for the home page will be associated with /homepage.html. On January 1, if you decided to call your home page "Welcome to our store," all new data after January 1 will be listed for "Welcome to our store."

- SiteCatalyst considers the following three paths as the same to avoid fragmenting the page name.

  - http://example.com/folder

  - http://example.com/folder/

  - http://example.com/folder/index.html

  - http://example.com/folder/index.htm

> **Note:** To avoid losing historical data when switching from a URL to a page name, you could use classifications to classify both the URL and the page name to the same name. Via this methodology, the classified name would reflect on both new and historical data.

Data discrepancies between reports

If you're reviewing the visit metric for the pages report, the manual addition of all visits will be greater than the sum indicated. The visit count indicated next to the page reflects the visits in which the page was viewed. So when multiple pages are viewed in a single visit, each of those pages gets incremented in a visit.

Code implementation and console settings

The pages report has the following settings:

- References data is assigned to `s.pageName` variable.

- SAINT classification can be enabled on a page name to classify that dynamically instead of using site sections and hierarchy.

Report: Analyze visit trends

Navigate to Site Content > Site Sections Report. This report focuses on trying to report data at a higher level than pages. For websites with a lot of pages, having information about site sections is more valuable.

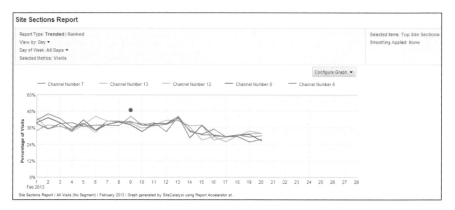

Key insights

Analyzing visit trends to site sections can help answer questions such as:

- **What site section content are visitors finding more engaging?** The analysis that we did for the pages report can be replicated at the site section level for websites with a high number of pages. Instead of using page as the level of granularity, you can use site sections to gauge interest in a group of pages.

- **How are visitors traversing between site sections?** Before you can analyze this, you'll need to ensure that you or your company's SiteCatalyst admin have contacted ClientCare to enable pathing on site sections. Once that's done, you'll be able to review how visitors are hopping between different site sections and their pathing preferences.

Interpretation of report data

In interpreting the data with respect to unique visitors to your site, keep the following in mind:

- If you have multiple site sections, the visits and unique visitors to each section will be greater than the total visits or visitors to the site.

- If the pages are misclassified in the site sections, the data will be incorrect.

- Data cannot be rectified retroactively.

Code implementation and console settings

The Site Content > Site Sections reports are based on values added to `s.channel`.

Report: Analyze visit trends by hierarchy

Navigate to Site Content > Hierarchy Report. This report focuses on estimating traffic to each section and levels within them for your site. It's important to understand the difference between hierarchies and levels. There are five hierarchy variables: s.hier1, s.hier2, s.hier3, s.hier4, and s.hier5. Within each hierarchy variable, the level of the hierarchy can be indicated by a list separated by delimiters. When Adobe enables this, you get 10 levels, but you can request up to 98 levels.

Imagine that you have a global company in 25 countries; you would want to track each country separately and compare their performance on page views, visits, or visitors. Here's what your hierarchy settings might look like:

- Hier1 could be your company.

- Hier2 could be the country.

- Hier3 could be the pages.

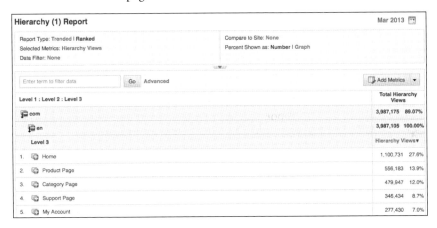

Key insights

Analyzing visit trends can help answer questions such as:

- **How are content groups performing?** View how content groups within your site are doing based on page views, visits, or visitors.

- **How does the performance of one sublevel compare to others?** You can compare the performance of one level in a hierarchy versus another. For example, if you have a retail site, you compare the toys sold in the infant section to toys sold in the teen section.

- **How does level data correlate with other segments or finding methods?** Hierarchy reports with different amounts of levels: Similar to correlations, hierarchies must account for all page views across all levels. If you have an image request with a hierarchy that only goes two levels down, and another that goes three levels down, viewing the level three hierarchy report will show "unspecified" to account for the image request with only two levels.

▶ **Tip:** It is not advisable to attempt to remove "unspecified" from hierarchy reports, as this would require that every page on your site contain the exact same number of levels. Since this essentially defeats the purpose of implementing hierarchies in the first place, it is recommended to simply ignore these breakdowns in reporting.

Interpretation of report data

In interpreting the data with respect to unique visitors to your site, keep in mind that SiteCatalyst provides a built-in method for visitors to track hierarchies. By specifying the hierarchy "depth" (the default is 10 levels), visitors may view the overall hierarchy, as well as the position and data for specific pages in the selected hierarchy. You may specify names for your hierarchies and, depending on the service level you have purchased, view hierarchies according to page views, visits, and visitors.

Code implementation and console settings

● **Note:** Hierarchy variables are not available for segmentation.

These settings apply to the hierarchy report:

- Add data to five hierarchies: `s.hier1`, `s.hier2`, `s.hier3`, `s.hier4`, `s.hier5`.
  `s.hier1='Level1,Level2,...Level10';`

- The Hierarchy Report in SiteCatalyst is not a default report . You would need to call ClientCare to enable hierarchies.

- You are limited to 255 characters total.

Task: Understand use of rich media content

You just paid top dollar to have that jazzy rich media content created. Now, how do you show that the spend was worth it? You can add your analytics tags for the rich media content. All rich media, like videos and Flash, require special tagging.

Report: Analyze video overview

Navigate to Videos > Video Overview Report. This report will tell you the videos viewed, videos completed, the total amount of time it was viewed, and the video segment views. Apart from that, you can also look at the average views per video, the average completes per video, and the average time watched per video flow.

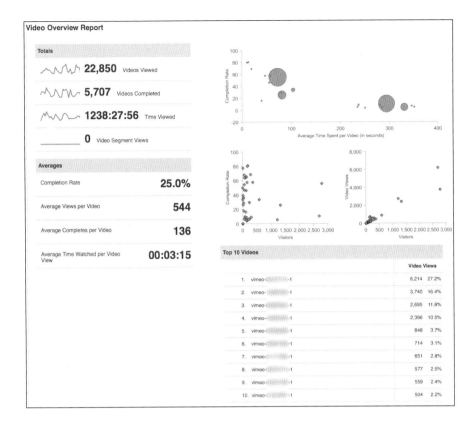

Key insights

Analyzing reports of video views can help answer questions such as:

- **Are visitors interested in video content?** Gauge the popularity of different videos by determining how many views each of the videos received. If the videos are reinforcing content on some pages, you can compare and contrast whether most visitors prefer text content, video content, or both.

- **What kind of videos are visitors interested in?** Check with your company's SiteCatalyst admin to see if classifications are set up for the videos. Classification of videos into different categories will help you determine the types of video preferred by the visitor demographics.

- **How much time are visitors spending on video versus text content?** Compare and contrast the time spent on text content versus video content.

Interpretation of report data

In interpreting the data with respect to video views, keep the following in mind:

- The total video time includes all time spent on videos in an entire visit, not just the total time per video view; for example, if a visitor views the same video three times in a single visit, then this visitor's time spent on video data will reflect a value three times longer than the video itself.

- The time spent on video report is the total amount of time spent on a video during a visit, including the time that the video is paused or played back while the visitor is viewing other pages on your site.

- If a video was started, paused, and started multiple times, it will still count as one view.

- If you don't see any video reports in your SiteCatalyst reporting section, check with your company's SiteCatalyst admin. It needs to be specifically enabled in the admin section.

Code implementation and console settings

- In the admin console, the Video Tracking Settings option lets you enable or disable all video tracking, including reports and all video settings.

- To track videos, you need one custom traffic variable (s.prop), three custom conversion variables(eVars), and four success events. One of these eVars must have full subrelations enabled.

- Custom traffic variable: video name

- Enable pathing on custom traffic variable—video name

- Custom conversion variables

  - Video name

  - Segments—these expire at page view

  - Content type—values are video or page; these expire at page view

- Custom events

  - Video time—Counter event that counts the number of seconds spent watching video since last request

  - Video views—Counter event that tracks the number of video views

  - Video completes—Counter event that tracks video ends

  - Video segment views—Counts the number of video segment views

  Determine milestone events to track. For example, if you want to track how many visitors viewed 25 percent, 50 percent, 75 percent, and 100 percent of the video, you would need to track four separate events.

Report: Analyze videos

Navigate to Video > Videos Report. This report indicates the number of video views, video completes, video time viewed, and video segment viewed.

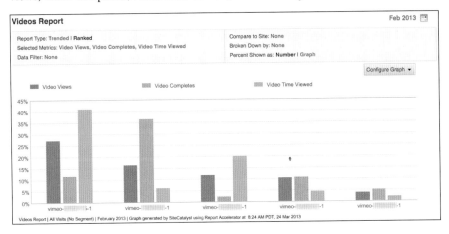

Key insights

Analyzing reports of videoscan help answer questions such as:

- **Are visitors engaging with the videos?** The video visits report lets you compare visits where video was viewed versus total visits.

- **What kind of videos are visitors interested in?** Check with your company's SiteCatalyst admin to see if classifications are set up for the videos. Classifying videos into different categories will help you determine the types of video preferred by visitors.

Interpretation of report data

In interpreting the data with respect to video visits at your site, remember that even when multiple videos are viewed in a single visit, it's counted as one visit with a video view.

Code implementation and console settings

Apart from the video tracking setup discussed earlier, no additional setup is required for this report.

If you would like to credit the video view as an influencing factor preceding the conversion, you can enable participation metrics.

Report: Analyze video detail

Navigate to Video > Video Detail Report. This report indicates detailed information about video-segment views, average completion, and fallout for a single video.

Key insight

Analyzing reports of video detail can help answer questions such as:

- **How much do visitors really engage with the videos?** The video detail report focuses your attention on how many times the video was watched completely, and where did the visitors stop or pause it. Having this information will help you to decide on the optimal length of the video for your audience.

Interpretation of report data

In interpreting the data with respect to video detail, remember that the video segments are video milestones defined by you in terms of percentages.

Code implementation and console settings

Apart from the video-tracking setup discussed earlier, no additional setup is required for this report.

Report: Analyze video events

Navigate to Video > Video Events > Video Time Viewed Report. This report indicates how much time visitors spent watching videos.

Navigate to Video > Video Events > Video Views Report. This report indicates how many times the videos were watched.

Navigate to Video > Video Events > Video Completes Report. This report indicates how many times the videos were watched for their entire duration.

Navigate to Video > Video Events > Video Segment Views Report. This report indicates how many segments of the videos were watched.

Key insights

Analyzing the videos your visitors viewed can help answer questions such as:

- **What videos are being watched, and for how much time?** The video events suite of reports lets you compare visitors' interest in videos. If you've enabled multiple events to track milestones of the videos viewed, you can gauge how much attention an average visitor on your site devotes to videos. This will inform future decisions on the optimal length of your videos.

- **What channels are driving more video views?** Using breakdowns, the video reports can be segregated by channel information. This will help you correlate whether a particular campaign or channel drove more visitors toward video engagement. Future campaigns on that channel can then be optimized with videos.

- **Which videos drove more conversion?** Using participation metrics, the video may be given credit for any conversion after the video was viewed. This will help determine the influence of the video on conversion.

- **At what point of the visit is the video viewed?** Using average video depth metrics, you can understand the average depth in which the video was viewed. This will help determine the order in which the videos were viewed.

Code implementation and console settings

Apart from the video tracking setup discussed earlier, no additional setup is required for this report.

Report: Analyze video variables

Navigate to Video > Video Variables > Segments Report. This report analyzes the custom variables assigned to video.

Key insight

Analyzing the video flows can help answer questions such as:

- **If you have multiple videos on your site, in what sequence do visitors prefer to engage with the videos?**

Code implementation and console settings

Apart from the video tracking setup discussed earlier, no additional setup is required for this report.

Task: Understand path analysis

Path reports help you analyze the clickstream data or the browsing patterns that any visitor has on your site. Based on the patterns you see, you can optimize your site and the flow of pages to keep the visitor engaged and more likely to convert (make a purchase, sign up for a newsletter, or whatever you have identified).

Path analysis helps you:

- Understand clickstream data of usage patterns.

- Look for commonly used paths and sequence.

- Identify where visitors lose interest in your site.

- Analyze usage patterns over time.

- All pathing reports and metrics such as single access, entries, visits, and exits are visit-based. With SiteCatalyst 15's improved processing methodology, even visits without a tracking cookie can be calculated.

Report: Analyze next page flow and previous page flow

Navigate to Paths > Pages > Next Page Flow. From the selected page, the branches extend to the right, denoting the next page that was viewed. There are five branches with the size of the width, denoting the percentage of path views. From the second-level branch, there are five third-level branches. You can expand the number of branches to view up to ten second-level branches and five third-level branches.

Navigate to Paths > Pages > Previous Page Flow. From the selected page, the branches extend to the right, denoting the previous page that was viewed.

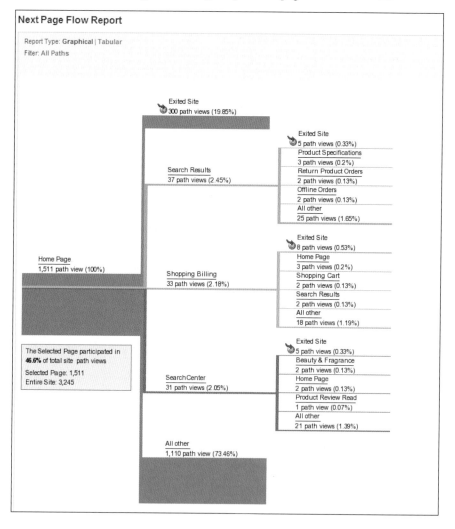

Key insights

Analyzing your visitors' page flow can help answer questions such as:

- **What steps are taken most frequently before or after viewing a selected page? What route does a visitor take when entering a page on your site?** Running the next page flow and the previous page flow will help you understand what steps are being taken after viewing a page. This will help optimize the path to conversion.

- **What are the popular site paths?** Optimize your site path design to funnel your traffic to a desired goal page.

- **Where are you losing customers?** You can identify what paths visitors are taking instead of reaching your desired goal pages. The report also highlights when visitors exit your site.

- **Which pages feed visitors to important pages on your site?** Analyze a signup page, for example, in order to understand which of your site pages is most effectively driving your visitors to sign up or subscribe to your services.

Interpretation of report data

In interpreting the data on page flow, keep the following in mind:

- Instances are the same as path views in the next and previous page flow report.

- A path view indicates the number of times a page was viewed in that specific sequence, constrained to the displayed paths.

- If there are more than 100,000 unique paths, the paths that contain only one instance are removed. There are two exceptions to this rule: (1) Single page visits (entered site, page, exited site) are never removed, and (2) if a report shows only two steps (entered site, page), then no paths are removed.

- The term "path view" is used to indicate the number of times a page was viewed, given the constraints of the displayed path(s); in other words, this metric reports the number of page views for the given page that occurred within the selected path. For example, consider the following path:

  Product Detail Page > Home Page > Search Results Page

  The home page may have 10,000 total page views, but the path views metric will return only those views of the home page that occurred as a part of this specific three-page path. This number may be much lower than 10,000 because only a fraction of visitors view this particular path.

Code implementation and console settings

No special variables are required to track pathing of pages.

Report: Analyze next page and previous page

Navigate to Paths > Pages > Next Page. The next page report provides detailed site path analysis by showing you the pages on your site that visitors viewed after seeing a selected page on your site.

Navigate to Paths > Pages > Previous Page. The previous page report provides detailed site path analysis by showing you the pages on your site that visitors viewed before seeing a selected page on your site.

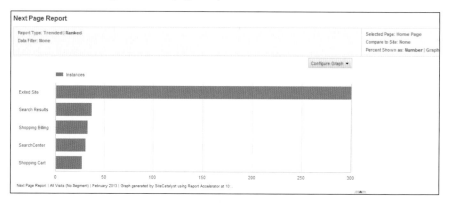

Key insight

Analyzing next and previous pages can help answer questions such as:

- **Which pages precede or succeed key pages on your site?** This helps you determine which pages lead to conversion or precede an error.

Code implementation and console settings

No special variables are required to track pathing of pages. To enable pathing on any other traffic variable, contact ClientCare.

Report: Analyze fallout

Navigate to Paths > Pages > Fallout. You can use the fallout report to determine how many visitors depart the site at specific points as they navigate through the website. With the fallout report, you can view the percentage of visits that drop out after a certain page.

Key insights

Analyzing the fallout at your site can help answer questions such as:

- **Where are prospects abandoning the path within a specific path?** The fallout report is useful to understand at which step visitors fall out of the sequence of pages you wanted them to visit. This is eye opening when you're looking for

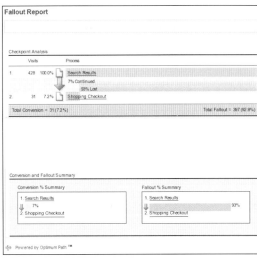

reasons to optimize. Once you figure out the page where you're losing them, you can use the next page path report to understand what they are doing next.

- **How is the conversion in a specific conversion funnel path?** The fallout report helps you analyze where you're losing visitors in a conversion funnel.

- **Of the people who went to your trial signup page, how many signed up?** Understand the way visitors navigate your site and the path they take so you can tailor your messaging and sales delivery to elicit favorable results.

- **What percentage of people used internal search and how many converted?** Understand the correlation between multiple events in your site.

Interpretation of report data

In interpreting fallout data, keep the following in mind:

- By default, fallout report data is limited to pages.

- To enable pathing on traffic variables, contact ClientCare.

Code implementation and console settings

No special variables are required to track pathing of pages. To enable pathing on any other traffic variable, contact ClientCare. Once you enable pathing on any custom traffic variable (s.prop), you can gauge the fallout for that variable.

Note: Pathing reports are not available via the Excel integration toolbar.

Report: Analyze full paths

Navigate to Paths > Pages > Full Paths. This report displays the all the paths that visitors use to navigate your website.

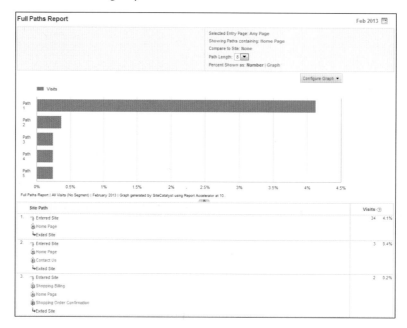

Key insights

Analyzing full paths in this way can help answer questions such as:

- **What are the most popular paths that contain a certain page?** In the full paths report, select Configure > Report, and click Showing paths containing to select the page you want to analyze. When the report reloads, the item listed highest in the report will be the most popular path that includes the page you selected.

- **How does each visitor engage your site?** Determine not only entrances and exits, but also every page in between to better evaluate your site's size and relevance in relation to initial customer interest.

Interpretation of report data

In interpreting the full path analysis data, keep in mind that there will be as many paths listed as the visitors take, so take the most popular ones and ignore the long tail of pages.

Code implementation and console settings

No special variables are required to track pathing of pages. To enable pathing on any other traffic variable, contact ClientCare.

Report: Analyze path finder

Navigate to Paths > Pages > Path Finder. This report lets you analyze fragmented paths based on different predefined patterns or custom patterns. Path fragments are a subset of the pages visited during a visit. SiteCatalyst has two types of pattern objects: anchors and wild cards. Anchor objects restrict the path fragments to people who entered the site, landed on a specific page, exited the site, and so on. Wild cards give you the flexibility of defining a blanket step that covers a visit to any page.

Key insights

Analyzing path finder can help answer questions such as:

- **What are the most popular entry-path fragments following the home page?** Path fragments are subset of the pages visited during a visit.

- **What are the most popular paths following the home page, whether or not the home page was an entry page?** Determine the navigation path that most visitors follow, this could help you understand the intent of their visit.

- **What are the most popular path fragments prior to exiting the site?** Determine the paths the visitors are taking prior to exiting the site. For example, this will help you understand if they are completing any macro- or microconversions or multiple internal searches before exiting your site.

- **What are the most popular path fragments that lead to a specific page, such as the shipping policy page?** This will also help you understand the pages that are influencing conversion.

▶ **Tip:** If the preferred navigation path is circular, Page A > Page B > Page A, that suggests that content could be moved from Page A to Page B to enhance usability.

Interpretation of report data

In interpreting the path finder data, keep in mind that SiteCatalyst allows up to four pages of depth (that is, steps) in the path finder report. There are discrepancies between page views and path view metrics. Path views are counted only for visitors with persistent cookies enabled, and hence slightly lower than page views. Path views do not count reloads, but page views do.

Code implementation and console settings

No special variables are required to track pathing of pages. To enable pathing on any other traffic variable, contact ClientCare.

Report: Analyze path length

Navigate to Paths > Pages > Path Length. This report displays the depth of each visit to your site by percentage and by total count. Average visit depth is determined by the ratio of the page views to the number of visits for the chosen calendar period.

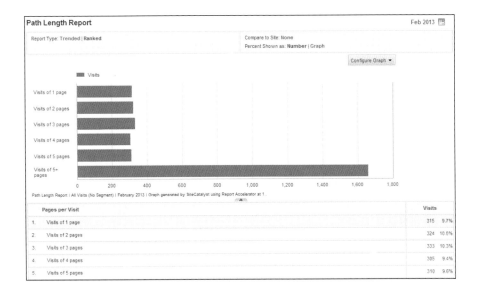

	Path Length Report		Feb 2013

Report Type: Trended | **Ranked**

Compare to Site: None
Percent Shown as: **Number** | Graph

	Pages per Visit	Visits	
1.	Visits of 1 page	315	9.7%
2.	Visits of 2 pages	324	10.0%
3.	Visits of 3 pages	333	10.3%
4.	Visits of 4 pages	305	9.4%
5.	Visits of 5 pages	310	9.6%

Key insights

Analyzing path length can help answer questions such as:

- **What is the average number of pages visitors traverse on your site? How does that compare to the total pages on the site?** Your site probably has hundreds of pages. Most visitors are hardly interested in most of them. This will give you an insight into the number of pages that are regularly viewed by your visitors.

- **How many visitors traverse more than or greater than the average path length?** Path length can be misleading metric in the sense that a visitor can be searching for some content on your site and end up visiting more pages. Unfortunately, she may exit the site as a frustrated visitor despite visiting more pages than your average visitor.

- **What messaging can be given to visitors at the average path length to keep them engaged longer?** If the visitor has seen a few pages and you cannot gather their intent, you could serve them a quick survey to understand the intent of their visit or have them chat with your customer representatives to determine their needs.

Note: The finding that only a few pages are viewed regularly does not imply that you should remove the rest of the pages from your site.

Code implementation and console settings

No special variables are required to track pathing of pages. To enable pathing on any other traffic variable, contact ClientCare.

Report: Analyze page summary

Navigate to Paths > Pages > Page Analysis > Page Summary. The purpose of this report is to summarize the information about a single page as a precursor to in-depth analysis of a specific page.

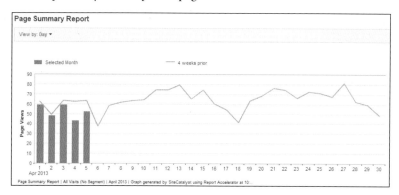

Key insights

Analyzing page summary reports can help answer questions such as:

- **What did visitors do before and after viewing this page?** The navigation section identifies where your visitors were before viewing the selected page, and where they went after viewing the selected page. The metrics section displays numerous metrics related to the selected page.

- **How many entries did the page have from referring and non-referring pages?** The left side of the graphic shows information about the entry pages. The top percentage relates to referrer pages (pages outside your ecosystem), and the bottom number relates to non-referrer pages (pages inside your ecosystem).

- **How many exits did the page have from referring and non-referring pages?** The percentages on the right side of the graphic refer to exit pages, of which there are two kinds. The top percentage relates to a complete exit of the domain, while the bottom percentage relates to an exit to another page in the domain.

Code implementation and console settings

No special variables are required to track pathing of pages. To enable pathing on any other traffic variable, contact ClientCare.

Report: Analyze reloads

Navigate to Paths > Pages > Page Analysis > Reloads. This report indicates the number of reloads. A reload is page information sent twice or more sequentially even if the visitor clicks on a custom link or download inbetween. This can happen when the visitor clicks on the Refresh button or clicks the Back button on the browser.

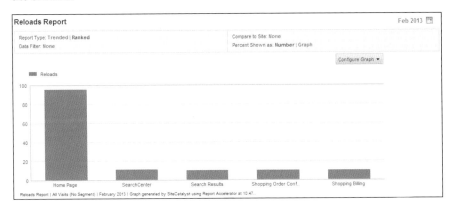

Key insight

Analyzing reloads in this way can help answer questions such as:

- **What pages are loading slowly or not loading?** Pages that load slowly or don't load due to JavaScript errors on the page can be identified with this report. Most visitors will refresh the browser or exit the site when the page does not load quickly or loads partially. This will help you identify:

  - Pages that are too heavy in size (requiring more trips from the server)

  - Pages with JavaScript errors that cause them to load partially

  - Pages that have rich media content and are slow to load on certain connection types

Interpretation of report data

In interpreting the reloads data, keep the following in mind:

- If the visitor viewed two pages with the same page name consecutively, this would be interpreted as a reload, even if the page URLs were different.

- Page views are attributed to the date of the actual page view, while reloads are attributed to the date the visit was closed, which may be different; that is, the visit began before midnight and ended after midnight.

- A page that has a form that posts back to itself would show as a page reload.
- If you have your SiteCatalyst code—s.t()—at the bottom of the page, you may not track reloads if the first page view never fired the SiteCatalyst tracking pixel.

Code implementation and console settings

If you are using page names, ensure that any two pages that could potentially be loaded in sequence don't have the same name.

Report: Analyze time spent on page

Navigate to Paths > Pages > Page Analysis > Time Spent on Page. This report measures the amount of time a visitor spent on the page. Of course, we can't tell if he hopped up to get coffee or was reading every word.

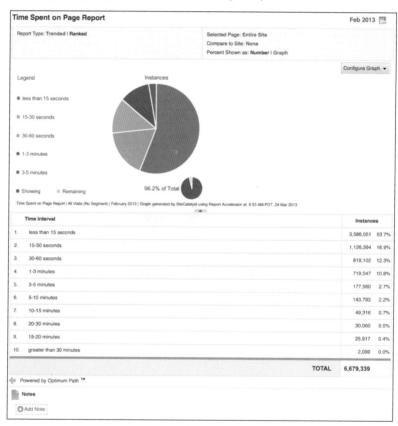

Key insights

Analyzing time visitors spend on pages can help answer questions such as:

- **How long do visitors stay on your individual website pages?** The time on page reports is literally what it says: the amount of time spent on the page. Intuitively, the longer a visitor was on the site, the more interested he was in the content. However, SiteCatalyst cannot account for eyeball time on the site. So this data should be used very directionally and only in conjunction with other reports. Any insights from this data should be verified with A/B tests or usability tests.

- **Which site content/promotions trigger visitor interest?** This informs you about what type of content visitors prefer. If you have a lot of content compared to the video hours, your data will look skewed, so use your best judgment while drawing insights on reports like this. They are very dependent on your website design and architecture.

Interpretation of report data

In interpreting the time spent on page data, keep the following in mind:

- This report has the same data as the average time spent on page metric.

- Time spent on page is calculated as the difference between two events. Each time interval starts or ends when it encounters a unique value or when a visit ends. However, it is not impacted by reloads, so the time interval will continue when there is a reload(s). Time spent on the page is also not impacted by pages that do not set that variable. Since page name is set on every page, time spent on page is calculated for every page (except reload), but when you're trying to determine the time spent on page for a custom traffic variable, the time interval is calculated between the pages where this traffic variable is set.

- There will be very few visits in the Greater than 30 minutes tally. This is possible if the visitor refreshes the page; this resets the visit expiration but does not reset the time interval. Other than that use case, since a visit expires after 30 minutes of inactivity, they won't be included in the Greater than 30 minutes bucket.

Code implementation and console settings

No special variables are required to track average time spent on page.

Report: Analyze clicks to page

Navigate to Paths > Pages > Page Analysis > Clicks to Page. This report displays the number of clicks visitors make to reach any selected page, along with the number of visits that match each number of clicks to the page.

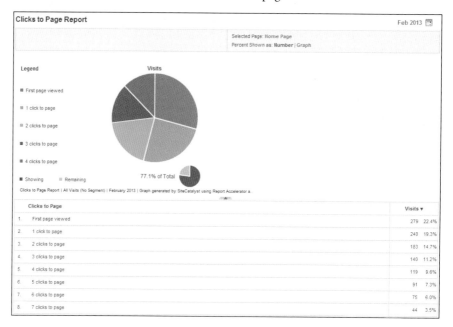

Key insight

Analyzing clicks to page can help answer questions such as:

- **Are the pages you want the visitor to view easy to find?** If the visitor takes more than 10 clicks to reach a page, the page could be really hard to find or the visitor may not need it immediately. If the pages you want the visitor to view are taking more clicks to find, you may want to make the links to that page more prominent in your landing pages or the subsequent pages.

Interpretation of report data

"Clicks to page" is the same as "page depth."

Code implementation and console settings

No special variables are required to track clicks to pages. To enable pathing on any other traffic variable, contact ClientCare.

Task: Understand landing pages preferences

Entry and exit pages give you an idea of the common pages through which visitors prefer to enter or exit your site. This will give you some insights on how you can engage visitors to stay longer in your site's ecosystem. You can use these reports to understand preferred landing pages, look for common exit pages, and to analyze entry and exit patterns over time.

Report: Analyze entry pages

Navigate to Paths > Pages > Entries & Exits > Entry Pages. This report provides the list of landing pages visitors use to land on your site.

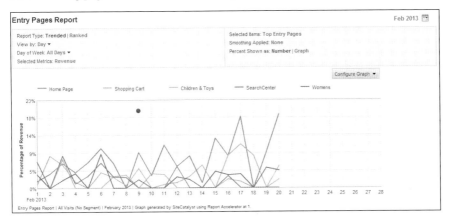

Key insights

Analyzing entry pages can help answer questions such as:

- **Is your vanity URL or a special landing page for the campaign successful in driving traffic to your site?** If you've created a vanity URL, you can analyze how much traffic is being sent to that landing page. The entry pages report counts only visits where the page in question is the entry page.

- **When a given page is the entry page, how often do visitors leave the site without accessing any other pages?** You can determine whether an entry page is optimized to serve the specific needs of the visitor to your site. A high bounce rate or a single access might indicate that the landing page needs to be optimized to better address specific needs.

Code implementation and console settings

No specific implementation detail is required to track entry pages. It is automatically tracked using `s.pageName`.

Report: Analyze original entry pages

Navigate to Paths > Pages > Entries & Exits > Original Entry Pages Report. This report displays reports success metrics based on the entry page of the visitor's first visit to your site as opposed to the visitor's entry page on the visit during which the success event occurred.

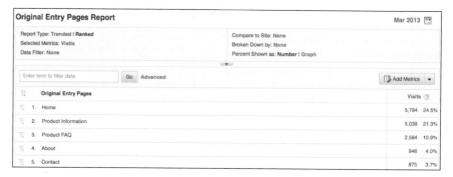

Key insight

Analyzing original entry pages can help answer questions such as:

- **What was the first experience the visitor had on your website?** This report tries to correlate the visitor's first experience and impression of your site to his propensity to convert.

Interpretation of report data

The first visit is based on persistent cookies, so if the visitor does not accept cookies, this data may be skewed.

Code implementation and console settings

No specific implementation detail is required to track original entry pages.

Report: Analyze exit pages

Navigate to Paths > Pages > Entries and Exits > Exit Pages Report. This report provides an overview of the last page the visitor viewed before exiting your site.

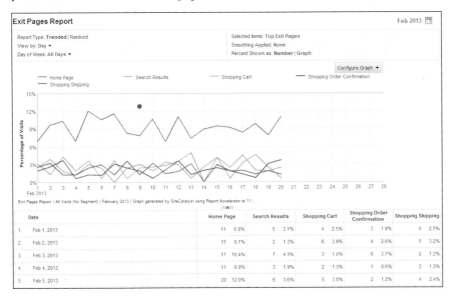

	Date	Home Page		Search Results		Shopping Cart		Shopping Order Confirmation		Shopping Shipping	
1.	Feb 1, 2013	11	6.9%	5	3.1%	4	2.5%	3	1.9%	4	2.5%
2.	Feb 2, 2013	15	9.7%	2	1.3%	6	3.9%	4	2.6%	5	3.2%
3.	Feb 3, 2013	17	10.4%	7	4.3%	3	1.8%	6	3.7%	2	1.2%
4.	Feb 4, 2013	11	6.9%	3	1.9%	2	1.3%	1	0.6%	2	1.3%
5.	Feb 5, 2013	20	12.0%	6	3.6%	5	3.0%	2	1.2%	4	2.4%

Key insight

Analyzing exit pages can help answer questions such as:

- **Which page has a maximum number of exits?** This report shows how many visitors left your site from a given page.

  ● **Note:** Maximum exits, by itself, may not provide many actionable insights. If your landing page has a login button and the visitor logs off after engaging with your site, we assume that the visitor is then redirected to the landing page. Of course, since the visitor is finished, he exits your site from the landing page. Now your landing page looks like it has a high exit rate!

Interpretation of report data

If your page has links that direct the page to another website, even if you open the external website in another tab or browser the page looks like it has a lot of exits.

Code implementation and console settings

No specific implementation detail is required to track exit pages.

Task: Understand navigation

Analyzing custom links and buttons is crucial to seeing how your visitors engage in the site. With pathing reports, you can determine the pages that a visitor visited, but with custom links, you can get a deeper insight into the links, tabs, or rich content the visitor engaged with. Also, some of these links or tabs don't refresh the page, so having navigation tracking would be particularly useful. Also, thinking about downloads, it would be great to know which kind of content is preferred for downloading. That said, let's take a closer look below.

Report: Analyze custom links

Navigate to Site Content > Links > Custom Links. This report provides the list of links that visitors prefer on your site.

Key insight

Analyzing custom links in this way can help answer questions such as:

- **Which links and types of links do your visitors prefer?** The popularity of links can give you insight into the type of content visitors are looking for. Also, if you have redundant links or buttons, this report will give you an idea of visitor preferences.

Code implementation and console settings

In the s.tl() call, remember to pass the link type as "o."

If you want to capture the page name on which one of these visitor actions occurred, Adobe recommends setting a custom traffic variable to capture the page name on all pages, and then capturing the page name in this same custom traffic variable on custom links, file downloads, and exit links.

Report: Analyze downloads

Navigate to Site Content > Links > Downloads Report. This report provides an overview of which files are being downloaded on your site.

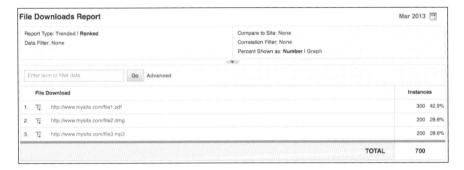

Key insights

Analyzing downloads in this way can help answer questions such as:

- **Which files are downloaded most frequently from your site?** This gives you an idea of which files your visitors prefer to download.

- **Which file formats are preferred by your visitors?** For example, visitors may trust an Adobe PDF file for a download more than a video download.

- **Are certain files downloaded more often during specific time periods?** The business and calendar seasonality can help you determine the optimal content for your files. For example, in the last quarter of the year, your visitors may be interested in downloading holiday recipes.

Interpretation of report data

In interpreting data on downloads, keep the following in mind:

- Downloads do not stop a visit from being single access.

- Pathing reports include only the one page, not the download.

- These are really download intents, as we can't measure whether the file was completely downloaded or even if there is a 404 error on the file being downloaded. Also, you would need to write custom code to determine if the visitor opened the file that was downloaded.

Code implementation and console settings

You can enable custom link tracking on the link that launches the download, then set the link type to download.

If the link does not contain a file name with an extension listed in the `s.linkDownloadFileTypes` variable, it will not be tracked, so ensure that the file type list is comprehensive for all file formats.

> **Note:** Validate that all formats for a given document are required. For example, perhaps you are currently translating your user manuals into twelve languages and making them available via your website. With file-download reporting, you'll know how often each user manual version is downloaded and can assess the business value of continuing to translate the user manual into all twelve languages.

Report: Analyze exit links

Navigate to Site Content > Links > Exit Links Report. An exit link is the link that a visitor clicks on to leave the ecosystem of your site. Exit links are different from exit pages.

Key insight

Analyzing exit links can help answer questions such as:

- **Which sites are your visitors visiting after your site?** This will help you determine which competitors your visitors are comparing your products to. You can also determine which websites you might want to negotiate an affiliate program with.

Interpretation of report data

In interpreting data on exit links, keep the following in mind:

- Custom link tracking hits are not counted as page views. This prevents an artificial inflation of the page view metric of the page with the links.

- Exit links are in context to the s.linkInternalFilters setting.

- SiteCatalyst calculates exit rates by time. When a visitor leaves your website for 30 minutes and does not continue to another tagged page in the website, SiteCatalyst considers the visit as closed.

- Exit links do not appear in any pathing reports. Pathing reports are determined by page views.

Code implementation and console settings

The parameter s.linkLeaveQueryString determines the logic used by exit links. If s.linkLeaveQueryString=false, exit links are determined using only the domain, path, and file portion of the link URL. If s.linkLeaveQueryString=true, the query string portion of the link URL is also used to determine an exit link.

If you see a large number of internal links being counted as exit links, check the `s.linkInternalFilters` variable. If an internal site is being listed as an exit link, it needs to be added in the internal filter list. If an external site is incorrectly missed in the exit links, the internal filters variable may be too generic and needs to be more explicit. For example, if any link that contains a.com is listed in the internal filter, then even true exit links like area.com will be considered internal to your site (since it contains a.com).

For manual custom link tracking, an `s.tl()` request must be fired with the middle parameter set to "e."

For an automatic custom link tracking:

- `s.trackExternalLinks` must be set to true.

- The link the visitor clicked on must not match any values within the `s.linkInternalFilters` variable.

- If `s.linkExternalFilters` is implemented, the external link must match at least one of the values set in this variable.

Conclusion

This chapter has covered a lot of ground on analyzing visitor engagement. The visitor's experience will have a high impact on his motivation to convert on your site.

- **Is the visitor having a good experience on your website?** This can be determined by the visitor's behavior on the site. A visitor normally has a good experience if he's able to complete the personal goal he had in mind when he came to your site. If the visitor gets an error on the page, the site loads too slowly, or the content does not engage him, you'll see a high bounce rate and lower conversion.

- **Does the visitor find the content engaging? How much time is he spending on it?** Understanding how the visitor is engaging with the site and how much time he's spending on the content will give you an idea of which content is most influencing his decisions.

- **How is the visitor navigating through your site? What paths or links does he prefer?** Following the visitor's path can give you insights into the purpose of his visit. Also, it gives you an idea of the sales cycle stage he is in.

- **Is he viewing any videos or rich media content?** This sheds light on the visitor's demographics and his propensity to engage with video and rich media content.

- **Which landing pages are preferred by the visitor? What's the bounce rate and exit rate on those pages?** This will give you insights into which landing pages need to be optimized to meet the customer expectations.

Next, we'll review the persuasion reports to understand which content at your site has the highest impact on the visitor. How are you feeling so far?

Review questions

1   How many traffic variables can you enable pathing on?

2   Does it matter which vendor is hosting your videos?

Review answers

1   This depends on your contract with Adobe. You could ask your company's SiteCatalyst admin or have your supported user call Adobe ClientCare.

2   As long as the video-hosting provider can send you information on the video name, time, and the actions taken on the videos, you should be able to track that using SiteCatalyst. This is generally accomplished through an API.

6 PERSUASION ANALYTICS

Lesson overview

In this lesson, you'll learn to analyze persuasion data. This chapter will help you understand which web pages truly have an impact on persuading your visitors to make that decision to convert. Think of persuasion as a visitor trying to decide between brands or different products to buy.

Goals of this section are:

- Understanding pages that influence in your website
- Determining the influence of technology
- Determining the influence of mobile technology on the data quality

 This lesson will take 30 minutes to complete.

Once a visitor is engaged, she still needs to be persuaded to make the final leap. The persuasion stage of the marketing funnel helps you find out which pages, product review ratings, or other content elements are successfully influencing your visitor's behavior.

Task: Define KPIs

We've been through quite a few of these—setting goals and KPIs should be second nature to you by now! For persuasion metrics, your business goal may be to increase revenue by 25 percent for the fiscal year. Examples of KPIs for persuasion could be:

- **Page influence visit rate**

  Page influence visit rate = Number of visits to pages that influence ÷ Total visits

  The page influence visit rate outlines the visits in which a page of influence was visited to the total number of visits. This helps you determine the extent to which the pages that influence are even visited. If the bulk of your visitors do not visit these pages, they may not be very useful after all.

- **Conversion from page influence**

  Orders from page influence = Number of orders after visits to pages that influence ÷ Total number of orders

  Units from page influence = Number of units purchased after visits to pages that influence ÷ Total number of orders

  Revenue from page influence = Revenue from orders after visits to pages that influence ÷ Total revenue

  The order to visitor rate highlights how many orders resulted from a visitor. It helps you determine the average number of visitors it takes for a conversion. The purpose of these KPIs is to determine the key metrics centered around pages that influence on your site. The first determination you are trying to make is whether the pages *you* think have an influence on the visitors truly have an influence on their buying decision or not.

- **Reviews ratings**

  Review rating = Number of good reviews ÷ Total number of reviews

  For products that you are selling, you could ask visitors to record their thoughts using product review. Getting more reviews would be the KPI. This would indicate the quality of the products you are selling and, more importantly, how it meets the customer needs.

Real-world example

Imagine that you work in marketing at a manufacturer of retail goods. Your company sells through resellers as well as direct via your website. People come to your site to learn about your products and, in some cases, purchase direct. You've been tasked with increasing your direct sales. To persuade visitors, you do the following on your product detail pages:

- Promote free ground shipping.
- Promote your fantastic return policy.
- Implement a product review system and start encouraging buyers to leave reviews.

Well on your way to success, you must report on the performance of these changes you made on your product detail page. The following KPIs can be used to show this performance relative to the goal:

- Add to cart trend/velocity
- Product review count and average by product in relation to velocity

If you have the resources, it's optimal to A/B test the changes in order to show direct lift as a result of the changes, with all things being equal (cyclical sales, and so on).

The next logical step is to determine which Adobe SiteCatalyst reports can help you understand the factors that affect the KPI. Deepen your analysis by looking at the data with multiple metrics. Then sharpen your insights by segmenting the data. Segments can include any custom traffic variable, any custom conversion variable, and any SiteCatalyst Attribute Importing and Naming Tool (SAINT) classification. Following are a few suggestions you can use to segment the conversion (this list is not meant to be exhaustive):

- By geosegmentation
- By channel
- By campaign
- By new and repeat visitor
- By first-time or return customer
- By referrer
- By mobile devices
- By nonmobile devices

Task: Determine page influence

Persuasion analytics are geared toward pages that the marketing team identifies as transitioning the prospect from the "learning and orienting" phase to deciding to buy. (Refer back to Chapter 1, "Preliminary Work," for a refresher on the stages of the marketing funnel.)

To track persuasion analysis, it is assumed that pages are tracked as such. The focus of the assessment is:

- Measuring visitor engagement with the persuasion page group
- Determining the correlation of those pages with conversion

Table 6.1 summarizes the metrics for pages that persuade.

Table 6.1 Persuasion reports and metrics

FOCUS	MEASURES	SITECATALYST REPORT	METRICS
Pages that persuade	Content Influence	Site content > Pages > Page type (created in SAINT classification)	Single access Participation metrics Time on page

Report: Understand pages that persuade

Navigate to Site Content > Pages > Page Type. This report will not appear by default. A SAINT classification file must be uploaded to categorize these pages. For example, pages can be classified as landing pages, learning and orienting pages, persuading pages, and conversion pages. The purpose of this report is to filter the pages that persuade and determine the extent to which they have an impact in your site.

Key insights

Running a page type report can help answer such questions as:

- **What is the effectiveness of the pages that were identified as "persuading"?** By finding the traffic for Page Type = Persuading pages, you can determine the pages that influence the visitor's conversion. Pathing reports can help determine how many times the conversion decision was influenced by this decision.

- **What content within the persuasion pages is engaging visitors?** By determining the videos and links that visitors are most engaged in, this analysis can provide guidance on the content within the pages that are compelling.

Interpretation of report data

In interpreting the page type reports, keep in mind that your data can be skewed if the right pages are not identified as the pages that persuade. And remember that just because a visitor visited a page, it doesn't guarantee that her decision was influenced merely by viewing the page.

Code implementation and console settings

A SAINT file with this classification needs to be loaded to classify the correct page names or page URLs as persuasion pages.

Real-world example

You work in marketing for a SaaS product (software as a service). You've invested money acquiring traffic and now you need to make sure that this traffic is qualified and engaged. The following KPIs can be leveraged to make that determination:

- Video views
- Time on site (or time on specific types of pages)
- Whitepaper downloads

Task: Determine technology influence

Understanding technology helps you gauge the influence of technology on the sales cycle. The crux of technology analytics is:

- How does technology affect visitor experience?

- What are the visitor's technical preferences? For those technical pages, does your website render well on her computer or device?

Table 6.2 highlights the metrics that help you understand a visitor's technology preferences.

Table 6.2 Technology reports and metrics

FOCUS	MEASURES	SITECATALYST REPORT	METRICS
Web technology influence	Understand visitor use of technology	Visitor profile > Languages	All key metrics
		Visitor profile > Technology > Browser	All key metrics
		Visitor profile > Technology > Browser types	All key metrics
		Visitor profile > Technology > Browser width	All key metrics
		Visitor profile > Technology > Browser height	All key metrics
		Visitor profile > Technology > Operating systems	All key metrics
		Visitor profile > Technology > Monitor color depths	All key metrics
		Visitor profile > Technology > Monitor resolutions	All key metrics
		Visitor profile > Technology > JavaScript	All key metrics
		Visitor profile > technology > JavaScript	All key metrics
		Visitor profile > Technology > JavaScript version	All key metrics
		Visitor profile > Technology > Cookies	All key metrics
		Visitor profile > Technology > Connection types	All key metrics
Video preferences	Analyze video players (Only in Version 14)	Video > Video players	Video views
		Video > Video by players	Video views
		Video > Video details by players	Video views
Understand performance	Understand bots	Site Metrics > Bots > Bots	All key metrics
		Site metrics > Bots > Bot pages	All key metrics
	Understand servers used	Site content > Pages report > Servers	All key metrics

Report: Understand visitor browser preferences

Navigate to Visitor Profile > Technology > Browser. This report identifies the browser used by your visitors.

Navigate to Visitor Profile > Technology > Browser Types. This report categorizes the browsers visiting your site into their major families.

Navigate to Visitor Profile > Technology > Browser Width. This report measures the browser's viewable area. It excludes scroll bars, and will be altered if the window size is changed.

Navigate to Visitor Profile > Technology > Browser Height. This report measures the browser's viewable area. It takes into account and excludes the title bar and bookmarks bar, and can be altered if the window size is changed.

Navigate to Visitor Profile > Languages. This report indicates the language settings on the browsers that were used to navigate your site. English languages also have multiple rows to indicate British English, US English, and Canadian English, among others.

Navigate to Visitor Profile > Technology > Operating Systems. This report indicates the operating system used by your visitor.

Navigate to Visitor Profile > Technology > Monitor Color Depths. This report refers to the number of colors that can be displayed on the screen.

Navigate to Visitor Profile > Technology > Monitor Resolutions. This report refers to the number of pixels that can be displayed going across and down the screen.

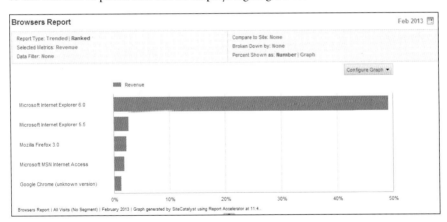

Key insights

Analyzing the technical preferences of your site can help answer questions such as:

- **Which browsers should your website support?** This data gives you an understanding of your audience's web sophistication level and can help you understand which browser and version you need to optimize. This will also help you prioritize testing for your website.

- **Is your site's screen height width maximized for visitor experience?** Even though a visitor may have her monitor resolutions at one setting, she may not have her browser window maximized to that setting. The browser height and width reports help you optimize for the visitor's preferred settings.

- **Is your site tailored to people speaking languages other than US English?** If you see increased visits but less conversion from France, visitors there may need a different experience. If the fallout rate is substantially high, they could need a more tailored, substantial visitor experience like a site translated in a regional language.

- **Is your site optimized for the popular operating systems used by your visitors?** If you see increased visits from a particular operating system, you can design and optimize for it.

- **Are your site colors and images optimized for best visitor experience?** If you can identify the most used monitor color depths and monitor resolutions, you can design and optimize your images and colors for it.

Interpretation of report data

In interpreting the data with respect technical preferences, keep the following in mind:

- SiteCatalyst uses a lookup table to populate the browsers report. After any major browser update, you may see "Unknown Version" until Adobe retroactively fixes the data.

- If you see a browser you don't recognize, it could potentially be from browser plugins that let visitors manually alter the user-agent string. The user-agent string has the browser information.

- Language settings are set by default by many browsers. Although uncommon, this can be altered by the visitor, which has the potential to impact this report data.

Code implementation and console settings

This data is based on the information sent by the browser in the user-agent string and does not require any implementation in SiteCatalyst.

Report: Understand technology impact

Navigate to Visitor Profile > Technology > Java. This report monitors visitors with Java enabled.

Navigate to Visitor Profile > Technology > JavaScript. This report monitors visitors with JavaScript enabled.

Navigate to Visitor Profile > Technology > JavaScript Version. This reports tells you the version of JavaScript used by visitors.

Navigate to Visitor Profile > Technology > Cookies. This report indicates whether the visitor has enabled cookies in the browser.

Navigate to Visitor Profile > Technology > Connection Types. This report indicates whether your visitors are using a modem, DSL, or cable modem. If the information cannot be determined, it is classified as unknown.

Navigate to Site Content > Pages Report > Servers to understand which server is getting maximum traffic on your site. This will help to do load balancing on your servers.

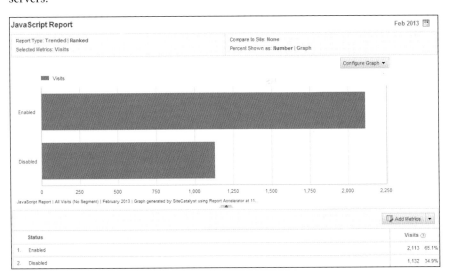

Key insights

Analyzing visitor profiles can help answer questions such as:

- **What is the level of technical sophistication of visitors to your site?** If JavaScript is enabled on most visitors' browsers, you can use JavaScript on your site.

- **What is the accuracy of reports?** If JavaScript is enabled on most visitors' browsers, your reports will be more accurate. Identify the version of JavaScript with which your site should be compatible.

Interpretation of report data

In interpreting visitor profile data, keep the following in mind:

- SiteCatalyst uses a JavaScript function to grab browser settings to determine the connection type. If the visitor's browser does not support JavaScript, or has JavaScript disabled, or does not support JavaScript, the connection type will be listed as unknown.

- If a visitor fires an image request from an unknown browser source such as an executable program or programs her own browser in Linux, and JavaScript functionality is not available, technology reports will show "none" to indicate this information could not be gathered.

- "None" can also occur if your implementation code is placed into the <head> tags of your web page, since the page has not fully loaded yet on the browser. If the code is placed in the <body> tags, this issue will be resolved.

Code implementation and console settings

This data is based on the information sent by the browser in the user-agent string and does not require any implementation in SiteCatalyst.

Report: Understand video player preferences (Version 14 only)

Navigate to Video > Video Players. This report indicates which version of the video players is being used to watch videos on your site.

Navigate to Video > Video by Players. This report segments the videos by the video players.

Navigate to Video > Video Details by Players. This report gives you a breakdown of the video segments by the video players, with details to give a higher granularity.

Key insight

Analyzing reports of video player preferences can help questions such as:

- **Which video players are popular?** You can optimize videos for popular players by understanding this data.

Report: Understand bots

Note: IAB bot filtering rules are a quick way to start detecting bots.

Navigate to Site Metrics > Bots > Bots. This report tells you the bots that have viewed your site.

Navigate to Site Metrics > Bots > Bot Pages. This report tells you which pages at your site have been viewed by bots.

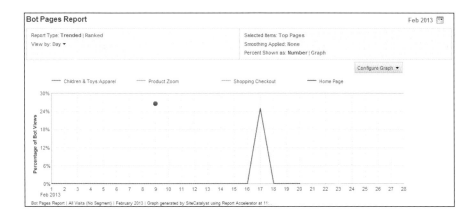

Key insight

Analyzing reports of bots to your site can help questions such as:

- **Is your site is frequently scanned by bots?** Bots can be identified by the user-agent string as well as IP address or IP address range, and the bot traffic can be excluded.

Interpretation of report data

In interpreting bot data, keep the following in mind:

- Bots can be explicitly identified or Adobe gives you the option of excluding any bots or spiders identified by Interactive Advertising Bureau (IAB).

- If a bot has artificially inflated your report numbers, the bot report cannot fix the data retroactively.

Code implementation and console settings

This data is based on the information sent by the browser in the user-agent string identifying the bot and does not require any code implementation in SiteCatalyst.

You need to set up bot rules in the admin console. See the Appendix for more details.

Task: Determine mobile influence

Understanding mobile influence on your website helps you gauge the influence of devices and technology on the sales cycle. Questions that can be answered by mobile analytics include:

- How does mobile technology affect the visitor experience?

- What are the visitor's mobile device and technology preferences? For those pages, does your website render well on different devices?

Table 6.3 presents the reports and metrics for mobile.

Table 6.3 Mobile reports and metrics

FOCUS	MEASURES	SITECATALYST REPORT	METRICS
Mobile devices influence	Understand visitor use of mobile devices	Mobile > Devices	All key metrics
		Mobile > Device type	All key metrics
		Mobile > Manufacturer	All key metrics
		Mobile > Screen size	All key metrics
		Mobile > Screen height	All key metrics
		Mobile > Screen width	All key metrics
		Mobile > Cookie support	All key metrics
		Mobile > Image support	All key metrics
		Mobile > Color depth	All key metrics
		Mobile > Audio support	All key metrics
		Mobile > Video support	All key metrics
Mobile technology influence	Understand visitor use of mobile technology	Mobile > DRM	All key metrics
		Mobile > Net protocols	All key metrics
		Mobile > Operating system	All key metrics
		Mobile > Java version	All key metrics
		Mobile > Bookmark URL length	All key metrics
		Mobile > Mail URL length	All key metrics
		Mobile > Browser URL length	All key metrics
		Mobile > Device number transmit (ON/OFF)	All key metrics
		Mobile > PTT	All key metrics
		Mobile > Decoration mail support	All key metrics
		Mobile > Information services	All key metrics
		Visitor profile > Technology > Mobile carrier	All key metrics

Report: Understand mobile devices

Navigate to Mobile > Devices. This report displays the visits from different types of devices.

Navigate to Mobile > Device Type. This report categorizes visits from different devices.

Navigate to Mobile > Manufacturer. This report segregates visits from different mobile manufacturers.

Navigate to Mobile > Screen Size. This report displays both screen height and width.

Navigate to Mobile > Screen Height. This report displays only the screen heights of the mobile devices.

Navigate to Mobile > Screen Width. This report displays only the screen width of the mobile devices.

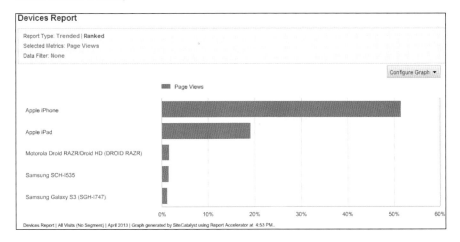

Key insight

Analyzing the total visits from mobile devices to your site can help answer questions such as:

- **Is the site optimized for mobile viewing?** Determining the device from which the traffic originated will help you optimize the visitor experience.

Code implementation and console settings

This data is based on the information sent by the browser in the user-agent string and does not require any implementation in SiteCatalyst.

Report: Understand technology support

Navigate to Mobile > Cookie Support. This report determines whether the mobile device accepts cookies.

Navigate to Mobile > Image Support. This report groups devices by the image types supported.

Navigate to Mobile > Color Depth. This report groups devices by the number of colors supported.

Navigate to Mobile > Audio Support. This report groups devices by the audio formats supported.

Navigate to Mobile > Video Support. This report groups devices by the video formats supported.

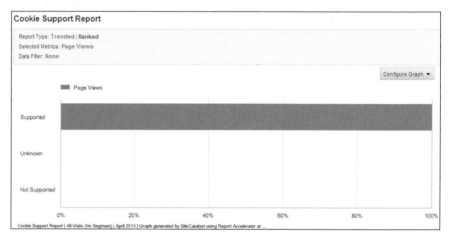

Key insight

Analyzing the technology support to your site can help answer questions such as:

- **What is the optimal design for your mobile site?** Knowing the technology support of your mobile site will help you determine how to design your site. If most visitors lack cookie or image support, you'll need to adopt more text-based content. With audio and video support, you could give visitors a richer media experience.

Interpretation of report data

In interpreting the mobile data, keep in mind that the sum of the groups will be greater than the total shown at the bottom of the report since the visits can be attributed to multiple groups.

Code implementation and console settings

This data is based on the information sent by the browser in the user-agent string and does not require any implementation in SiteCatalyst.

Report: Understand other mobile settings

Navigate to Mobile > DRM. Digital Rights Management (DRM) is a system that was invented by the Open Mobile Alliance. This alliance represents mobile phone manufacturers, mobile manufacturers, and mobile network and information technology companies. The standard specifies three main methods: forward lock, combined delivery, and separate delivery. This report groups visits from mobile devices based on its DRM standard.

Note: The other mobile settings reports are listed for the sake of completeness, but with the changing mobile technology, they are not very useful.

Navigate to Mobile > Operating System. This report interprets the visits from different mobile operating systems.

Navigate to Mobile > Java Version. This report provides information on the Java version.

Navigate to Mobile > Bookmark URL Length. This report tells you the maximum URL length permitted by devices in use by visitors.

Navigate to Mobile > Mail URL Length. This report tells you the maximum mail URL length permitted by devices in use by visitors.

Navigate to Mobile > Device Number Transmit (ON/OFF). This report tells you how many visitors have devices that transmit their device numbers.

Navigate to Mobile > PTT. This report tells you how many visitors have devices that have the Push to talk (PTT) feature.

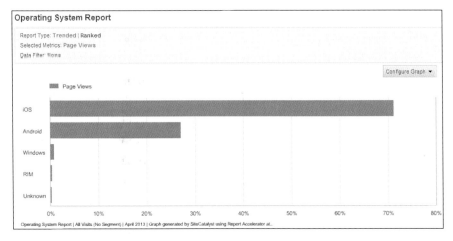

Navigate to Mobile > Decoration Mail Support. This report reports Deco-mail, a mobile functionality that allows rendering of HTML on mobile for MMS. This is more popular in Japanese devices.

Navigate to Mobile > Information Services. This report shows the information services supported by the device.

Navigate to Visitor Profile > Technology > Mobile Carrier. This report lists the carriers used by visitors on mobile devices.

Key insights

Reports on visitors' mobile settings can help you answer questions such as:

- **Is your site optimized for popular mobile technology?** Based on the popular mobile devices and technology visitors use to access your site, determine whether your site is rendering well on those devices.

- **Does your site provide the optimal visitor experience?** Since different mobile devices have different resolutions and colors, your digital assets will need to be optimized for each of them.

Code implementation and console settings

This data is based on the information sent by the browser in the user-agent string and does not require any implementation in SiteCatalyst.

Conclusion

Persuasion reports help you validate some key information about your visitors:

- **What is the influence of your key pages on your conversion?** This helps you understand the success of your strategy for your key pages.

- **How do technology choices on visitor's desktop and/or laptop affect your user experiences?** This helps you understand the popular technology choices that visitors to your site have made. It helps you conclude if your site can cater to that audience.

- **How do technology choices on mobile devices affect your user experiences?** This helps you understand the mobile technology choices visitors to your site have made. It helps you conclude if your site can support those visitors.

- **How do bots impact the data on your site?** Bots can artificially inflate your traffic numbers. Knowing the bots identity and preventing the bot traffic from skewing your numbers can help you from making wrong decisions based on data.

Next, we'll review the conversion reports and track the KPIs, the reports, and metrics. Take a well-deserved break!

Review questions

1 Does Adobe offer a list of known bots?

2 Is the video players report available in SiteCatalyst 15?

Review answers

1 Not really. However, Adobe has recently made it easy to exclude the IAB list of known spiders and bots. Your admin can simply check the Enable IAB Bot Filtering Rules box and click Save. The traffic from these agents will be collected in SiteCatalyst, but will be sectioned off. It will not be included in your traffic or conversion data, but you will incur a server call.

2 The video players report has been deprecated in Version 15.

7 CONVERSION ANALYTICS

Lesson overview

In this lesson, you'll learn to analyze conversion data. Almost everyone in an organization has an eye on conversion to assess the monetary impact of marketing and technology decisions. So this is an important topic for all.

The goals of this section are:

- Understanding what to measure to determine the success of converting customers

- Determining which Adobe SiteCatalyst reports to run to determine gross and net revenue

- Determining the issues that impact the data and the implementation details that affect data quality

 This lesson will take 45 minutes to complete.

Once a visitor starts the conversion process on your site, you want to sell and cross-sell as many products to him as possible. Optimizing your cart, your products, and your checkout process can help you over the final hurdle of turning a visitor into a customer.

Task: Define goals and KPIs

As with all analytics, we begin by defining goals and setting KPIs. For conversion metrics, your business goal may be to increase revenue by 25 percent for the financial year. Examples of KPIs for conversion could be:

- **Focus on purchases**

    The purpose of these KPIs is to determine the key metrics centered around orders on your site. There are several aspects you could compare the orders with, such as checkout rate.

    Order to checkout rate = Number of orders ÷ Number of checkouts

    The order to checkout rate gives you an idea of how many orders resulted from an average checkout. If you have few items in your orders for each checkout, then that might be an opportunity for you to cross-sell when the visitor is viewing his cart.

    Order to visit rate = Number of orders ÷ Total visits

    The order to visit rate tells you how many orders resulted from a visit. This data can help you determine the average number of visits it takes for a conversion.

    Order to visitor rate = Number of orders ÷ Total visitors

    The order to visitor rate highlights the number of orders that resulted from a visitor. It helps you figure out the average number of visitors it takes for a conversion.

    Average Units Per Order = Total number of units ÷ Total number of orders

    This highlights how many units result from an order. It helps you determine the average number of units a visitor buys in a single order.

- **Increase microconversions and decrease microconversion abandonment**

    An example of a microconversion might be signing up for a newsletter subscription or downloading a white paper, as opposed to making a purchase on your website.

    Microconversion 1 visit rate = Number of microconversion 1 completions ÷ Total number of visits

    The microconversion visit rate helps you understand how many visits a microconversion was completed in. If not many visits result in a microconversion, consider revaluating the purpose of the microconversion or moving it to a more visible place on the site.

    Microconversion 1 visitor rate = Number of microconversion 1 completions ÷ Total number of visitors

Real-world example

You work in an ecommerce website business that specializes in selling multiple products across a wide range of categories: toys, clothes, accessories, home furniture, and home goods. Your business goal is to increase revenue on categories and products that have the highest turnover. You have several conversion KPIs that tie into your business goal:

- Conversion rate by product category. This could be further segmented by product ID: for each product, apart from the conversion rate, how often are they returned?

- Cart optimization by product category by region (segmented by product ID). Trended over time, how often are visitors purchasing, and which geographical location prefers each product?

- Which products are cross-sold the most? How can you optimize that by geographical location?

- Which branded and nonbranded keywords contribute most to the purchase?

The microconversion visitor rate tells you how many visitors are taking the steps you have identified as microconversions. The learning is similar to the microconversion visit rate if the same visitor is not expected to complete the microconversion task multiple times.

$$\text{Microconversion 1 completions} = \text{Number of microconversion 1 completions} \div \text{Number of conversions started}$$

$$\text{Microconversion 1 abandonment} = (\text{Number of conversions started} - \text{Number of microconversion 1 completions}) \div \text{Number of conversions started}$$

Microconversion completions help you understand the abandonment and fulfillment of the conversion. If you see a high abandonment rate, consider reevaluating the information you're seeking from the user in a microconversion.

- **Optimize cart conversions**

  If your business model has shopping carts, this next set of KPIs may apply to you:

  Cart open rate = Number of cart opens ÷ Total visits

  The cart open rate helps you gauge the visitor's propensity to convert.

  Cart add rate = Number of cart additions ÷ Total number of cart opens

  The cart add rate tells you the number of products the visitor is interested in.

  Cart removal rate = Number of cart removals ÷ Total number of cart opens

The cart removal rate tells you the number of times the visitor changed his mind and removed an item from his cart. An ad hoc analysis could shed some light on any trends that are negatively impacting the visitor's decision. Segment the visits in which there were cart removals, then do a path analysis between the events cart add and the cart removal.

Cart checkout rate = Number of checkouts ÷ Total number of cart opens

The cart checkout rate helps you understand how successful you were in keeping the visitor's interest in buying between the time he opened a cart and checked out.

Cart abandonment rate = (Number of cart opens – Number of cart checkouts) ÷ Total number of cart opens

The cart abandonment rate helps you understand the potential to improve conversion between the time the visitor opened a cart and checked out.

- **Get insights on cost**

  Cost is probably one thing that is common across verticals and irrespective of the microconversions and macroconversions. Ideally, when you compute costs, add all your marketing expenses, your development costs, and vendor costs. Ensuring that will give you a more realistic return on investment (ROI).

  Cost per acquisition = Total cost ÷ Total number of units

  Cost per visit = Total cost ÷ Total number of visits

  Cost per visitor = Total cost ÷ Total number of visitors

  The cost per acquisition, visit, and visitor gives you an idea of how much you're spending on an average visit or visitor. It will also help you gain perspective when you're looking at the ROI.

- **Increase gross revenue**

  Gross revenue is the amount of money you charge the customer for your products.

  Gross revenue per visit = Total gross revenue ÷ Total visits

  Gross revenue per visitor = Total gross revenue ÷ Total visitors

  Gross order value = Total gross revenue ÷ Total orders

  The gross revenue per acquisition, visit, and visitor tells you how much you're earning with every visit or visitor. It will also help you gain perspective when you're looking at the ROI.

- **Increase return on investment**

  The ROI compares the revenue you generate and the cost associated with it.

  Visit ROI = Gross revenue per visit ÷ Cost per visit

  Visitor ROI = Gross revenue per visitor ÷ Cost per visitor

  Order ROI = Gross revenue per order ÷ Cost per order

  Unit ROI = Gross revenue per unit ÷ Cost per unit

  If the ROI is 1, you're earning the same amount that you're spending. If the ROI is less than 1, you're spending more than you're earning. If the ROI is greater than 1, you're spending less than you're earning, which is great!

- **Estimate loss of revenue**

  You can estimate how much revenue is lost from errors and abandonment:

  Revenue loss from errors = Number of visits with page not found errors × Revenue per visit

  Revenue loss from abandonment = Number of cart abandonments × Revenue per visit

  Putting a numeric value on revenue loss can help build a sense of urgency and priority within your organization to address these issues.

The next logical step would be to understand which SiteCatalyst report or reports can help you understand the factors that affect the KPI. Deepen your analysis by looking at the data with multiple metrics. Then sharpen your insights by segmenting the data. Segments can include any custom traffic variable, any custom conversion variable, and any SiteCatalyst Attribute Importing and Naming Tool (SAINT) classification. Following are a few suggestions you can use to segment the conversion (this list is not meant to be exhaustive).

- By geosegmentation
- By channel
- By campaign
- By new and repeat visitor
- By first-time or return customer
- By referrer
- By mobile devices
- By nonmobile devices

Table 7.1 presents metrics and reports that can help you evaluate conversion performance. The reports listed are covered in more detail later in the chapter.

Table 7.1 Conversion reports and metrics

FOCUS	MEASURES	SITECATALYST REPORT	METRICS
Purchase focus	Purchases	Site metrics > Purchases > Purchases conversion funnel	Product views Cart additions Checkouts Orders Units Revenue
	Revenue	Site metrics > Purchases > Revenue	Revenue
	Orders	Site metrics > Purchases > Orders	Orders
	Units	Site metrics > Purchases > Units	Units
Cart focus	Cart conversion funnel	Site metrics > Shopping cart > Cart conversion funnel	Instances Carts Checkouts Orders Revenue
	Number of carts	Site metrics > Shopping cart > Carts	Selected by default
	Number of cart views	Site metrics > Shopping cart > Cart views	Selected by default
	Number of cart additions	Site metrics > Shopping cart > Cart additions	Selected by default
	Number of cart removals	Site metrics > Shopping cart > Cart removals	Selected by default
	Number of checkouts	Site metrics > Shopping cart > Checkouts	Selected by default

(continues on next page)

Table 7.1 Conversion reports and metrics (continued)

FOCUS	MEASURES	SITECATALYST REPORT	METRICS
Product focus	Product focus	Products > Product conversion funnel	Product views Cart additions Checkouts Orders Units Revenue
		Products > Products	Cart views Cart additions Cart removals Checkouts Orders Units Revenue
		Products > Cross-sell	Cart views Cart additions Cart removals Checkouts Orders Units Revenue
		Products > Categories	Cart views Cart additions Cart removals Checkouts Orders Units Revenue
Customer focus	Funnel complete	Site metrics > Custom events > Event number specified by your admin	Selected by default
	Funnel abandonment	Site metrics > Custom events > Event number specified by your admin	Selected by default
	Form submits	Site metrics > Custom events > Event number specified by your admin	Selected by default
	Form abandonment	Custom conversion > Variable specified by your admin	

● **Note:** For macroconversions that are purchase-oriented, SiteCatalyst has some predefined reports that you can use. For microconversions that are specific to you organization, consult your admin.

Task: Manage macroconversions (purchase focus)

Macroconversions are the main goals of your website—the ones that align with the primary goals of your site, like generating revenue. Microconversions are the secondary and tertiary goals of your site, such as signing up for an email subscription.

Report: Understand purchase conversion funnel

Navigate to Site Metrics > Purchases > Purchases Conversion Funnel. The purchase conversion funnel is a basic conversion funnel that initially shows visits (report-specific), carts, checkout, orders, units, and revenue.

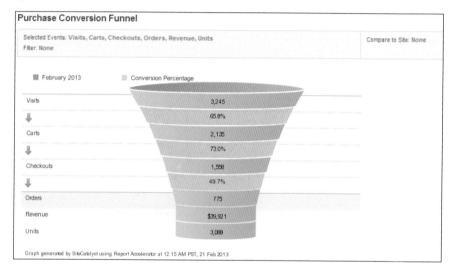

Key insights

Understanding the purchase conversion funnel can help answer questions such as:

- **What's the conversion rate of your visits?** This helps you determine the quality of the traffic to your site. You can understand the ratio of visits that resulted in an order.

- **How many visits resulted in an order?** This can also help you evaluate your site's traffic quality.

- **What's the total number of purchases or orders?** The purchase conversion funnel report focuses on the total orders that were placed. If multiple products or multiple units are bought in a single order, this report will show only one instance of that.

- **What's the conversion funnel for a specific product?** To learn this, apply a filter to select the variable that stores the product name. Better still, run the Products > Products Conversion Funnel report discussed later in this chapter.

Interpretation of report data

In interpreting the data with respect to purchase conversion at your site, keep the following in mind:

- "Visits (report-specific)" is a subset of the "total visits" metric that occurs in custom conversion reports.

- It indicates the number of visits using the filters assigned on that reports.

Code implementation and console settings

The product variable needs to be set in conjunction with an event. A semicolon is the delimiter between the variables for a product:

```
'Category;Product;Quantity;Price'
```

However, when you want to set multiple products, those should be separated by a comma. If your delimiters are incorrect, or the fields are in the wrong order, the data won't populate correctly in the product variable. Since the default delimiters used are commas and semicolons, the data populated in the products variable cannot include any commas or semicolons (before the products variable is created). Also, all HTML characters, such as registered symbols or trademarks, should be removed from the product name.

Note the comma between the two data sets in the second line of the following code example:

```
s.events="purchase";
s.products="Running;Shoe;1;69.95,Running;Socks;10;29.99";
s.purchaseID="1234567890";
```

Relevant events to set with products are scOpen, scView, scRemove, scCheckout, purchase, and prodView, but any custom event can be set. Also, if the event variable is not set with the products string, prodView event is set by default.

The category value in the product variable is created when a product is first recorded and persists for the entire month. All subsequent success events recorded for the product will automatically be credited to the category that was first assigned. This can cause unexpected results, so Adobe recommends assigning categories in SAINT classification for product categories.

Real-world example

You work in an ecommerce company that sells kids' toys and clothes. At some point you realize that the revenue is listed lower in SiteCatalyst than your accounting books. Also, when you're looking at the cross-sell reports, most products seem to cross-sell to themselves. You want to know what went wrong, so you enlist the help of an implementation specialist, who determines the following:

- The purchase event is probably set right, since you're seeing some revenue.

- The parameters might not be set correctly for situations in which a visitor buys multiple units of the same product. While setting the `s.products` variable, the units parameter must be updated with the total number of units purchased for the product, and the revenue must be updated with the total amount paid for all the units of the product. So, for example, if a person bought two Monopoly games, then the units will be set to two and the revenue should be set to 40 (assuming one game of Monopoly costs $20). This will also resolve the cross-sell issue caused by listing the same product twice in the `s.products` variable.

In terms of revenue, be aware of the following:

- Be sure to strip currency symbols ($) from the price.

- Revenue is impacted by the value passed in `s.products` variable.

- It is also impacted by the currency setting for the report suite.

- The revenue reports round the decimal places for a time period based on the currency set in the report suite. It does not round each individual product or hit. So if you add the sum of daily revenue, it might be slightly off compared to the weekly revenue.

- You can create a calculated metric and a report that does not round revenue to the nearest whole currency.

- When more than one product is present in the `s.products` variable, all the revenue information will be summed up toward the revenue report; for example:

  `s.products="Mens;Shoes;1;25.50,Womens;Shoes;1;34.50"`

  would pass $60 in revenue to SiteCatalyst.

- Revenue will not be multiplied if the visitor buys multiple units of a single product. For example, `s.products="Womens;Shoes;3;25.00"` will list revenue of $25 instead of $75 (three pairs of shoes for $25 a pair). So the correct way to pass that information would be:

  `s.products="Womens;Shoes;3;75.00"`

You can create a serialized event by passing a unique value in a purchaseID variable, so that the revenue data is not inflated if a page is reloaded or the same purchase information is sent multiple times.

Quantity refers to a unit that is driven by the value passed in the s.products variable. When you sell two units of the same product, you could see the same product as being cross-sold because the product is being passed in twice in the product string; for example, ';product;1;1.99,;product;1;1.99'. Instead, this should be passed in as ;product;2;1.99 to indicate two units of the same product.

Report: Understand revenue

Navigate to Site Metrics > Purchases > Revenue. This report specifies the total revenue you have earned. The revenue will be your gross revenue and will not include any adjustments stemming from returns or cancellations.

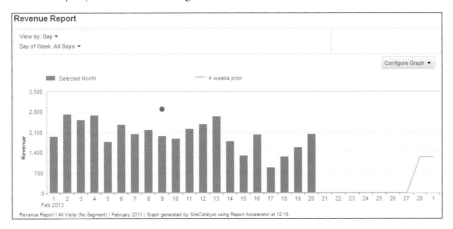

Key insights

Understanding revenue can help answer questions such as:

- **What is the total revenue generated by your website and digital efforts?**
  The key insight from this report is the total revenue generated from your website. This number may or may not tie accurately with your back-end database due to the way that SiteCatalyst handles decimals.

- **Which events trigger high revenue?** Determine which events influence the revenue trends. Some of the campaigns or market conditions can positively or negatively impact the revenue. You can isolate that now.

Interpretation of report data

In interpreting the data with respect to revenue at your site, keep the following in mind:

- Revenue will be the gross revenue received from the web without taking into account cancellations and returns.

- To show decimals in revenue, create a calculated metric where the formula section contains "Revenue" and the calculated metric is set to "Currency" with two decimal places.

- Excluded IP addresses may be placing orders that may increment your database numbers, but not the SiteCatalyst revenue numbers.

- Time zone differences between the database and the setting in SiteCatalyst can create subtle differences in the date credited with the revenue.

- The revenue report rounds the total amount for a time period to the nearest currency value. It does not round the decimals for each individual product or hit. SiteCatalyst rounds each day to the nearest whole currency, so the sum of each day will be off by a very small amount when compared to the monthly total.

Code implementation and console settings

The settings and implementation for understanding revenue are similar to those for purchase conversion:

- The data will populate only if the purchase event is set. If the event is set on the confirmation page, the data will be sent to Adobe only after the page successfully loads.

- Serialize the purchase event using a purchase ID (a unique value or order ID that is passed in with a purchase event in order to prevent the double-counting of orders).

- The same parameters are passed in the s.purchase variable as mentioned in the revenue section above.

- When more than one product is present in the s.products variable, all the revenue information will be summed up toward the revenue report; for example

  s.products="Mens;Shoes;1;25.50,Womens;Shoes;1;34.50"

  would pass $60 in revenue to SiteCatalyst.

- Revenue will not be multiplied if the visitor buys multiple units of a single product. For example, `s.products="Womens;Shoes;3;25.00"` will have a revenue of $25 instead of $75 (three pairs of shoes for $25 a pair). So the correct way to pass that information would be:

  `s.products="Womens;Shoes;3;75.00"`

- Hourly breakdowns of revenue are based on the report suite's time zone.

Report: Understand orders

Navigate to Site Metrics > Purchases > Orders. This report specifies the total number of orders in the selected time period. This gives you an idea of number of orders placed. An order can consist of multiple units of the same product or multiple products.

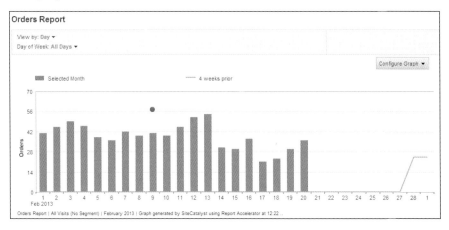

Key insights

Analyzing reports of orders placed at your site can help answer questions such as:

- **How many orders are generated by your website?** You'll be able to determine the number of orders generated by your digital efforts. This number may or may not match your back-end database if you're not passing a `purchaseID` variable.

- **Which events trigger high or low orders?** Determine which events influence the order trends. Campaigns or market conditions can positively or negatively impact the orders. You could be losing orders when a visitor abandons his shopping cart or the conversion funnel. So, it's important to identify the contributing events to the high and low points of order activity on your site to remedy or enhance those order trends.

Interpretation of report data

In interpreting the data with respect to orders placed on your site, keep the following in mind:

- If you switch the allocation to linear after collecting data for some time, orders and units need to accept decimal numbers to receive partial credit for purchases. Due to Adobe's data warehouse architecture, the data is now stored in a separate table that allows for decimals. The impact on the SiteCatalyst user is that the interface will lose the historical data for orders and units.

- Units and orders won't match if multiple units of a product are sold in a single order.

- An order is defined as a completion of a purchase. SiteCatalyst counts orders as the number of times the purchase event is fired.

Code implementation and console settings

There are no special settings for the orders report.

Report: Units

Navigate to Site Metrics > Purchases > Units. This report specifies the total number of units ordered in the selected time period. Since each order can contain multiple units and a mix of different products, units help you optimize inventory.

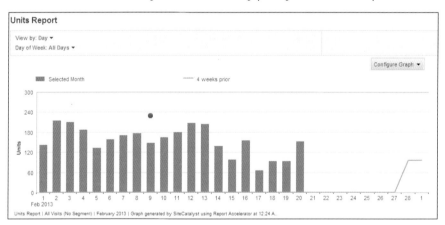

Key insights

Analyzing reports of units ordered from your site can help answer questions such as:

- **How many units are visitors purchasing per order?** Determine the trends of units sold.

- **What inventory should you plan for?** This report shows the total units that were ordered for the selected time period. The units metric reveals general inventory movement, which is helpful because there can be many units purchased per order.

- **What is the seasonality of your product(s)?** Identify the highs or lows of unit movement.

- **Which events correlate with the inventory flow?** Pinpoint the events or properties that contribute to the inventory flow on your site.

Interpretation of report data

In interpreting unit data, keep the following in mind:

- Units can be greater than orders since multiple units of a single product or multiple products can be ordered in a single order.

- If you purchase two products from two different categories, both categories will show one order each, summing to two orders (although there was only one order), but the number of units against each product will be correct.

Code implementation and console settings

The settings below apply to the unit report:

- The data will populate only if the purchase event is set.

- Serialize the purchase event using a purchase ID (a value that is passed in with a purchase event to prevent the double-counting of orders).

- The units data needs to be set in the `s.products` variable.

Task: Manage macroconversions (cart focus)

Almost all of us are familiar with the online shopping cart. It's a great way to add items to your cart for consideration before you are ready to check out. As an eCommerce site owner, you will always be looking for ways to optimize the shopping cart experience for your user and evaluate how best you can get them to add more items, cross-sell related items, and dissuade them from removing items. This section is focused heavily on just that!

Report: Understand cart conversion funnel

Navigate to Site Metrics > Shopping Cart > Cart Conversion Funnel. The default events are instances, carts, checkouts, orders, and revenue.

This report helps you analyze key conversion ratios. By changing the calendar dates, you can analyze key conversions like instances to orders, carts to orders, and checkouts to orders. You can also review revenue averages like average revenue per instance, average revenue per cart, average revenue per checkout, average revenue per order. You can also review order averages like average orders per instance, average orders per cart, and average orders per checkout.

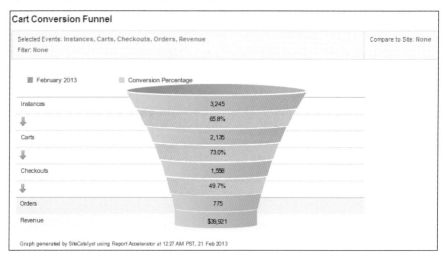

Key insights

Analyzing the cart conversion funnel can help you answer questions such as:

- **What's the likelihood of a visitor starting a cart order?** The cart open to order ratio should give you an insight into this. If the ratio is too small, there may be an issue either with your cart process or with the SiteCatalyst events being set.

- **If a visitor removes items from his cart, how likely is he to check out?** The cart removals to order ratio should give you a preview of this data. If a visitor who removes products from his cart does not have a high tendency to order, he can be targeted again with an email campaign.

- **If a visitor adds an item to his cart, how likely is he to add another?** Since SiteCatalyst tracks the cart adds as a counter event, you may not be able to segment the visits where the cart addition event was incremented more than once. So to understand this, you could look at visits in which units were greater than one or in which there were multiple products.

- **What is the average dollar value that a visitor spends on the site?** This helps you determine the average dollar value that an average visitor spends. Then you could compare your high spenders with your low spenders to see any patterns they exhibit as a group.

Interpretation of report data

In interpreting the data with respect to cart conversion, keep the following in mind:

- The lack of cart metric data in conversion reports could indicate that the shopping cart events have not been implemented on your site or have not been implemented correctly.

- Cart indicates how many times the `scOpen` event is set.

- Cart additions indicate how many times the `scAdd` event is set.

- Cart removals indicate how many times the `scRemove` event is set.

- Checkout indicates how many times the `scCheckout` event is set.

- Orders indicate how many times the `purchase` event is set.

- For events, if no success event is set, `prodView` is set by default.

Code implementation and console settings

The following settings apply to the cart conversion reports:

- For cart, set the `scOpen` event.

- For cart additions, set the `scAdd` event.

- For cart removals, set the `scRemove` event.

- For checkout, set the `scCheckout` event.

- For orders, set the `purchase` event.

- For events, if no success event is set, `prodView` is set by default.

- If your checkout funnel has more steps than the built-in events, you can use a custom success event.

Report: Understand number of carts

Navigate to Site Metrics > Shopping Cart > Carts. This report shows you the number of shopping carts that were opened by clicking on the cart or adding the first item purchased to the cart during the chosen time period.

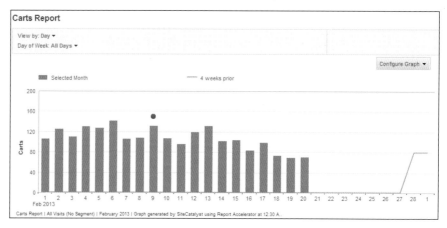

Key insights

Analyzing the number of carts can help answer questions such as:

- **On what pages do visitors tend to think of carts?** Run the pages report and choose the carts metric to find out which pages contribute the most or least shopping carts.

- **At what point is the visitor ready to engage with a cart?** Correlate the carts report with time spent on the site to understand how much time is spent on the site before the visitor uses a shopping cart.

- **How many times does a visitor come to the site before using a shopping cart?** After you run the carts report, you could segment the data by the "first-time visits" to get an idea of the engagement with the cart in the very first visit.

- **What are the patterns, highs, or lows in the number of carts opened on your site?** The carts report shows you the number of shopping carts that were opened during the chosen time period. The report is populated with an additional instance every time the scOpen event is passed into SiteCatalyst from the pages of your site.

- **How many times does a visitor view his cart without adding an item to it?** For this report, you could run the carts report and then segment by visits in which the event scAdd is set.

Interpretation of report data

In interpreting the data with respect to the number of carts, keep in mind that a shopping cart is usually opened when a customer selects an item for purchase, but it can occur without an item as well.

Code implementation and console settings

The number of carts report is impacted by the number of times the scOpen event is set.

Report: Understand number of cart views

Navigate to Site Metrics > Shopping Cart > Cart Views. This report lets you see the number of times shopping cart contents are viewed by your customers.

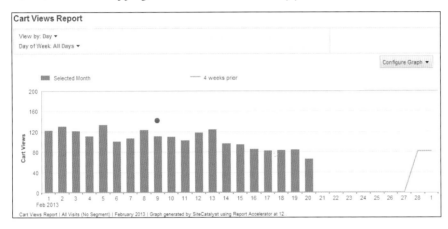

Key insights

Analyzing cart views can help answer questions such as:

- **On what page types do visitors most often view their cart contents?** Segmenting the cart views by different page types (landing pages, engagement pages, and pages of influence) can tell you what types of pages motivate visitors to add to their carts.

- **How many cart views result in cart removals or cart additions?** You could segment this data by visits in which the event cart removal occurred. You could also segment this data by the visits in which the event cart additions occurred.

Interpretation of report data

In interpreting the data with respect to cart views, keep in mind that if a product variable is set, but no cart view event is set, then the cart view variable will not be incremented.

Code implementation and console settings

The cart views report is impacted by the number of times the scView event is set.

Report: Understand number of cart additions

Navigate to SiteMetrics > Shopping Cart > Cart Additions. This report shows the number of times that items were added to the cart. It can be broken into the number of additions at product-level granularity.

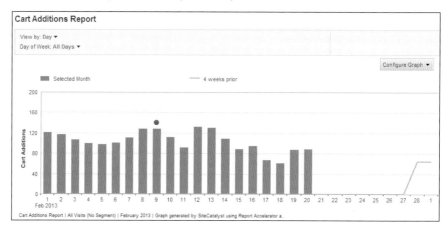

Key insights

Analyzing reports of cart additions can help answer questions such as:

- **Of the times that the cart is viewed, how many times does the visitor add to the cart?** Run the cart additions report and segment by the events in which the cart was viewed. This will help you correlate cart additions with cart views.

- **Which products or product families are added the most?** If you break down this report by products > categories, you can determine which product families are added the most.

- **What other factors drive cart additions?** You can also break down the cart additions by traffic sources, campaigns, visitor profiles, visit number, and so on.

Interpretation of report data

In interpreting the data with respect to cart additions on your site, keep the following in mind:

- The cart addition report tells you the number of times the cart addition event was set, irrespective of the number of products that were added.

- If multiple products are added in a single cart, each product will be attributed as a cart addition.

Code implementation and console settings

The settings below apply to cart additions reports:

- The `s.products` variable needs to be updated with the product, units, and revenue information.

- Event `scAdd` should be assigned to the `s.events` variable.

Report: Understand number of cart removals

Navigate to Site Metrics > Shopping Cart > Cart Removals. This report shows how many products were removed from shopping carts during the selected time period.

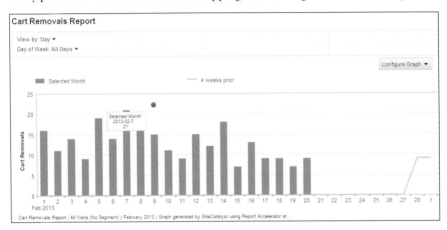

Key insights

Analyzing reports of cart removals can help answer questions such as:

- **Of the times that the cart is viewed, how many times does the visitor delete an item from the cart?** Run the cart removals report and segment by the events in which the cart was viewed. This will help you correlate cart removals with cart views.

- **Which products or product families are deleted the most?** You can break down the cart removals report by products or product categories to understand which product or product family is deleted the most.

- **Which factors drive the most traffic that results in cart deletions?** You can also break down the cart additions by traffic sources, campaigns, visitor profiles, visit number, and so on.

- **How much revenue is lost from cart removals?** Calculate the lost revenue by multiplying the revenue per visit and multiplying that by the number of cart removals.

Interpretation of report data

In interpreting the data with respect to cart removals on your site, keep the following in mind:

- The cart removals report tells you the number of times that the cart removals event was set, irrespective of the number of products that were deleted.

- If multiple products are removed at the same time, each product will be attributed as a cart removal.

Code implementation and console settings

The settings below apply to cart removal reports:

- The s.products variable needs to be updated with the product, units, and revenue information.

- Event scRemove should be assigned to the s.events variable.

Report: Understand number of checkouts

Navigate to Site Metrics > Shopping Cart > Checkouts. This report indicates how many times visitors arrive at the checkout stage of a purchase. Checkout stage still gives a visitor the option of not ordering.

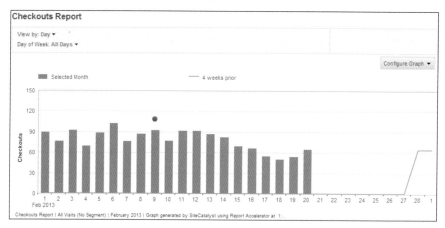

Key insights

Analyzing reports of checkouts can help answer questions such as:

- **How often do visitors reach checkout but not buy anything?** This can be gathered by comparing the number of checkouts to the orders. If you see a high discrepancy here, check your SiteCatalyst implementation as a potential source of data quality. If that seems right, one way to identify the issue would be to segment those visitors and survey them.

- **How much revenue is lost from items checked out versus ordered?** The difference (or delta) between the number of checkouts and the number of orders can give you the potential number of visits in which there was a loss in revenue. For this, you could multiply the average revenue from a visit to get an approximate dollar amount.

Interpretation of report data

In interpreting the data with respect to number of checkouts, keep in mind that visitors who check out need not necessarily complete an order. Hence, the number of checkouts will be higher than the number of orders.

Code implementation and console settings

The settings below apply to checkouts reports.

- The `s.products` variable needs to be updated with the product, units, and revenue information.

- Assign the value `scCheckout` to the `s.events` variable to indicate a checkout.

Task: Manage macroconversions (product focus)

These reports look at your sales with a product focus to help you determine how each product you offer is selling. This can help you adjust your product mix.

Report: Understand product conversion funnel

Navigate to Products > Product Conversion Funnel. This report displays the product views, cart additions, orders, units, and revenue. This should have the same data as the other funnels filtered by a specific product.

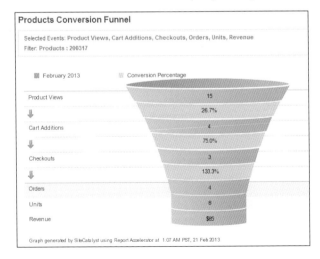

Products Conversion Funnel

Selected Events: Product Views, Cart Additions, Checkouts, Orders, Units, Revenue
Filter: Products : 200317

| | February 2013 | | Conversion Percentage |

Product Views	15
	26.7%
Cart Additions	4
	75.0%
Checkouts	3
	133.3%
Orders	4
Units	8
Revenue	$85

Graph generated by SiteCatalyst using Report Accelerator at 1:07 AM PST, 21 Feb 2013

Key insights

Analyzing reports on the product conversion funnel can help answer questions such as:

- **Which products have a higher conversion rate?** By choosing one product at a time, you can determine which product has a higher conversion rate.

- **Which products are ordered with multiple units in the same order?** Determine which products have a higher run rate of being ordered in bulk or in multiple units at the same time. Using the filter option in SiteCatalyst, you can choose the SKU numbers or the product ID you would like to review.

Interpretation of report data

In interpreting the data with respect to products, keep in mind that multiple products may be ordered in a single order. So the number of orders in the product conversion funnel will be inflated compared to the Orders report.

Code implementation and console settings

As a reminder, the category value in the product variable is created when a product is first recorded and persists for the entire month. All subsequent success events recorded for the product will automatically be credited to the category that was first assigned. This can cause unexpected results, so Adobe recommends assigning categories in SAINT classification for product categories.

Use semicolon delimiters to separate data of a single product and a comma to segregate data between two products.

Report: Understand products

Navigate to Products > Products. This report gives you statistics on the success of each product sold on your site.

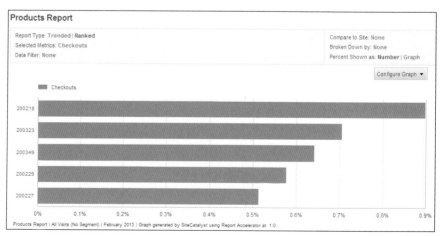

Key insights

Analyzing reports on products can help answer questions such as:

- **What products are being viewed, added, deleted, or ordered on your site?**
  This report gives you insights into which products have the highest conversion
  so you can plan your inventory accordingly.

Interpretation of report data

In interpreting the data with respect to your products, keep in mind prodView
event is available only in this report and the product category report.

Code implementation and console settings

In products reports, if no success event is set, the prodView event is set by default.

Report: Understand product cross-sell

Navigate to Products > Cross-Sell. This report shows the products that have a high
propensity to be ordered together. If two products are strongly associated, you
might consider suggesting one item to customers who are buying the other.

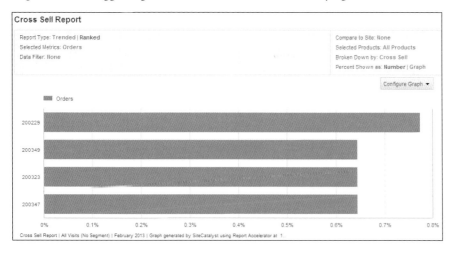

Key insights

Analyzing reports of product cross-sell at your site can help answer questions
such as:

- **Which products have a higher tendency to be sold with others?** This report
  breaks down one product ID with other product IDs that are ordered together.

- **Which products can you recommend to other visitors similar to these
  visitors?** The cross-selling report helps you determine which other products are
  of interest to visitors. This helps you build a robust recommendation engine.

Interpretation of report data

In interpreting the cross-sell data at your site, keep the following in mind:

- The cross-sell report is essentially a subrelation report, so you can't perform a breakdown by other variables, including product categories and classifications.

- The report does allow the user to perform subrelations, but this breaks down the individual product line items, not the cross-sell data, by the selected other variable.

Code implementation and console settings

The settings below apply to cross-sell reports:

- The values passed in the products variable are considered a cross-sell only when the purchase event is set.

- If your implementation lists multiple units of the same product separately, then the same product will be considered as a cross-sell. For example, if you set

```
s.products=";product A;1;2.00,;product B;1;3.50,;product A;2;4.00"
s.events="purchase"
```

  then product A will appear on its own cross-sell list.

- If your implementation lists multiple units of the same product together, then the same product will not be considered as a cross-sell. A more correct implementation of this purchase is shown in the example below:

```
s.products=";product A;3;6.00,;product B;1;3.50"
s.events="purchase"
```

  Then product A will not appear on its own cross-sell list. This is the correct way of implementing the purchase variable.

Report: Understand product categories

Navigate to Products > Categories. The categories report aggregates the success of products by categories or by product families. This data is especially helpful for sites that have products that fall into distinct groupings, such as clothing for men versus clothing for women. Performance of product groups can give you insight about what type of products audiences are finding your site, or what type of products your company is known for among consumers.

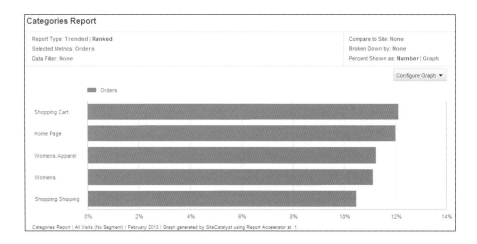

Key insights

Analyzing product categories at your site can help answer questions such as:

- **Which product categories are overperforming?** Sometimes dominance of a particular category means that you're not getting the message out about your other offerings.

- **Which product categories are underperforming?** Perhaps you're not promoting these products, they're hard to find on your site, or they simply don't appeal to your audience.

Interpretation of report data

In interpreting the data with respect to product category report, keep the following in mind:

- If multiple products are assigned to the same category, any purchase of either of these products will increment the category count by one.

- This data can be misinterpreted if there is a large difference in the number of products within each category and the revenue each of these products generates.

Code implementation and console settings

The category value in the product variable is created when a product is first recorded and persists for the entire month. All subsequent success events recorded for the product will automatically be credited to the category that was first assigned. This can cause unexpected results.

▷ **Tip:** To avoid this issue, Adobe recommends assigning categories in SAINT classification for product categories.

Task: Manage macroconversions and microconversions (custom events)

The primary goal of your website is a macroconversion. Secondary, tertiary, and other goals are microconversions. Microconversions are baby steps toward a macroconversion. An example of a macroconversion could be buying a product on your site, while examples of microconversions could include recommending products to others, contacting the sales team, or subscribing to an RSS feed.

Report: Review conversion funnel fulfillment and abandonment

Navigate to Site Metrics > Custom Event > Custom Event Funnel. If your funnel has three steps—the first page requesting the visitor's personal information, the second asking for credit card information, and the third confirming the order—then get the event numbers from your admin to determine the steps in the event funnel.

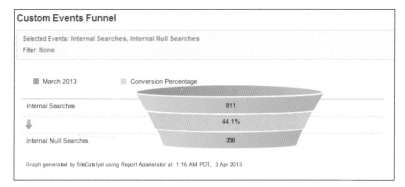

Key insights

Analyzing reports of microconversions can help answer questions such as:

- **How many visitors who start the funnel actually fulfill it?** Compare the number of visitors who start the funnel and the number of visitors who complete it. This will give you an idea of the conversion and abandonment rate of your microconversion.

- **How many visitors who start the funnel go on to abandon it, and at what step?** This insight is pertinent if you have a multistep funnel and you're trying to determine at which step your visitors abandon the funnel most often.

Interpretation of report data

In interpreting microconversion data, keep in mind that if the page is refreshed, the event is incremented again.

Code implementation and console settings

The settings below apply to microconversions reports.

- Assign predetermined event numbers for each funnel step to `s.events`.

- Your admin can help you with this data.

Report: Review form fulfillment and abandonment

This report indicates either the field in which the visitor abandoned or the field after which the visitor abandoned the form. Ask your admin about which variables collect that data.

Key insights

Analyzing reports of microconversions can help answer questions such as:

- **Which form fields have maximum abandonments?** With the help of this report, you can determine which conversion funnel, if you have multiple ones, outperformed the others. If a form has a high abandonment in the SSN field, it probably leans to the fact that people might not be comfortable sharing that information with you. You could consider asking for other information, or listing your privacy policy or security policy next to it.

- **Which forms have the highest abandonment?** By comparing the form starts to the form complete ratio, you can compare completions across multiple forms. This will help you determine which funnel is preferred by the visitors.

Interpretation of report data

In interpreting the data with respect to forms at your site, keep in mind that depending on the how the implementation is done, the forms data can indicate which field was the last filled. The abandonment could truly be on the field after the last filled field.

Code implementation and console settings

The settings below apply to form reports:

- SiteCatalyst 14 had a forms plugin. Adobe now recommends writing form variables directly into SiteCatalyst variables. Note that you should not write any PII data to SiteCatalyst.

- For the form name, prefix the page name as a best practice. This guards against page code being accidentally copied over.

Conclusion

All of these reports will help you determine next steps in focusing your analytics effort:

- **What are the total units, orders, and revenue generated on your site?** This helps you understand the total revenue and inventory-related questions.

- **How is the cart being used on your site?** The cart is a temporary place where the visitor considers buying your products. These reports will help you determine which pattern or sequence of steps pushes toward an order as opposed to the visitor abandoning his cart.

- **What products are being sold in high volume or cross-sold?** The product-related reports highlight the products and categories that are popular among your visitors. The audience that you're actively targeting and the visitor demographics on your site may be different. These reports will help you bridge that gap.

- **Are the microconversions successful?** This question may be pertinent if you're tracking any microconversions, such as newsletter sign-ups or registrations. Since SiteCatalyst has no default variables or reports for these, they must be configured.

Next, we'll review the retention reports and track the KPIs, the reports, and metrics. We are nearing the finish line!

Review questions

1 How can you break down conversion by geosegmentation?

2 Will the number of units and orders match?

Review answers

1 With advanced segments, you can create a segment for the country you are interested in and then segment by it.

2 No, if you are selling multiple units in an order, the number of units sold will be greater than the number of orders. If the orders are greater than units, it is evidence that you have an implementation error.

8 RETENTION ANALYTICS

Lesson overview

In this lesson, you'll learn to analyze retention data. This will be particularly insightful if you sell products on your site.

The goals of this section are:

- Understanding what you need to measure for retention analytics

- Determining the Adobe SiteCatalyst reports to run based on your analysis needs

- Identifying the issues that impact the data and the implementation details that affect the data quality

 This lesson will take 30 minutes to complete.

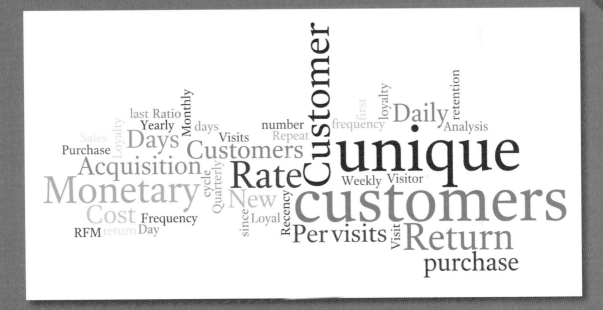

The cost of acquiring a customer is high for most businesses. So once you have one, you want to encourage her loyalty and maximize the revenue she brings to your site. Reward your customer's loyalty by understanding the recency, frequency, and monetary aspects of analytics.

Task: Define goals and KPIs

At this point your visitors are aware of your site, they've come to your site, and (we hope) they've been engaged by your content. Now the challenge is to retain them as return or even frequent visitors or customers. For retention metrics, your business goal may be to increase revenue by 25 percent for the financial year. Your intent with the retention KPI is to determine how much of that can be generated from your existing customer base. Examples of KPIs for conversion could be:

- **Recency focus**

  The purpose of these KPIs is to determine how long it takes visitors to convert.

  Same day (0 days) purchase rate = Revenue from same-day purchase as first visit ÷ Total revenue

  The same-day purchase rate determines how much revenue comes from conversion in the very first visit.

  Medium time period (1–5 days) = Revenue from medium time period purchase rate (1–5 days) purchase ÷ Total revenue

  The medium time period (1–5 days) purchase rate determines how much revenue comes from conversion in the medium term of five days. This formula can vary based on your sales cycle.

  Long time period (6 or more days) = Revenue from long time period (6 or purchase rate more days) purchase ÷ Total revenue

  The long time period (six or more days) purchase rate determines how much revenue comes from conversion in the long term of six or more days. This formula can vary based on your sales cycle.

- **Frequency focus**

  The frequency focus outlines the new and repeat visits to the site.

  Return visits ratio = Number of return visits ÷ Total number of visits

  The frequency focus helps you determine the ratio of new to return visits on your site. This will help you create a more personalized visitor experience.

- **Monetary**

  These KPIs compare the monetary purchases made by a new customer (first-time buyer on your site) with those made by a second-time or repeat buyer. The final comparison is with loyal customers who have purchased more than twice.

  New customer monetary rate = Revenue from new customers ÷ Total revenue

  New customer order rate = Orders from new customers ÷ Total orders

  New customer units rate = Units from new customers ÷ Total units

  First, we evaluate first-time customers on the spectrum of three metrics: revenue, orders, and units.

  Repeat customer monetary rate = Revenue from repeat customers ÷
  Total revenue

  Repeat customer order rate = Orders from repeat customers ÷ Total orders

  Repeat customer units rate = Units from repeat customers ÷ Total units

  Then, we evaluate repeat customers on the same spectrum of three metrics.

  Loyal customer monetary rate = Revenue from loyal customers ÷ Total revenue

  Loyal customer order rate = Orders from loyal customers ÷ Total orders

  Loyal customer units rate = Units from loyal customers ÷ Total units

  And finally, we evaluate loyal customers on the same spectrum of three metrics.

- **Insights on cost**

  When computing costs, we ideally add all marketing expenses as well as development and vendor costs. We then break that down by targeted marketing campaign costs, as follows:

  Cost per acquisition of new customers = Total cost ÷ Total number of units
  by new customers

  Cost per visit of new customers = Total cost ÷ Total number of visits by
  new customers

  Cost per new customer = Total cost ÷ Total number of new customers

  We begin by evaluating first-time customers on the spectrum of three metrics: cost per acquisition, cost per visit, and cost per visitor.

$$\text{Cost per acquisition of repeat customers} = \text{Total cost} \div \text{Total number of units by repeat customers}$$

$$\text{Cost per visit of repeat customers} = \text{Total cost} \div \text{Total number of visits by repeat customers}$$

$$\text{Cost per repeat customer} = \text{Total cost} \div \text{Total number of repeat visitors}$$

Then, we evaluate repeat customers on the same spectrum of three metrics.

$$\text{Cost per acquisition of loyal customers} = \text{Total cost} \div \text{Total number of units by loyal customers}$$

$$\text{Cost per visit of loyal customers} = \text{Total cost} \div \text{Total number of visits}$$

$$\text{Cost per loyal customer} = \text{Total cost} \div \text{Total number of loyal visitors}$$

Finally, we evaluate loyal customers on the same spectrum of three metrics.

The cost per acquisition, visit, and visitor give you an idea of how much you're spending on an average new customer as compared to a repeat customer or a loyal customer. It will also help you gain perspective when you're looking at the return on investment.

Table 8.1 suggests a few reports you can run and some pertinent metrics to better understand the data. When you need data with higher granularity, you could use some of the suggested segments. Segments can include any custom traffic variable, any custom conversion variable, and any SiteCatalyst Attribute Importing and Naming Tool (SAINT) classification. Following are a few suggestions you can use to segment the conversion (this list is not meant to be exhaustive):

- By geosegmentation
- By channel
- By campaign
- By new and repeat visitor
- By first-time or return customer
- By referrer
- By mobile devices
- By nonmobile devices

Table 8.1 Retention reports and metrics

FOCUS	MEASURES	SITECATALYST REPORT	METRICS
Recency		Visitor retention > Sales cycle > Days since last purchase	
Frequency	Number of visits to conversion	Visitor retention > Return frequency	Number of instances against the visit number frequency table
		Visitor retention > Visit number	Visit number
		Visitor retention > Return visits	Only return visits; excludes first-time visits
		Visitor retention > Daily return visits	Visits
Monetary	Understand sales cycle	Visitor retention > Sales cycle > Customer loyalty	Visits Visitors Bounces Revenue Orders Units
		Visitor retention > Sales cycle > Days before first purchase	
		Visitor retention > Sales cycle > Daily unique customers	
		Visitor retention > Sales cycle > Weekly unique customers	
		Visitor retention > Sales cycle > Monthly unique customers	
		Visitor retention > Sales cycle > Quarterly unique customers	
		Visitor retention > Sales cycle > Yearly unique customers	

Task: Understand recency

Retention analysis is based on recency, frequency, and monetary (RFM) analysis. It's a marketing technique that is based on the 80-20 Rule (http://en.wikipedia.org/wiki/Pareto_principle), which can be applied to your business to suggest that 80 percent of your business comes from 20 percent of your customers. Recency examines how recently a customer has purchased. Frequency determines how often a customer makes a purchase. Monetary examines the customer spend. In the first task, the focus is on recency.

Report: Understand days before first purchase

Navigate to Visitor Retention > Sales Cycle > Days Before First Purchase. This report shows the number of days that pass between the first time a customer visits your site and when she actually makes a purchase.

	Days Before First Purchase	Orders		Units		Revenue	
1.	Same Day	195	47.6%	386	44.4%	$40,501	47.4%
2.	1 Day	16	3.9%	28	3.2%	$3,505	4.1%
3.	3 Days	8	2.0%	26	3.0%	$1,700	2.0%
4.	46 Days	1	0.2%	2	0.2%	$1,600	1.9%

Key insights

Analyzing the days before first purchase report can help answer questions such as:

- **How long does it take the visitor to convert on your site?** This report helps you determine how long a visitor takes to convert on your site for the very first time. If you have a high number of same-day purchases, your site has a high conversion rate for first-time visitors. The longer it takes for a visitor to convert, the more cost associated with that acquisition.

- **Which factors accelerate the purchase decision?** For visits in which the visitor converted on the same day that she made a purchase, it would help to understand patterns of paths she used.

- **Which channels are sending a high number of same-day purchases?** For visits that generate purchases the same day or less than three days before conversion, figure the channel that's sending that high-quality data.

- **How many days after the first visit is the optimal time to convert visitors?** This will help you figure out when you can best target visitors for remarketing or provide additional offers or a different experience.

Interpretation of report data

In interpreting the data about days before purchase, keep the following in mind:

- Purchases that are made the same day as the first visit will appear as "Same Day."

- The report lists all the days from the same day to second day to as many days as the slowest visitor took to convert.

- This report doesn't take into account how the visitor may have reached your site, or how many page views or visits she may have made between the time of the first page view of the first visit and the order.

▶ **Tip:** You can also segment the visitors who have been on your site more than a certain number of times, and choose the optimal number for your business. You can then reach out to this group via an email campaign to find out how else you can engage and convert them. Another option is to identify them for an inline chat session with your customer representatives.

Code implementation and console settings

The settings below apply to days before first purchase reports:

- Since this is a visit-based report, noncookied users will not be counted.

- This report will also have skewed data for visitors who have deleted their cookies between their first visit to the site and purchase.

Note: The "days since last purchase" report is not available in SiteCatalyst, but it is available in Adobe's Data Warehouse product. It will help to determine the most common number of days that pass between repeat purchases.

Task: Understand frequency

This set of reports analyzes the correlation between the frequency of the visits and repeat customer conversion. Frequency means literally "how often" do you see the customer returning to your site. Your goal, if your business supports the repeat buyer model, is to increase the frequency of visitors and in turn their conversion.

Report: Understand return frequency

Navigate to Visitor Retention > Return Frequency. Based on the time lapse between visits, this report shows the number of visitors who returned to your site in one of the following categories: less than 1 day, 1–3 days, 3–7 days, 7–14 days, 14 days to 1 month, and longer than 1 month.

Note: 1–3 days goes up to 2.999999999 days while 3–7 days starts at 3.00000 days.

Therefore, a visitor with a return frequency of three days fits into the 3–7 day category. SiteCatalyst measures the return frequency by using cookies to gauge the amount of time that has elapsed between an initial visit and any return visits to your website.

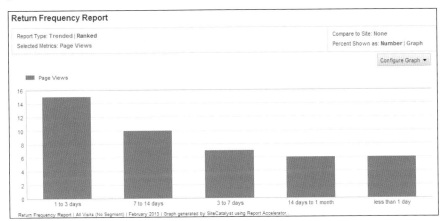

Key insights

Analyzing reports of return frequency can help answer questions such as:

- **What is the frequency of customer return visits?** This insight will help you understand how frequently customers are returning to your site, which will help you evaluate your site's appeal and relevance to visitors over time. You could specifically target repeat customers with special offers and personalized content based on their product preferences.

- **Which pages are customers engaging in?** This insight will help you understand whether visitors are finding the content and products alluring enough to return to your site periodically. The second course of that evaluation would be which pages they're interested in. There are two obvious caveats to this. First, if you're selling high-end products like jewelry, visitors won't be shopping for them very often. Second, if your business routinely requires customers to pay their premium or their bill, they'll have no interest in your website per se. They're simply there to pay the bill and leave.

- **What channels are customers using to return?** Prospects and customers always behave differently in the sense that prospects are trying to make up their mind, whereas return customers have a sense of loyalty and understanding of your products already.

Interpretation of report data

In interpreting the data with respect to return frequency, keep the following in mind:

- This report counts only returning visits; first-time visits are not reflected. For example, if a visitor comes to your site for the first time on January 1, then twice on January 3, the visitor's January 1 visit will not be included in this report.

- The data in the return frequency report is based on the visit, not the visitor. So a visitor may be counted multiple times in multiple reporting intervals if she comes often. For example, if a visitor comes for the first time on January 1, then twice on January 3, the visitor's January 1 visit will not be included in this report. But the January 3 visit will be counted twice in the 1–3 days report.

- Since this is a visit-based report, visitors who have not enabled cookies will not be counted.

Code implementation and console settings

No settings or code changes are required for the return frequency report.

Report: Understand return visits

Navigate to Visitor Retention > Return Visits. This report displays the number of visits from previous visitors to your site.

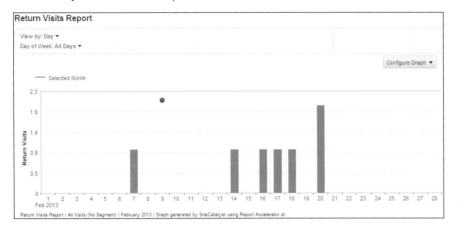

Key insights

Analyzing reports of return visits can help answer questions such as:

- **How many return visits is your site receiving? How does that compare to new visits?** This report is primarily used to understand the intent of return visitors. You can compare their behavior with that of new visitors.

- **What's the ratio of return visits to new visits?** This ratio of new to return visits is primarily used to understand how much new traffic you're acquiring. If you have strong revenue contribution from repeat customers, your preference for return visits would be high. However, if you have weak contribution from repeat customers, then you would need a high acquisition rate of new visits.

Interpretation of report data

In interpreting the data with respect to return visits to your site, keep the following in mind:

- This report is configured to count both visitors who have enabled cookies and visitors who have not enabled cookies by using their user-agent string and IP address.

- This report does not contain line items and can be viewed only in trended format.

Code implementation and console settings

No settings or code changes are required for the return visits report.

Report: Understand daily return visits

Navigate to Visitor Retention > Daily Return Visits. This report provides the number of visitors who came back to your site in the same day.

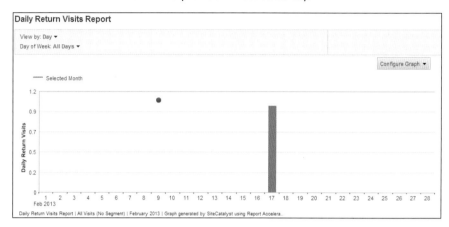

Key insight

Analyzing reports of daily return visits can help answer questions such as:

- **How many daily return visits does your site get?** This is pretty much the only data you'll get from this report: how many daily return visits you get. It's good news for you if visitors are converting multiple times. Other uses of this report could be to determine the presence of malicious attacks if you're suddenly seeing more daily return visits.

Interpretation of report data

In interpreting the data with respect to daily return visits to your site, keep the following in mind:

- This report focuses solely on visits and no additional metrics are provided.

- The visitor must visit twice in the same calendar day to be counted.

Code implementation and console settings

No settings or code changes are required for the daily return visits report.

Report: Understand unique customers

Navigate to Visitor Retention > Sales Cycle > Daily Unique Customers. This report identifies the number of different people who make purchases from your site during one day.

Now run the reports of other durations to get an overview of unique customers on your site:

- Navigate to Visitor Retention > Sales Cycle > Daily Unique Customers.

- Navigate to Visitor Retention > Sales Cycle > Weekly Unique Customers.

- Navigate to Visitor Retention > Sales Cycle > Monthly Unique Customers.

- Navigate to Visitor Retention > Sales Cycle > Quarterly Unique Customers.

- Navigate to Visitor Retention > Sales Cycle > Yearly Unique Customers.

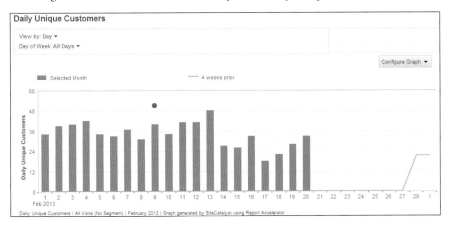

Key insight

Analyzing reports of unique visitors who make purchases at your site—including the more specific reports for unique daily through unique yearly visitors—can help answer questions such as:

- **How many unique customers visit the site daily?** This data should give you an idea of the unique number of customers you get across the selected time period.

Interpretation of report data

In interpreting the data with respect to unique visitors to your site, keep in mind that the report lists the total number of unique customers based on the date granularity you select (weekly, daily, and so on).

Code implementation and console settings

The settings below apply to unique customer reports:

- A unique customer is a person who makes a purchase from your site for the first time within the time frame you selected.

- If multiple purchases are made in the selected time frame, only one unique customer value is stored.

- Daily unique customers is impacted by the time zone setting (but from 12:01 a.m. to 12:00 a.m.) in the report suite.

- Daily, weekly, monthly, quarterly, and yearly unique customers are calculated based on the calendar setting in the report suite.

Task: Understand monetary

"Know thy business," and in this case your sales cycle. How long does it take for a visitor to first acknowledge that they need a product from your site and then be persuaded into converting on your site? Normally, you will notice a faster sales cycle for cheaper products and products that are considered part of consumer essentials.

Report: Understand customer loyalty

Navigate to Visitor Retention > Sales Cycle > Customer Loyalty. This report helps you identify purchases by new customers (first-time purchase), return customers (second-time purchase), and loyal customers (third purchase or more).

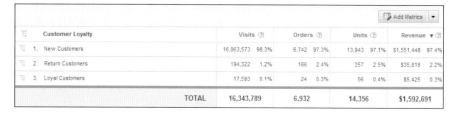

	Customer Loyalty	Visits ⑦		Orders ⑦		Units ⑦		Revenue ▼⑦	
1.	New Customers	16,063,573	98.3%	6,742	97.3%	13,943	97.1%	$1,551,448	97.4%
2.	Return Customers	194,322	1.2%	166	2.4%	357	2.5%	$35,818	2.2%
3.	Loyal Customers	17,593	0.1%	24	0.3%	56	0.4%	$5,425	0.3%
	TOTAL	16,343,789		6,932		14,356		$1,592,691	

Key insights

Analyzing reports of customer loyalty can help answer questions such as:

- **How much traffic and revenue is generated by loyal customers?** To understand the monetary impact of repeat customers, you can evaluate customers who bought once (new customer), twice (return customer), or more than three times (loyal customer).

- **What patterns of web usage do new, return, and loyal customers exhibit?** You can create a segment with a container of a visitor where customer loyalty equals "new." You would need two more segments for return and loyal customers. Using these segments, you can compare the pathing and preferences of these three separate segments.

- **What's the ratio of loyal customers to return customers to new customers?** A deeper dive into these numbers will help you gauge which segment of loyal customers are spending the most on your site.

Interpretation of report data

In interpreting the data with respect to customer loyalty at your site, keep the following in mind:

- When you run the customer loyalty report, if you see only new customers listed in the report and are missing return and loyal customers, it's because the purchase variable and event have not been set.

- With the Purchase Event, you can run the Customer Loyalty Report and select purchase-related metrics such as revenue, orders, and units for returning and loyal customers.

Code implementation and console settings

Refer to the discussion of the purchase conversion funnel in Chapter 7, "Conversion Analytics," to review settings such as the product variable, category value, revenue and product quantity settings, and creating serialized reports.

Report: Understand visit number

Navigate to Visitor Retention > Visit Number. This report helps you comprehend how many visits it takes your visitors to convert, if you add the orders metrics to the report.

	Visit Number	Orders ⑦		Units ⑦		Revenue ▾ ⑦	
1.	1st Visit	171	41.7%	344	39.5%	$36,203	42.4%
2.	2nd Visit	61	14.9%	108	12.4%	$12,138	14.2%
3.	4th Visit	25	6.1%	70	8.0%	$6,360	7.4%
4.	3rd Visit	24	5.9%	50	5.7%	$4,743	5.5%
5.	6th Visit	8	2.0%	18	2.1%	$2,155	2.5%

Key insight

Analyzing visit number reports can help answer questions such as:

- **What is the optimal number of visits it takes to convert a visitor to a customer?** Based on the distribution of data across visit numbers, you can determine the optimal number of visits it takes for a visitor to convert. You could also segment and target visitors.

Code implementation and console settings

The settings below apply to visit number reports.

- If the visitor arrived twice at your site, she would be counted in visit one category and visit two categories.

- If the visitor deletes her cookies or uses another device, she would be seen as visit number one again.

- This report tells the visit number that occurred during the time period selected. For example, if a customer's first visit is in September and her second visit is in October, when you look at the October report, the customer will be reported in the second visit since it was her second visit in October.

- The visit number report does not include visitors without cookies, so these metrics will be extremely close—if not identical to—return visits.

Conclusion

Retention analytics are for sites that support repeat customers—having customers visit and buy again.

- **What is the importance of recency?** The recency reports analyze the time it takes for a visitor to convert since she first arrived your site.

- **How frequently do visitors come to your site?** This helps you understand the sustained interest in your brand and your products by repeat and loyal customers. Also, frequency reports analyze the correlation between the frequency of the visits and repeat customer conversion.

- **What's the revenue from new customers versus loyal customers?** This helps you determine the revenue contribution from new customers, return customers, and loyal customers.

We have covered every stage of the marketing funnel. In the next chapter we will review how we tie SiteCatalyst data with other vendor data.

Review questions

1   Is the return visits report dependent on visitors enabling cookies?

2   Why would you not see any data for return and loyal customers when you run the customer loyalty report?

Review answers

1   This report is configured to count both visitors who have enabled cookies and visitors who have not enabled cookies by using their user-agent string and IP address.

2   If the purchase variable and event have not been set, you may not be able to see data for return and loyal customers in the customer loyalty report.

Lesson overview

In this lesson, you'll learn how to analyze external analytics data. The primary issue with analytics data is that most companies have multiple sources of data in disparate tools and databases. This lesson teaches you ways to see all the key elements of the offline data in Adobe SiteCatalyst.

The goals of this section are:

- Understanding what you need to integrate data with offline data
- Determining the SiteCatalyst reports to run based on your analysis needs
- Determining the issues that impact the data and the implementation details that affect the data quality

 This lesson will take 30 minutes to complete.

Once you've optimized the visit for each aspect of the marketing funnel, it's important to get a holistic view that ties all your analytics data together. Follow your customer from the awareness stage all the way to the retention stage to understand his life cycle with your business.

Task: Define KPI

In most companies, web data is collected in SiteCatalyst or a comparable web analytics tool. The data primarily describes acquisition and web usage data until the visitor makes a purchase. You may use other tools to help you understand visitor sentiments, such as "voice of the customer" survey products like ForeSee or iPerceptions. You might use Test&Target testing. Your product team may inform you that the order fulfillment data is in their proprietary, back-end database. Your email campaigns may be run by a third-party vendor like Responsys or ExactTarget. Now they have a lot of data regarding the email campaigns you run. Do you see the issue? You have all this data in different systems and you need it all together to analyze it holistically.

First things first: let's set the KPIs. For external data metrics, your business goal may be to increase revenue by 25 percent for the financial year. Your intent with the retention KPI is to determine how much of that can be generated from your existing customer base. Examples of KPIs for retention could be:

- **Increase net revenue**

  Gross revenue is the amount of money the customer is charged for your products.

  Net revenue per visit = (Total gross revenue − Cost of digital advertising − Revenue loss from cancellations − Revenue loss from returns) ÷ Total visits

  Net revenue per visitor = (Total gross revenue − Cost of digital advertising − Revenue loss from cancellations − Revenue loss from returns) ÷ Total visitors

  Net order value = (Total gross revenue − cost of digital advertising − Revenue loss from cancellations − Revenue loss from returns) ÷ Total orders

  Net revenue per acquisition, visit, and visitor reflects deeper than gross revenue per acquisition since it removes false revenue from cancellations and returns.

- **Increase return on investment**

  The return on investment (ROI) compares the revenue you generate and the cost associated with it.

  ROI = (Net revenue − Total cost) ÷ Total cost

  If the ROI is 1, you're earning the same amount that you're spending. If the ROI is less than 1, you're spending more than you're earning. If the ROI is greater than 1, you're spending less than you're earning, which is great!

- **Loss of revenue**

  This step will help you estimate how much revenue is lost from errors and abandonment.

  Net revenue loss from errors = Number of visits with page not found errors × Revenue per visit

  Net revenue loss from abandonment = Number of cart abandonments × Revenue per visit

  Putting a numeric value on revenue loss can help build a sense of urgency and priority within your organization to address these issues.

Now that we have a few KPIs in hand, let's look at the SiteCatalyst reports that can help us get the data for them. In some places, you may need to further segment them to get deeper dives.

> **Note:** All integrations require custom conversion variables and custom events. This chapter will help you gauge how many variables you may need.

Table 9.1 presents the types of external data you might want to examine, the suggested dimensions, and the metrics to compare. The suggested dimensions in the table below are the values that will need to be written to both SiteCatalyst and the other vendor product simultaneously so that they match up.

Table 9.1 External data analytics integration and metrics

CATEGORY	TYPE	SUGGESTED DIMENSIONS	METRICS
Ad	Generic ad server	Tracking codes	Impressions
			Views
			Clicks
			Cost
	Generic email campaign server	Tracking code	Number of messages sent
		Email subscriber ID	Number of messages opened
		Email creative ID	Total delivered
			Bounces
			Clicks
			Subscribers
			Unsubscribed
	Generic pay per click	Tracking codes	Impressions
		Ad groups	Clicks
		Keywords	Total cost
		Match type	

(continues on next page)

Table 9.1 External data analytics integration and metrics (continued)

CATEGORY	TYPE	SUGGESTED DIMENSIONS	METRICS
CRM	Generic call center	Products	Seconds on phone
			Total sales
			Number of calls
	Generic customer support	Customer ID	Number of new incidents
			Seconds spent on incidents
			Number of resolves incidents
			Incidents still open
Customer satisfaction	Survey data	Date	Respondents counts
			Surveys served
			Surveys started
			Surveys completed
Site performance	Generic site download speed	Page name	Number of measurements
			Total download time for all measurements
Online purchases	Product returns		
	Product cost		
	Product status		
Leads and quotes	Lead generation	Products	Offline orders
			Offline units
			Offline revenue
	Online quote	Products	Offline orders
			Offline units
			Offline revenue
	Offline channel data		
Website usage	SiteCatalyst web beacons	NA	NA
	WebServer log files*		

* Gets basic visit and visitor information only. Gives the option of choosing the following web server log formats: NCSA Common (Apache Default), NCSA Combined (Apache), W3C Extended (IIS 4.0 or later), and MS IIS Logs (IIS 3 or later).

Task: Integrate external data at transaction level

Transactions are purchases that a visitor makes on your site. This data is stored using the `s.products` variable. You may be using an external proprietary database to track your orders, their shipment, cancellations, and returns. So in order to assess the number of units sold or revenue generated, it's crucial to see the returns and cancellation data in SiteCatalyst. Let's dive into more details below.

Report: Product returns and cancellations

If you're integrating product data with offline data, navigate to Products > Products Conversion Funnel. Alternatively, for any report, add user-defined metrics like the number of cancellations, number of returns, revenue loss from cancellations, or revenue loss from returns. The revenue loss can be indicated with a negative number. Then a calculated metric can be defined as the net revenue (the default revenue metric in SiteCatalyst) minus the user-defined metric of revenue loss in cancellations and revenue loss in returns.

Key insights

Analyzing reports of returns and cancellations can help answer questions such as:

- **Which product has the highest number of returns?** When you run the Products > Products Conversion Funnel report, you can choose an event that is imported into SiteCatalyst and select user-defined metrics like number of cancellations or number of returns. Knowing the products with the highest number of returns or cancellations can help you address the quality of the product.

- **How much revenue is lost with returns and cancellations?** Going back to the Products > Products Conversion Funnel report, you can choose an event that's imported into SiteCatalyst and select user-defined metrics like revenue loss from cancellations or revenue loss from returns. This will help you give more realistic numbers when you're ready to report to senior management.

- **What's the net revenue (gross revenue, returns, cancellations)?** Integrating the back-end data helps you identify the true net revenue generated from the web. You could subtract from the gross revenue the revenue lost from cancellation or returns. If you have a high number of returns, the gross revenue may be misleading.

Interpretation of report data

In interpreting the data with respect to product returns at your site, keep the following in mind:

Note: You'll need to contact Adobe customer support to enable the s.transactionID variable.

- s.transactionID variable is specific to the visitors. Every time an s.transactionID variable is updated, a snapshot of every persistent variable along with VisitorID at the time is taken. So any persistent variable at that point in time can be tied to the offline data you upload, including the entire lifetime of a visitor.

- If s.transactionID was not recorded in the same image request to Adobe as the purchase event and variable, there will be no way to completely tie the online SiteCatalyst data to the offline data.

- If you record purchases without setting the s.transactionID variable and import a data batch with transaction IDs, SiteCatalyst will view them as new purchases and won't be able to join that data with the existing data.

- s.transactionID data is not available directly in SiteCatalyst for reporting.

- s.transactionID must be unique across all systems. Integration data sources will not function as expected if a unique s.transactionID is seen twice.

- By default, s.transactionID values are remembered for 90 days. If your offline interaction process is longer than 90 days, contact an Adobe representative to have the limit extended.

Code implementation and console settings

The settings below apply to reports that add metrics for cancellation and returns, including the next report on product cost:

- If you're recording s.transactionID for multiple systems, like purchases and leads, make sure the value in s.transactionID is always unique. This may be accomplished by adding a prefix to the ID, like lead_1234 and purchase_1234.

- If you want to report on transactionID values, replicate the s.transactionID value in a custom conversion variable.

- You'll need to use data sources to import the data.

Report: Product data with product cost

If you're integrating product data with offline data, navigate to the Products > Products Conversion Funnel. Alternatively, for any report, add user-defined metrics like product cost. Product cost includes any cost associated with the product creation. Then a calculated metric can be defined as the net revenue (the default revenue metric in SiteCatalyst) minus the user-defined metric of product cost apart from returns and cancellations.

Key insight

Analyzing reports with product cost can help answer questions such as:

- **What is the ROI?**

  Return on Investment = (Gross revenue – Total cost) ÷ Total cost

  Integrating back-end data helps you identify the true net revenue generated from the web. You can subtract from the gross revenue the revenue lost from cancellation or returns. If you have a high number of returns, the gross revenue may be misleading. Also, removing the product cost from the revenue can help you arrive at the true ROI.

Interpretation of report data

In interpreting the data with respect to ROI, keep the following in mind:

- If the ROI is positive, the revenue is greater than your costs, meaning that your website is profitable.

- If the ROI is negative, the costs are greater than your revenue, meaning that your website is taking a loss.

- If the ROI is zero, your revenue is the same as your costs, meaning that your website is not adding much to the bottom line.

Code implementation and console settings

The code implementation for product cost is the same as that for product returns and cancellation listed above.

Report: Order data with status

For the s.transactionID, you would also have an Order Status.

Key insight

Analyzing reports of order status can help answer questions such as:

- **How many instances are there of each order status? Are orders delivered greater than cancellations?** Grouping orders by order status can give you an idea of where orders are in terms of order fulfillment.

Interpretation of report data

In interpreting the data with respect to order status, keep in mind that order status denotes the status for the records that have data in the SAINT classification. If there is a `s.transactionID` that does not have a corresponding order status in the SAINT file, it will be classified as none.

Code implementation and console settings

For order status, set up SAINT classification on the custom conversion variable that replicates the `s.transactionID` data. Import data from the back-end database that clarifies the current status of the order as, for example, to be shipped, shipped, cancelled, or fulfilled.

Task: Integrate external data at the customer level

SiteCatalyst lets you review web usage by a visitor and describe each of his visits and his patterns of behavior on the site. You might have another database that tracks repeated purchases that the visitor makes. Knowing the visitor from his very first purchase to his most recent one may help you determine his loyalty. His loyal journey with your company and your products may give you ideas about how to give those visitors the royal treatment!

Report: Integrating and running reports with `visitorID`

Use this option when you want to join the data in SiteCatalyst and an offline database when the granularity is at the visitor level.

Key insights

Integrating and analyzing `s.visitorID` reports can help answer questions such as:

- **How many times does the visitor renew his subscription for a membership?** Based on the visitor ID, you can correlate visitor activity on the web with the post-web data in a separate database.

- **What's the visitor's value over X years?** By aggregating the visitor's payments over time, you can determine the visitor's lifetime value to your business.

Interpretation of report data

The interpretation of the data depends on the data that's pulled from another data source.

Code implementation and console settings

For visitor ID reports, set the `s.visitorID` to match the customer ID of the back-end database. This works only if you can identify your visitors from all pages of the site.

Task: Genesis Integration

Let's look at ways to integrate other tools with SiteCatalyst, which will let you see specific integrated data within SiteCatalyst. Adobe's internal tools, like Test&Target and Survey, can easily be integrated into SiteCatalyst using Genesis Integration. External tools like Facebook Demographics and BrightEdge can also be integrated via Genesis Integration.

Note: Genesis Integration is report-suite specific. So be sure you have selected the correct report suite before doing the integrations. Also, if you need integrations in multiple report suites, you may need to repeat the Genesis Integration on each of them.

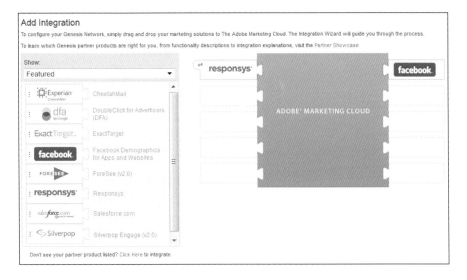

Integration and Report: Test&Target > Campaign

Navigate to Test&Target > Campaign. The other menu options are based on the SAINT classification set up by your admin. These reports outline which campaign and recipe the visitor experienced. Correlating that information with other information sheds lights on which user experience most visitors favor and which have a positive impact on their conversions.

Note: Don't confuse acquisition campaigns with test campaigns.

Key insights

Analyzing reports of Test&Target can help answer questions such as:

- **How did the visitors who were served the control user experience behave versus the visitors who were served the variant user experience?** Run the Test&Target > Campaigns Report. Remember to filter by your test name. Then, adding metrics like bounces, orders, units, and revenue will give you an in-depth look of how the control and variant test performed against each other on engagement and conversion aspects. This will help you pick a clear winner between the two. Don't forget to consider statistical significance when picking a winner.

- **Which demographics of visitors responded better to your test?** Segmenting the test campaign by available demographic information like geographical location or new or returning visitors can help you gain a deep understanding of whether demographics were a factor in the test.

- **What impact did the control and variant experiences have on conversion and revenue?** Understanding the number of conversions and revenue driven by the tests is a crucial piece of information to understand the winner of the test.

Interpretation of report data

In interpreting the data with respect to Test&Target, keep in mind that there could be variances in the numbers reported by SiteCatalyst and Test&Target:

- The SiteCatalyst report suite includes all visits and visitors to the ecosystem of pages included in the report suite. Test&Target includes only visits and visitors who are part of any testing campaign.

- SiteCatalyst visitors are based on persistent cookie expiry. Test&Target will have an inflated count of visitors since the visitor identification is reset after every conversion.

Code implementation and console settings

The settings below apply to Test&Target reports:

- Implement the `trackTnT` plug-ins.
- You'll need rights to view Test&Target reporting.
- The value set in the `s.tnt` variable is campaign ID, recipe ID, and the traffic type segregated by a semicolon delimiter.
- The value in `s.tnt` variable can be classified using SAINT. Other attributes can be added to classifications.

Report: Genesis > Email vendor name

Navigate to Genesis > (Name of your email vendor). Other menu options are based on the variables you've set up. The number of variables required for the integration depends on the vendor you're using.

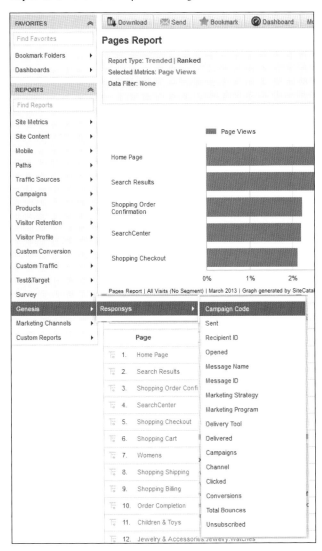

Key insights

Analyzing reports of email marketing can help answer questions such as:

- **Which email campaigns are driving more conversions?** Identify the email campaigns that drive more conversions by correlating the events metrics such as clicked.

- **Which subscriber is driving more conversions?** Identify the email campaigns that drive more conversions by correlating the subscriber information to the third-party vendor data.

- **Which segment of visitors can be targeted for remarketing?** To find visitors to remarket, create the following segments:

  - Visits in which visitors bounced

  - Visits in which visitors engaged but did not start conversion

  - Visits in which visitors started the conversion funnel but abandoned

  - Visits in which visitors added items to a cart, but did not check out

  - Visits in which visitors checked out, but did not order

  - Visitors who completed conversion

Interpretation of report data

In interpreting the data with respect to how many emails were delivered, keep in mind that the *emails opened* metric is subject to the email client capabilities. For example, Outlook does not load images automatically and so won't transmit the email opened information to your email vendor unless the recipient opts to download external images.

Code implementation and console settings

These settings apply to email campaign integration:

- Integrate the email client using Genesis Integration.

- Reserve one or two custom conversion variables depending on your integration.

  - Responsys requires two custom conversion variables.
    - Unique identifier of the email creative
    - Unique identifier of subscriber

  - Bronto needs only one custom conversion variable.
    - Unique identifier of the email message sent

  - Set the following events: sent, delivered, opened, clicked, unsubscribed, total bounces.

- Optionally, create the following segments for retargeting.

  - Product purchases

  - Product views

  - Cart abandonment

- Genesis Integration greatly simplifies this setup and is available for many vendors. If your email vendor is not a supported vendor, contact Adobe customer support. In the interim:
  - Update the variable `s.campaignID` with the value that uniquely identifies the campaign.
  - Update the custom conversion variable that uniquely identifies the subscriber.
  - Update the custom conversion variable that uniquely identifies the email creative.

Report: Genesis > CEM or VOC vendor name

Customer experience management (CEM) or voice of customer (VOC) products help you measure customer satisfaction and its correlation to conversion. SiteCatalyst and related products gather a lot of quantitative data. With VOC products, you get a chance to collect qualitative data on the visitor experience on your site.

Navigate to Genesis > (Name of your CEM or VOC Vendor). The other menu options are based on the SAINT classification set up by your admin.

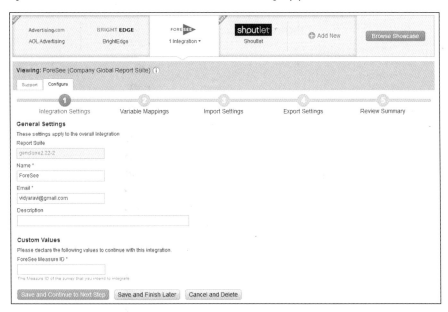

Key insights

Analyzing VOC reports can help answer questions such as:

- **What is the primary measure of the survey?** The primary measure of the survey is to get qualitative information on the voice of the customer, primarily, overall satisfaction, goal completion, net promoter score, and demographics analysis.

- **What are the primary areas of improvement requested by the survey respondents?** Identify the key pain points of visitors who responded to the survey. These areas of dissatisfaction can be prioritized based on their severity.

- **Which segment of visitors can be targeted for remarketing?** To find visitors to remarket, create the following segments:

  - Visitors with a high-net promoter score

  - Visitors with a low-net promoter score

- **What impact does the net promoter score have on your conversion?** Correlating the visitor information between SiteCatalyst and VOC products gives you an idea of the correlation between net promoter score and conversion.

- **If a visitor leaves you negative feedback, how likely is he to convert?** You can determine whether a visitor who leaves you negative feedback is falling out of your funnel due to a bad experience.

Interpretation of report data

In interpreting the data with respect to VOC campaigns, keep the following in mind:

- The `surveyID` will be set only in visits where the visitor was presented with a survey.

- The `respondentID` variable will be set only when the visitor responds to the survey, irrespective of the number of questions he responds to.

Code implementation and console settings

Two custom conversion variables must be set for VOC reports:

- A variable that uniquely identifies the survey

- A variable that uniquely identifies the respondent

Genesis Integration greatly simplifies this setup and is available for many survey vendors. If your survey vendor is not supported, contact Adobe customer support. In the interim:

- Update a `surveyID` to a custom conversion variable tracking survey data.

- Update a `respondentID` to a custom conversion variable tracking `visitorID`.

Report: Genesis > SEO vendor name

Search engine optimization (SEO) products help you measure the effectiveness of your organic search.

Navigate to Genesis > (Name of your SEO vendor). The other menu options are based on the SAINT classification set up by your admin.

Key insights

Analyzing reports of SEO products can help answer questions such as:

- **Which organic search keywords and phrases are driving more conversions?** Tracking conversions at keyword granularity will not only help you optimize your SEO efforts, but also influence your paid search efforts.

- **How do your organic search keywords and phrases compare with the performance of your indicated competitors?** Some SEO vendors provide competitor keyword data and tell you how your search terms compare in terms of rankings.

- **Which landing pages need to be optimized?** SEO tools also help you correlate the keyword to the landing pages. This will give some prioritization of key landing pages for organic search.

Interpretation of report data

In interpreting the data with SEO products, remember that in order to push non-ranked keywords to the bottom, BrightEdge sends in a sentinel value of 10,000 to represent non-ranked data. This is intended to push all non-ranked data to the bottom of the reports.

Code implementation and console settings

Integration with BrightEdge requires:

- Two custom conversion variables
  - Organic search term
  - Landing page URL
- Six events
  - Keyword rank
  - Search volume
  - Denominator
  - Optional keyword rank for competitors one, two, and three

Report: Genesis > Social media vendor

Note: It's important to note that none of this information is personally identifiable information (PII). See the sidebar in Chapter 4, "Acquisition Analytics."

Facebook Demographics can be integrated with using Genesis Integration to understand the demographics of the visitors who come to your site from Facebook. The following demographic information is available:

- Gender
- Age
- Education level
- Years of work experience
- Relationship status
- Friend count
- Current city, state, and country
- Home city, state, and country
- Friend app users

Key insights

Analyzing reports of social media can help answer questions such as:

- **Which Facebook campaign is driving the most traffic to the site and converting more visitors?** Having links from your Facebook campaigns to your site allows you to determine this.

- **How can you understand your Facebook audience to inform Facebook marketing campaign and ad spend decisions?** Having the demographic information from Facebook can help you determine the audience that's visiting your site and which digital marketing efforts might be most effective.

Interpretation of report data

In interpreting social media data, keep in mind that the data reflects only those who have agreed to share their demographics.

Code implementation and console settings

This integration can collect data from the following resources:

- Applications on Facebook.com (iFrame and FBML)

- Facebook for Websites (formerly Facebook Connect); this integration does *not* support Facebook fan pages.

- Any website that can execute JavaScript

- You'll need at least one unused `Commerce eVar`, and up to 12 optional `eVars`, available to collect Facebook demographics data.

Report: Genesis > CRM vendor name

Navigate to Genesis > (Name of your CRM vendor). Here you can specify an external customer relationship management system (CRM) from which you want to pull data, as long as it's in the current list of partners from Adobe. The other menu options are based on the SAINT classification set up by your admin.

Key insights

Analyzing reports from an external CRM can help answer questions such as:

- **Which offline or online campaigns are driving the most sales?** Correlating your digital marketing efforts to the sales pipeline gives you an idea of which campaign successfully drives visitors to sales completion.

- **What is the ratio of online to offline sales? Of the online sales, how much is contributed by the marketing efforts?** Since the CRM has cumulative sales information across online and offline channels, this integration offers the most accurate information about online and offline and compares the performance of both campaigns.

- **What is the sales cycle length by campaign and channel? Which campaigns are driving the shortest sales cycle?** You can also compare the sales cycle length across campaigns to derive the sales cycle applicable to your business. The shorter the sales cycle, the better the quality of the visitor for the business.

Code implementation and console settings

As an example, an outside Salesforce integration requires:

- Nine custom conversion variables that identify the following:

  - Party that needs to be attributed the lead

  - Opportunity

  - Customer account number

  - Creator of the opportunity

  - Last campaign responsible for generating the campaign

  - First campaign responsible for generating the campaign

  - Internal campaign responsible for generating the campaign

  - Retouch campaign responsible for generating the campaign

  - Multi-touch campaign responsible for generating the campaign

- Twenty events (33, including optional events for full integration), including counts of the following:

  - All opportunities

  - Opportunities that have progressed toward a lead

  - New opportunities when opportunity was closed

  - Opportunities identified as a potential for cross-sell when the opportunity was closed

  - Opportunities identified as a potential for upsell when the opportunity was closed

  - Opportunities won when the opportunity was closed

  - Opportunities lost when the opportunity was closed

  - Revenue generated in sales when the opportunity was closed

  - New opportunities of a new type

  - Opportunities of a new type identified as a potential for cross-sell

  - Opportunities of a new type identified as a potential for upsell

    - Amount of revenue generated in sales for the opportunity of a new type for a new customer

    - Amount of revenue generated in sales for the opportunity of a new type for a cross-sell

    - Amount of revenue generated in sales for the opportunity of a new type for a upsell

    - The count of campaigns that have been associated with this opportunity

- The count of lead-sourced campaign members that have been tagged as offline leads
- Total revenue for campaigns tagged as offline leads
- The cost of offline campaigns
- The budgeted cost of offline campaigns
- Total number of impressions for the offline campaign
- Total number of emails opened
- Marketing-sourced opportunities accepted by sales
- Marketing-sourced opportunities accepted by sales that have progressed to the next stage of the sales cycle

Task: Integration with external data sources

Your company probably has proprietary databases that you'd like to tap into for critical pieces of information. This section reflects on how to integrate with two of those as examples. That should give you enough information to work with any other databases you may have.

Report: Integrating customer support

Integrating call center data for the following metrics: time on phone, total sales, and number of calls for ordering products.

Key insights

Integrating and analyzing reports with advertising data to your site can help answer questions such as:

- **What's the web impact on customer support sales?** This insight will help you gauge the number of calls that the customer support team gets after using the web. If there's an increased number of calls to the call center for questions relating to the web, the questions posed to the customer service team should be evaluated to see where those can be addressed on the web using an FAQ.

- **What's the monetary impact on customer support sales?** This insight will help you determine the number of calls that the customer support team gets from visitors after they visit your site. If there's increased cost associated with the number of calls to the call center for questions relating to the web, that cost should be included while computing the net income.

- **Which products get sold more on the phone than the web?** If there are products that require the visitors to call customer support, special toll-free numbers can be reserved for each campaign to determine the campaign's performance. For example, Marchex and Ifbyphone are examples of providers who facilitate that.

Report: Integrating lead-generation data

If you're integrating lead-generation data with offline data, navigate to Site Metrics > Custom Event > Custom Event Funnel. Assuming you have user-defined custom events set up for tracking customer behavior, you can set up custom events for each step of the funnel to determine visitor abandonment of the multistep funnel.

Key insights

Integrating and analyzing reports of unique visitors to your site can help answer questions such as:

- **What are the leads to sales ratio?** Determine the leads to sales ratio by comparing how many leads get fulfilled as a sale.

- **How many leads were unqualified?** This will determine the quality of the traffic that converted to a lead. Segmenting this data by a referrer will point you to the referrer who sends the most unqualified traffic to your site.

Code implementation and console settings

For integrating lead-generation data you will need to store a unique identifier for the lead in a custom conversion variable and in your back-end system. Then use data sources to import lead generation data from your back-end system into SiteCatalyst for analysis.

Conclusion

External data analytics focuses heavily on joining external data to create a rich data set and draw insights across vendors. In this chapter, we've answered questions such as:

- **Why is it important to join data at the transaction level?** Joining data at the transactional level gives you an idea of the product sales cycle after initial purchase. It helps you quantify the net cancellations and returns.

- **What dimensions other than transaction and visitor can we join to external data?** As long as the same identifying data is captured on SiteCatalyst and the third-party tool or database, you should be able to join with any external data set. Note that the basic conditions of relational databases apply here.

We are almost near the finish line. Next we learn how to showcase the analysis you do with dashboards.

Review questions

1   What are some key issues with joining external data at the visitor level?

2   Can I integrate vendors that are not on Adobe's list?

Review answers

1   To join data at the visitor level, the visitor ID must be indicated in every page of the visitor's visit.

2   Yes. If you can find a common key that can be written to both systems at the time of the visit, you should be able to connect to any third-party vendor.

10 DASHBOARDS

Lesson overview

You've done all the analysis. Now you just need to package it up, tie a nice red ribbon around it, and deliver it to management. Adobe makes it easy to add those reports to your dashboard—a quick and easy way to present your findings. In this lesson, you'll learn to create dashboards within SiteCatalyst and find out how to include all your KPI information in them.

The goals of this section are:

- Understanding your audience and the business decisions they are looking to drive

- Determining the KPIs, SiteCatalyst reports, segments to run and analyze

- Determining the best way to present your findings catering to the audience

 This lesson will take 45 minutes to complete.

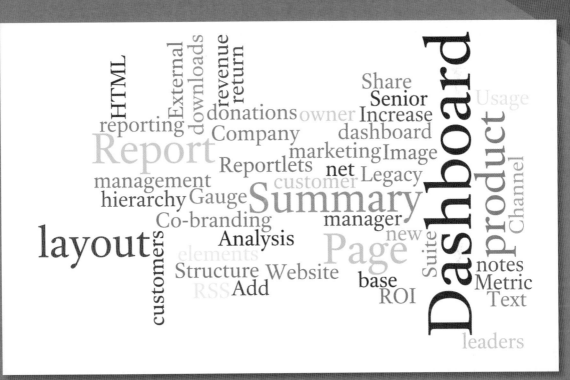

You've spent a lot of time and effort analyzing the numbers. Now you need to package the insights, making sure to tailor the level of detail to the intended audience, whether it's management or the marketing team. Don't simply report the data—leave that to scheduled reports, and focus on the analysis.

Ingredients of a good dashboard

A SiteCatalyst Dashboard is a collection of thumbnail-view reports. Each dashboard can have a maximum of 30 pages. Each page can have up to six "reportlets," so if the smallest reportlet is used for every page, a maximum of 180 reportlets can be created per dashboard. Dashboards can be copied from one report suite to another. They can also be shared among users or kept private.

Every good dashboard includes the business goal as a reminder as well as the KPIs that you and your company collaborated on. (Underscore the word *collaborated* in the previous sentence.) As you've probably noticed in both this book and your personal experiences, each business is different and each business question requires a completely different tool kit to evaluate and recommend analytics.

A KPI tells you how you're doing compared to what you planned to accomplish, but this is just one side of the story. There's a whole other side of analytics that's insight driven, that gives you data on your current pain points, which in turn drives your next steps.

When you need deeper insights in terms of data granularity, you might think of segments, subrelations, and correlations. Thankfully, with Adobe SiteCatalyst 15, you don't need to request correlations—they're automatically enabled across all variables.

Insights are your forte as an analyst. You are uniquely capable of looking at all the reports, segments, and KPIs, and understanding what steps the business could take to accomplish its goals. How are you currently presenting data and findings? How can you best communicate the value of your expertise and analytical talent? To start, let's look at the difference between reporting and analyzing.

Task: Know the difference between reporting and analysis

Reporting is when you present tons of data with no analysis of what needs to be fixed. The current industry trend is to use Excel's good, bad, and neutral colors to indicate performance in big data tables. But including every report or analysis you ever ran isn't a good idea: your audience will be overwhelmed and lose track of your key message.

Analytics is not the responsibility of the analyst alone! It's a joint responsibility of senior management, marketers, analysts, and a whole host of supporters from the engineering, quality assurance, data, and support teams.

The three quizzes that follow are structured for three key members of the analysis team. Take the quiz that matches your current role to determine whether you're reporting or truly analyzing.

Quiz for analysts

If your current job is that of an analyst, your role includes gathering data, running reports, and presenting your findings to your company. Take this quick test to see if you're reporting or analyzing in your current role as an analyst.

		YES	NO
1	Before you began the analysis, you and your team aligned on the approach to measure the KPI.	☐	☐
2	You have visited your website in the last 10 days and routinely get a walk-through from the website owner when anything changes.	☐	☐
3	You created a dashboard in collaboration with marketers, senior management, the engineering and quality assurance teams, or other analysts.	☐	☐
4	Your dashboard is no more than five pages long.	☐	☐
5	The dashboard addresses KPIs and reports for a business goal. You provide insights with next steps on how you can validate them using experiments or usability tests.	☐	☐
6	You have a dashboard for each audience with analysis pertinent to their business question.	☐	☐
7	You get a lot of questions on your dashboard when you present it.	☐	☐
8	You provide one or more follow-up analyses after you present the dashboard.	☐	☐
9	You validate the insights by running A/B tests and usability tests.	☐	☐
10	You support your findings with qualitative data from VOC surveys and benchmarking against competitors.	☐	☐

If you **answered no to at least seven of the ten questions** above, unfortunately you're reporting. Aren't you glad you bought this book? Jump to the next section to find out how to remedy that.

Quiz for marketers

If your current job is that of a marketer, your role is likely to ask questions—lots of them! Take this quick test to see if you're reporting or analyzing in your current role as a marketer.

		YES	NO
1	Before you began the analysis, you and your team aligned on the approach to measure the KPI.	☐	☐
2	You have visited your website in the last 10 days and routinely get a walk-through from the website owner when anything changes.	☐	☐
3	You have collaborated extensively with the analyst who created the dashboard for you.	☐	☐
4	You made a lot of effort to understand how technology and tracking implementation might impact the numbers you're looking at.	☐	☐
5	The dashboard addresses your burning business questions and provides options for your next steps.	☐	☐
6	You requested additional analysis and deep dives after reviewing the dashboard.	☐	☐
7	From the analysis, you get a fair read on your industry standing.	☐	☐
8	You have already communicated to the analyst on what the next dashboard should focus on.	☐	☐

If you *answered no to at least five of the eight questions* above, you are unfortunately aiding and abetting reporting! Help is on the way. Jump to the next section to find out how to remedy that.

Quiz for senior management

		YES	NO
1	You have a single document that outlines the business goal and maps the related KPIs.	☐	☐
2	The team meets to collaborate on findings from marketers, senior management, the engineering and quality assurance teams, or other analysts.	☐	☐
3	The dashboard comprehensively covers the goals and KPIs related to senior management and is tailored to your level.	☐	☐
4	You attend one presentation where a copy of the dashboard is presented with insights across the channel team, product team, marketing team, and analysts.	☐	☐
5	The dashboard has different analysis every week instead of just the numbers being refreshed.	☐	☐

If you *answered no to at least three of the five questions* above, your team is still reporting for the most part. The next section describes ways to fix that.

Task: Determine dashboard hierarchy and contents

Before you create a dashboard, ensure that the information in the dashboard aligns with its intended audience. Here are a few things you could consider.

Dashboard hierarchy

Consider the various roles on your team and the types of tasks they need to accomplish, and the reports to which they need access.

Senior management

Senior management needs an elevator pitch of how you're doing against the KPIs they set. If the risk of not achieving the target is high, then they need to know the options to course correct.

Key components of the dashboard could be a gentle reminder about the KPIs pertaining to company goals, how you're doing against them, projections of meeting or not meeting goals with confidence levels, steps to remedy the situation, and the ask from senior management for monetary or personnel resources. This might also be a good forum to escalate any issues like non-consensus on next steps from your presentations to the marketing or product teams.

Website owner or product manager and team

Website owners or product managers need deep insight into the marketing funnel to gauge which aspects of the website visitors are engaging with and what patterns they're showing for conversion. If the likelihood of hitting a target is low, then they need to know what their options are to course correct. When you design a dashboard for this audience, consider replicating information from the senior management dashboard for alignment. Then remind them about the product team's goals and KPIs, indicate how you're doing against them, share your projections for meeting or not meeting goals with confidence levels, and suggest steps to remedy the situation. Product managers need an overview of awareness, acquisition, and retention data, but they may also need a deep dive into engagement and conversion data.

Channel marketing leaders

Channel marketers need a deep insight into the quality of traffic that each channel is bringing to the site and their contribution to the conversion. They also focus on multichannel and cross-channel attribution (refer to Chapter 3, "Awareness Analytics"). After aligning them to the senior management KPIs, the key components of their dashboard might be a deep dive into awareness and acquisition data and their impact on conversion and retention, along with an overview of engagement data.

Channel marketers manage only specific channels and make decisions on those. They need deep insight into the awareness, acquisition, engagement, conversion, and retention data segmented by their specific channel.

Technical team

The technical team will need to be aware of the direction that your company is headed, but will be more interested in the influence of web technology and mobile devices in this mix.

Dashboard elements

Consider the various elements of the dashboard, including co-branding, the structure of your dashboard, and choosing the elements you need in your dashboard page layout.

Co-branding

Your site admin needs to set this up. Co-branding allows your company logo to be displayed on the pages of the dashboard along with Adobe's logo. You're probably wondering if you can remove Adobe's logo and just keep yours. The short answer is no. Hence, Adobe offers the option to co-brand.

Adobe provides some guidance on sizing your company logo. For best results in web browser output, upload a 100px × 30px image. For best results in PDF output, upload a 417px × 125px image.

Structure of the dashboard

The structure of the dashboard lets you divide the virtual page into different compartments. You can choose a 3 × 2 matrix or a 2 × 2 matrix. Once you create a matrix, you're not stuck with it. You can extend the matrix out.

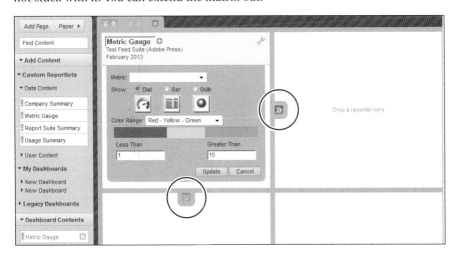

Page layout

Next, take a moment to choose one of the following page layouts based on the information you're trying to display:

Add "Custom Reportlets" > Data Content > Company Summary: If you have more than one report suite, each catering to a different business unit, then summarizing each business's success is as easy as dragging the company summary data content and selecting the reporting suites and metrics you need to report on.

You'll also notice a plus sign next to the name of the editable dashboard reportlet. That is basically to add a note.

Each note that you create in a dashboard will be given a serial number in the order it was created.

Add "Custom Reportlets" > Data Content > Metric Gauge: Metric gauge allows you to see how you're performing against a standard SiteCatalyst event, success metric, and calculated metric. You can choose the visual to be a dial, a bar, or a bulb. You can also choose the color range to indicate the threshold. You can indicate the threshold of tolerance based on the metrics chosen. The data in the metric you choose will be compared to the threshold limits you specified. Based on that, your metric gauge will indicate the good, neutral, and bad alarm in the dashboard. This is important for your key KPI or your macroconversion, because it allows you to have a laser focus on that and not get jumbled in all the data.

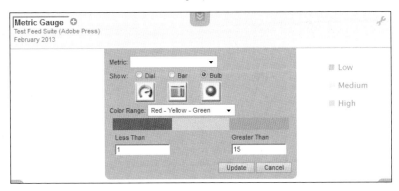

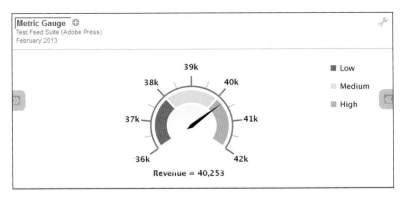

Add "Custom Reportlets" > Data Content > Report Suite Summary: The report suite summary reportlet lets you highlight the metrics you're focusing on with either the total or the dates when the metric was the highest or the lowest. Bounce rate is a report-specific metric that requires pathing data, and can be added to a dashboard only if pathing is enabled on that report suite. By default, only the pages report has pathing enabled.

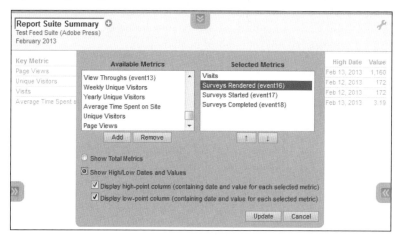

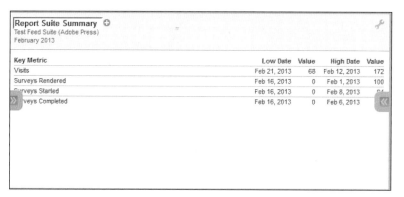

Add "Custom Reportlets" > Data Content > Usage Summary: The usage summary reportlet lets you highlight the reports that were run more often in SiteCatalyst. This may not be very useful while presenting on KPIs, but you can use it to track where the analysts in your team are spending the bulk of their time. This report has nothing to do with the KPIs.

Add "Custom Reportlets" > User Content > External Report: The user content is data from outside SiteCatalyst that can be imported in a dashboard using either XML technology or a CSV. This might be useful if you're trying to display data from third-party vendors or systems. If you choose the CSV option, the interface looks slightly different.

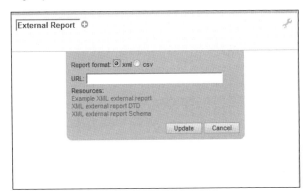

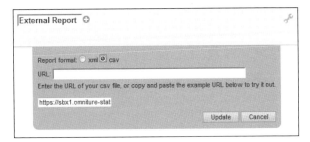

Add "Custom Reportlets" > User Content > HTML: The user content can also display HTML files. Downloaded or scheduled reports won't be able to see that HTML reportlet.

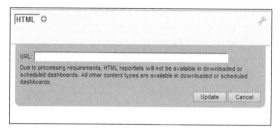

Add "Custom Reportlets" > User Content > Image: This might be a good option to display KPIs that you create in Excel. You can create an image and upload it into SiteCatalyst.

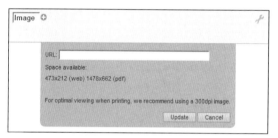

Add "Custom Reportlets" > User Content > RSS: RSS content from your site can also be uploaded here. If you like a blog by an expert on the market trends that impact your business, you could include that RSS feed here.

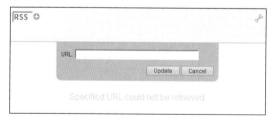

Add "Custom Reportlets" > User Content > Text: You can also add text and format it.

Add "My Dashboard" > Add Reportlets: You also have the option of adding any reportlet from previously created dashboards. So in the current month, if you want to refer to any analysis you did in the pevious month to show comparison, that is a great use case for this reportlet use.

Add "Legacy Dashboards" > Add Reportlets: You should also be able to display any data from legacy dashboards, if needed.

Note: Add only reports that will have a deep impact on the marketing efforts, which in turn will affect a KPI.

Task: Create SiteCatalyst dashboard examples

The whole point of a dashboard is that it should be a quick review of the status of your business. So it should ideally have a minimal number of pages. The first page could outline only high-level details, such as goals, KPIs, insights, and actions. Move any supporting reports from SiteCatalyst with references to the subsequent pages. The third level of granularity is the aggregated data and that should be in the appendix.

Following are some examples of approaching a business problem and understanding what KPIs might be good indicators for predicting success or failure to achieve your goal. There are also some tips on which reports to run, segment, and infer insights from.

The examples also offer some guidance on how to structure your dashboard to tailor the content and messaging for your audience.

Example 1: Increase net revenue from return customers

Your business goal for the financial year is to grow net revenue by 25 percent. Based on your analysis, you see that repeat customers are more likely to convert than new visitors. So now your goal is to get 17 percent of that net revenue growth from repeat customers and 8 percent from new visitors.

We already have a business goal. Now, you need determine the KPIs for a conversion of 17 percent from return customers. You could repeat this process for the new visitor with appropriate changes.

Conversion KPI 1

The primary macro goal is centered on net revenue:

$$\text{Net revenue} = (\text{Revenue} - \text{Cost} - \text{Returns}) \div (\text{Total revenue} - \text{Total cost} - \text{Total returns})$$

To get this data, create a calculated metric called net revenue. If you're uploading the cost and returns data in your SiteCatalyst, you may be able to do this calculation from within SiteCatalyst. Another option is to do it manually or simply compare gross revenue. To get this data, you could run the customer loyalty report.

To drill down on what type of return customers are buying more, you could segment the data by visitors from a particular geographical location, visits in which they went to a certain page, visits from a specific channel, and so on. Now you'll be able to report on the KPI to indicate whether it's green, yellow, or red (assuming those are your good, neutral, and bad colors) based on the acceptable thresholds you set. Why is it trending low or high? The answer would be the segment that contributed to the success or failure of the KPI. So now you know which segment to act on. The next step is to outline a plan to remediate that. Let's say the segment that did very well was repeat customers from California. Then your next steps could range between pouring more money and resources toward marketing efforts in California, targeting visits from California for special offers, or even doing nothing.

Conversion KPI 2

You'll also need a KPI for tracking net units to check if you need to adjust your price on each of the units or create a promotion offering deep discounts to meet your goal. Based on your margin, you can either adjust price or the quantity:

Net units = (Units sold − Returns − Cancellations) ÷
(Total revenue − Returns − Cancellations)

Again, you'll need to upload the cancellation and returns data in SiteCatalyst. If you're unable to do this, choose the manual option using an Excel file, or simply compare gross revenue. To get this data, you could run the customer loyalty report and add the units metric. You could segment like we did above and also look at which geographical location or type of demographics had the highest returns. So if you're trending low in terms of units, you could segment the visits in which there were returns and target those visitors with a survey or an email campaign that addresses their pain points.

Engagement KPI 3

You'll also need a KPI to determine whether you're engaging the visitors the right way:

Return customer bounce rate = Number of bounces ÷ Total visits

To get this data, you could run the Site Metrics > Pages Report and add the bounces metric. Now create a segment called Return Customer with a visitor container where Customer loyalty = Return. (For a refresher on segments, refer to Chapter 2, "Establish Business Strategy and KPIs.") Save that and apply that filter. Bingo! You have all the data you need.

You could also go through all the pathing reports with this segment in place to understand visitors' pathing preferences.

Acquisition KPI 4

You'll also need a KPI for tracking whether you're acquiring the right kind of visitors to your site.

Return customer visit ratio = Number of visits by return customers ÷ Total visits

To get data, you could run the Site Metrics > Key Metrics Report and add the visits metric. Now apply the Return Customer segment.

Now add your KPIs and insights to your dashboard!

Example 2: Increase ROI from the South African customer base for new product

You're launching a new product in South Africa and your business goal is to prove a ROI of 10 percent in the very first year of introducing a new product in this existing market.

The goal is very focused on a geographical location, so all the KPIs we create will be segmented for the traffic from South Africa. To create a segment, create a visit container where the geosegmentation country is South Africa.

Some assumptions in this case are that you have set up a calculated metric called ROI after you successfully upload the cost details with the data sources option.

Conversion KPI 1

Management is interested in gauging whether the company is making any profit from the new product being marketed. So think of ROI as:

ROI = (Total revenue − Total cost) ÷ Total cost

To get this data, create a calculated metric called ROI. If you're uploading the cost and returns data in SiteCatalyst, you may be able to do this. The other option is to do it manually or simply compare gross revenue. To get this data, you could run the Products > Products Report, and segment by the geosegmentation country you just created. Now the data is restricted to traffic from South Africa—that was easy! But this data now includes the revenue from all products sold in South Africa. So you'll need to filter by the new product you're interested in. To do this, click the filter link, select the products variable, and select the product name from the list that refreshes below.

Conversion KPI 2

You want to optimize the ROI, so the next step could be to figure the conversion rate:

Conversion rate = Total number of conversions ÷ Total number of visits

The conversion rate for visits from South Africa may be different from that of the country where your business is based. If you want to drill down on the funnel of that product, you could run Products > Products Funnel Reports. This will help you determine where you're losing customers (and revenue) in the funnel. Ensure that the geosegmentation country segment and product filters are still correct.

Engagement KPI 3

The next consideration is the engagement patterns of the visitors from South Africa. You may want to see if they're different from those of visitors from other countries:

Average bounce rate = Total number of bounces ÷ Total number of visits

Assuming you've set up site sections, you can see the bounce rate for the entire microsite (small subset of pages) by using Site Content > Site Sections and adding the bounces metric. If you haven't used site sections, the other option is to use SAINT classification and classify the pages as "Pages for South African audience." The next step will be to determine which pages contributed the most to that bounce rate, which means you need data at the page level. Just run Site Content > Pages > Pages Report and add the bounces metric. This will give you data for each page.

There! You are officially a pro now. You could also go through all the pathing reports with this segment in place to understand visitors' pathing preferences.

Acquisition KPI 4

Since you're focusing on the ROI aspect, the next step is to ascertain which channel is sending quality traffic and which channel has the most effective ROI.

Channel effectiveness ratio = Revenue from conversion from channels ÷ Cost from channels

To get data, you could run Campaign > Channel Name Report (assuming you've set up a SAINT classification identifying the type of channel the campaign represents). Now all you need to do is add the calculated metrics for ROI.

Now add your KPIs and insights to your dashboard!

Example 3: Increase donations for a nonprofit

Your goal is to increase donations to your nonprofit organization by 20 percent. Your analysis shows that most donations are local. The product team wants to know how to optimize the visitor experience to increase donations.

Conversion KPI 1

What are your average donations per visit?

Donations per visit = Total donations ÷ Total visits

First, you could track how much each visit is contributing to the donation pool. Run the Site Metrics > Purchases > Revenue report to get that data.

Engagement KPI 2

How often are visitors encountering pages not found?

$$\text{Average visits with errors} = \text{Total number of visits with a page not found error} \div \text{Total number of visits}$$

Run the Site Content > Pages Not Found report and see how many visits had an error. To evaluate how much the amount of donations was impacted by errors, multiply the visit number by the donation per visit amount. This should help you evaluate the potential donation loss.

Persuasion KPI 3

What pages are successfully connecting with donors?

$$\text{Page influence visit rate} = \text{Number of visits to pages that influence} \div \text{Total visits}$$

Requests for donations normally appeal to visitors' emotions. Assuming this site has multiple stories that tug at your heartstrings, you may want to find out which story was most successful. One way to do this is to compare visits to the pages that influence and the donations from those visits. If you run the Site Content > Pages Report > Page of Influence report and add the revenue metric, you can get that data.

The other analysis you may want to do is a Paths > Pages > Previous Page to check the page that was visited prior to the page that accepts donations.

Acquisition KPI 4

Which referring domain was most successful in getting visitors who wanted to donate to your site?

$$\text{Channel effectiveness ratio} = \text{Donations from referring domain} \div \text{Cost from channels}$$

To get this data, you could run the Traffic Sources > Referring Domain report and add the revenue metric.

Now add your KPIs and insights to your dashboard!

Example 4: Increase downloads

Your site offers the latest articles, videos, and podcasts from key experts in the industry. Your goal is to increase downloads of these files by 10 percent. Your content team is interested in understanding what type of content is popular among visitors and in what formats.

This section assumes that a separate event (event number 19) has been set to indicate file download. You could run the Site Content > Links > File Downloads report to see the total number of times each file is downloaded. But that data cannot be correlated to other custom traffic or custom conversion variables. This section also assumes the review ratings are being written to a custom conversion variable.

Conversion KPI 1

What are download visits and visitor rates?

Download visit rate = Total visits with downloads ÷ Total visits

Download visitor rate = Total visitors who downloaded ÷ Total visitors

First, let's determine how many downloads you get in ratio to a visit and a visitor. This will help you explain how common a download is as a goal in the first place.

Persuasion KPI 2

What is the download rate?

Downloads rate = Total downloads / Visits with at least one download

Assuming event number 19, run the Site Metrics > Custom Event > Custom Events 1–20 > Downloads report to get the total count of times the files were downloaded. Alternatively, use the total number of instances from Site Content > Links > File Downloads.

Persuasion KPI 3

What are the review ratings for downloads?

Favorable review rate = Total instances of reviews where you got a 4 or a 5 ÷
Total reviews

Use this KPI to indicate the number of times you got a favorable review for the file being downloaded.

You'll also need to find the favorite types of files being downloaded. To do this, you can run the Site Content > Links > File Downloads report, which will tell you the total number of instances of each file being downloaded. If you've replicated the name of the file downloaded in a custom conversion variable, you can further classify the files by download type and content type to ease your analysis of both of those. Then break down the popular files by the review ratings.

● **Note:** SAINT classification cannot be run for the Site Content > Links > File Downloads report.

Additionally, review the technology preferences of your visitor demographics to gain deeper insights.

Now add your KPIs and insights to your dashboard!

Task: Share the Dashboard

Sharing the dashboard is relatively easy in SiteCatalyst. You have a whole host of options to email the dashboard and reports to specific users or groups (publishing lists). You can schedule immediate, one-time delivery, or a future delivery on a recurring schedule.

The email functionality is very intuitive. The points below are lesser-known features related to the email functionality. All of these are also true for report sharing.

- Delivery of dashboards can be restricted to specific email domains. Check with your admin if any external email domain you are sending the dashboard to is included in that filter.

- Consider using digital signatures for key dashboards that share revenue and other sensitive information to ensure the dashboard file has not been altered.

- Choose the file type for sharing your dashboard: PDF or HTML.

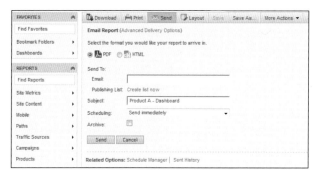

Conclusion

Dashboard creation is easy and very intuitive. This chapter should have helped you answer questions such as:

- **Can I add a couple of key reports to the dashboard and share them?** Adding key reports is a great idea for sharing multiple reports at the same time. However, emailing these to stakeholders may require additional due diligence to derive key insights and highlight only pertinent reports.

- **What is the maximum number of pages that you can add to a dashboard?** You can add a maximum of 30 pages to a dashboard.

Next we'll review what steps you can take to ensure you have a bulletproof implementation of SiteCatalyst.

Review questions

1   What time zone is used for report delivery?

2   What are the limits on the rows of data that can be downloaded?

Review answers

1   In SiteCatalyst, the time that you select for report delivery is based on the time zone specified in the given report suite's settings.

2   A maximum of 500 lines can be downloaded for Word, Excel, PDF, and HTML types; CSV gives you more, with a maximum of 50,000 lines. A data extract allows a maximum of 500,000 lines.

A IMPLEMENTATION DETAILS

Lesson overview

This book has emphasized the reporting and insight capabilities of Adobe SiteCatalyst, both of which require a good tracking framework to ensure accurate and high-quality results. This appendix explains some lesser-known facts about tracking and SiteCatalyst settings.

Joe Christopher, Director of Analytics at Blast Analytics & Marketing, shares his experiences with the popular plug-ins that are used in SiteCatalyst.

The goals of this section are:

- Understanding the preliminary work you need to do before a SiteCatalyst implementation

- Determining the SiteCatalyst implementation steps pertaining to your website code and the SiteCatalyst JavaScript library and variables

- Understanding the setting changes you need to make in SiteCatalyst

 This lesson will take 45 minutes to complete.

detection Security s.props groups search SAINT calendar aanouncements VISTA business suite Multi-suite s.eVars company procesisng rules plug-ins support publishing Call lists menus bot cycle tagging rules page-naming multi-suite roll-up channel-naming Calendar classifications ClientCare sub-domains domains paid metrics variables cookies sales report users

The value of your SiteCatalyst data depends on the way you implement it—as they say, "garbage in, garbage out"—so it's important to get the implementation right. Subtle differences in set up can affect the quality of the data, its interpretation, and the insights you gain from it.

Lay the groundwork

Do you already have SiteCatalyst in place? If so, you can just go through these steps and act on the ones you may have missed or the ones you think you may have a delta on. Otherwise, dive right in; there are a lot of steps involved in knowing and understanding a SiteCatalyst implementation. There could always be something that you can take away!

It's a good idea to spend some time learning how your business is set up online, which domains you own, and what pages are created under them. If your company is large and this task seems daunting, there are easier ways than chasing your web team in the hallways. You could either run a crawler that crawls your site and writes all the URLs to a CSV file, or you could potentially use your web logs to get a list of all the pages and domains you own.

Know your business's domains and subdomains

Skip this step if you own only one domain. If you own more than one, this is a very important step. Here's why:

- It determines the accuracy of your exit reports (exit reports let you see which domain the visitor hopped to after viewing your site, assuming they are still on the same browser).

- It helps to split traffic for each domain into a different report suite if you're using a VISTA rule to segregate based on domain.

- Each domain has its own cookie. Technically, this cookie is stored relative to the tracking domain. While not recommended, if you used the third-party cookie tracking domain, it would be the same visitor ID as you traverse domains. So it affects the custom conversion variables being set across domains in the same report suite.

Establish a web URL ecosystem

Consider using a tag management system to manage how you are tracking pages. Know the list of pages that are included in your website. This will help you determine the tags to be added and also explain the data with greater accuracy.

Tag management systems

A tag management system is a tool that can be used to manage all your tags in a central repository. Instead of having web tags on each web page, the tag management system abstracts the analytics implementation by using a standard line of code in all the pages and moving the analytics logic in a central tool. This reduces the dependency on the engineers for tagging. Also, marketers don't have to wait for a release cycle to see the tagging changes!

Irrespective of whether you have a tag management system or not, you could establish a Page URL Ecosystem—a comprehensive list of all URLs you are tracking. You could use this to identify the pages of influence using a SAINT classification—we'll come to that shortly. You could also use the pages list to determine site sections, hierarchy, and the type of page. This could also be used in your analysis when you are trying to determine how the visitors interacted with a section of the site or a certain type of a page.

Understand your business financial statements to architect report suites and decide on multisuite tagging

Understand how your business reports in the balance sheet, Profit & Loss statements, and the reporting requirements in your organization to arrive at the suitable report suite structure. For example, if your organization has two key businesses, selling widgets and clothes, and these two departments operate in silos, then you could consider having separate report suites for each of them and have a global report suite where you are multi-tagging.

Multisuite tagging gives you the ability to write the same data to multiple report suites. It has the ability to deduplicate visitors, provide pathing analysis across domains, display all pages across the other report suites, and provide accurate cross-site pathing and campaign data.

Rollup report suites are another option. The rollup suite is not an optimal choice if you are trying to determine the unique number of visitors across your company without duplication. The rollup suites simply add the visitors across all the report suites it is aggregating. Also, it provides no pathing reports to see cross-site pathing or cross-site campaign data. There is no way to correlate the data or see the pages report. In essence, it provides little value other than being a sum of multiple report suites.

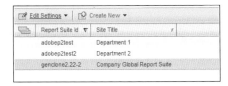

Understand business, sales cycle, and website goals

Understanding the business you're in is key for analytics. Ensure that you have a fair understanding of the business, your competition, and your sales cycle from your senior management. Then schedule a walk-through with the website owner to understand the nuances of the website—its goals and the pages that have a distinct URL, the ones that are pop-ups, created using iFrames, or even those that use AJAX calls.

If you have a three-step funnel and, if the second step is not a page with a distinct URL but an AJAX call, the code to set events and other SiteCatalyst variables will differ.

Establish business strategy and KPIs

Establish the business goals and KPIs (refer to Chapter 2, "Establish Business Strategy and KPIs"). Understand the overall business goal that the management has set and align the organization on the KPIs and how you plan to arrive at the data.

Also, when each business presents you with a business question that they are looking to resolve, follow the same practice of aligning them to the KPIs and the approach to collect and analyze data.

Establish common metrics

Create a common language for your company that is pertinent to the vertical and industry you are in. Review the calculated metrics that are shared within the organization and which ones are to be used for what purpose.

Establish personas

Based on your data, research and create personas of the visitors arriving at your site. These personas can be used later when you create segments. A persona is a description of a visitor who is your target visitor. Typically, you would base the persona on demographics or other characteristics. Develop multiple personas to create a spectrum of all the visitors you are targeting.

Understand your business calendar

The default calendar that SiteCatalyst uses is the Gregorian calendar, with the calendar year ranging from January to December. If your business, for example, follows the tax calendar from April to March, you could change these settings here. The changes will impact your weekly, monthly, quarterly, and yearly reports. The calendar also gives you the flexibility of splitting up the number of fiscal weeks in a quarter—it could be 5-4-4 or 4-5-4.

Ensure alignment across your organization

Alignment is often an overlooked step. In most organizations, the analytics team proposes a recommendation and is saddled with the responsibility of data quality and accuracy. Truth be told, data and analytics is not purely a function of the analyst, it is a culture that needs to be embedded in the organization. So it is important that the organization aligns on what KPIs it will use.

Decide on standards, variables, and plug-ins

Standards are key best practices to be adhered to by your analytics team, which will ensure smooth coordination and avoid potential problems.

Set up standards

You will need to understand your Solution Design document, set up a page-naming convention, and establish a channel-naming convention.

Solution Design Document

Typically, when SiteCatalyst is implemented, you are provided with a Solution Design document that tells the implementation story in a structured way. It answers the questions like "What is eVar1 used for, and how is it implemented in the code?" Your implementation should evolve over time. It requires ongoing maintenance to take advantage of new SiteCatalyst features or to adapt to properly track new types of conversions or features within your site. To keep track of these changes, ensure that your Solution Design document is kept up to date.

Choose a page-naming convention

Strongly consider a page-naming convention if you are planning on adding page names. There are three options for naming pages: the first is naming them exactly the same as the URL of the page or the canonical page URL, the second is naming the page through the Name Pages tool, and the third is to name them on the page with code.

Considerations when using URLs

- URLs are hard to read in the SiteCatalyst user interface, especially since they are truncated to the first 100 characters. In most cases, the majority of the first 100 characters are the protocol and domain information. So it is really hard to distinguish between pages in the user interface.

- Also, some companies may not follow a good URL structure. So two different departments having two different domains—http://abc.com/homepage.html and http://xyz.com/homepage.html—may be named as /homepage.html, and the data for both the pages cannot be segregated after collection with the page name.

- Also, it is recommended to use only paths without the domain name if you have a single domain. If you plan to use the URLs of the page, consider removing the protocol. This ensures that http://abc.com/a.html and https://abc.com/a.html are not treated as two separate pages.

- Querystring parameters, if included, treat the page with varying parameters in the URL as separate pages. This affects your pathing, traffic, and conversion reports—yes, I guess it is pretty much everything. If you have this issue, as remediation create a SAINT classification with a canonical URL.

- In some cases, even when URL parameters are excluded, http://abc.com/directory, http://abc.com/directory, and http://abc.com/directory/index.html are treated as three separate pages even though they are physically one page.

- Another point to stress is that URLs change over time due to SEO efforts and testing efforts. Historical analysis is difficult when your page URLs are changing.

Considerations when using the name pages tool

Familiarize yourself with the name pages tool in Admin > Admin Console. The name pages tool is a quick and temporary solution if you need to rename a page.

- This tool will only reflect pages that have been visited in the current month. Inactive pages or pages that have zero page views will not be listed here. So this tool cannot be used as an auditing tool for your pages.

- This tool takes default page name values from what is being set in s.pageName and not the URL of the page. So if the page name assigned in s.pageName changes, the value will reflect here.

- If two pages are updated here with the same name, their values will not be combined in the report.

- Classifications use the value assigned in s.pageName, but SAINT exports use the updated name from this tool.

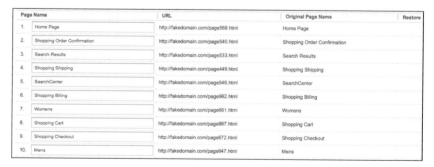

	Page Name	URL	Original Page Name	Restore
1.	Home Page	http://fakedomain.com/page569.html	Home Page	
2.	Shopping Order Confirmation	http://fakedomain.com/page540.html	Shopping Order Confirmation	
3.	Search Results	http://fakedomain.com/page533.html	Search Results	
4.	Shopping Shipping	http://fakedomain.com/page449.html	Shopping Shipping	
5.	SearchCenter	http://fakedomain.com/page546.html	SearchCenter	
6.	Shopping Billing	http://fakedomain.com/page962.html	Shopping Billing	
7.	Womens	http://fakedomain.com/page661.html	Womens	
8.	Shopping Cart	http://fakedomain.com/page997.html	Shopping Cart	
9.	Shopping Checkout	http://fakedomain.com/page672.html	Shopping Checkout	
10.	Mens	http://fakedomain.com/page647.html	Mens	

Considerations when using code to name pages

- The page name can be assigned in `s.pageName` through the code. If you have good due diligence in naming pages in the title of your page, you can leverage that to name your pages as well. Be cautious with that approach though. Title tags change because of SEO efforts, and you don't want your page name to change along with that as it prevents historical analysis over change periods. It's better to have a field in your CMS that is dedicated to the `pageName`.

- If no page name is listed, the URL of the page is assumed as the page name by default.

Page-naming conventions can be adopted from the hierarchy of your site. Try to mirror a combination of your balance sheet and your content management tool architecture. Suggested examples would be:

Department > Product a > Marketing site > Home page

Department > Product b > Product site > Learn page

The name pages tool is a quick and temporary solution if you need to rename a page prior to your next code release, but it's best to update the page name in the actual code.

Choose a channel-naming convention

Decide on a channel-naming convention to understand the channel the visitor came from. As a gentle reminder, the channel-naming convention would apply to external channels. Examples of external channels will include paid search, social, display, affiliate, SMS—any channel that can have a querystring parameter which describes the campaign run.

- Also, direct will not have a campaign ID. Bookmarked traffic will have a campaign ID, if it was saved with one, in which case you will see traffic from inactive campaigns. SiteCatalyst takes the total traffic and subtracts the visits from all different campaigns to arrive at the typed/bookmarked traffic.

- Organic traffic will not have a campaign ID. SiteCatalyst deduces organic traffic by taking the total traffic from search engines and isolating the traffic from paid search.

Set variables

You must set some default, configuration, automatic, direct, custom conversion, and custom traffic variables, as well as custom events, as covered next.

Set default variables

There are some default variables that need to be set in the code. Here is a quick look at what variables need to be set, but more importantly, why and where you will see them in the interface. These variables may or may not be contained in the s_code.js file. The variables list below are based on Adobe's Knowledge Base (**Table A.1**).

Table A.1 Default variables

VARIABLE	DESCRIPTION	REPORT
pageName	Uniquely identifies the name/URL of the page	Site content > Pages
	Mandatory; otherwise defaults to the page URL	
	Recommended approach is to explicitly set the page name without relying on the title tag	
channel	The section of the site	Site content > Site sections
	Optional variable	
server	Domain of the page where the page is hosted	Site content > Servers
	Optional variable	
hier1 - hier5	Hierarchy *variables*, used to record visits and visitors for a hierarchically structured site	Site content > Hierarchy 1
		Site content > Hierarchy 2
	Optional variable	Site content > Hierarchy 3
		Site content > Hierarchy 4
		Site content > Hierarchy 5
campaign	The value is based on the URL parameter(s) that is reserved for tracking marketing campaigns	Campaigns > Tracking code
	Value needs to set in the code	
products	Variable to track the product being purchased and other ecommerce information	Products > Products
	Can be used only in conjunction with cart and purchase events	
purchaseID	Variable that uniquely identifies a purchase and serializes it	Not visible in the user interface. Need to replicate the information in a custom conversion variable
	Optional variable	
	Can be used only in conjunction with a purchase event	
state	State name or ID, to be used on the order confirmation page, in conjunction with the purchase event	Visitor profile > Visitor state
	Optional variable and available only if the visitor inputs the value	
	Can be tracked only if visitor enters his state information.	

(continues on next page)

VARIABLE	DESCRIPTION	REPORT
zip	Zip code, to be used on the order confirmation page, in conjunction with the purchase or other event Optional variable and available only if the visitor inputs the value Can be tracked only if visitor enters his zip code	Visitor profile > Visitor zip/postal code
linkName	Optionally used to identify the name of a link for sending in custom, download, or exit link data Optional variable to be used in conjunction with linkType	Site content > Links > Exit links Site content > Links > File downloads Site content > Links > Custom links
linkType	Used to identify the type of link: custom, download, or exit Optional variable to be used in conjunction with linkName	Site content > Links > Exit links Site content > Links > File downloads Site content > Links > Custom links
s_objectID	A ClickMap *variable* used to uniquely identify links on a page Optional variable to be used for clickMap tracking	Site content > Links > ClickMap
pageType	Used on 404-page not found error pages; optional variable to track only 404 errors	Site content > Pages not found
pageURL	Variable used to override the URL of the page before it is recorded in SiteCatalyst Optional variable	Not in the user interface
referrer	Used to override a page's referrer before it is recorded in SiteCatalyst Optional variable	Traffic sources > Referrers
transactionID	Primary key to tie offline data to an online transaction Optional variable	Not visible in the user interface. Need to replicate the information in a custom conversion variable
visitorID	Visitors identified by the visitorID *variable*, or by IP address/user agent Set by default by SiteCatalyst	Not in the user interface

Configuration variables

Configuration variables, which control data collection, are contained in the .js file, but they are not considered data collection elements. Configuration variables are not included in any SiteCatalyst report, but they may affect the data that SiteCatalyst collects or the appearance of the reports. Configuration variables are based on the data that Adobe shares in its Knowledge Base and that is presented in **Table A.2**.

Table A.2 Configuration variables

VARIABLE	DESCRIPTION
s_account	If you are writing to a static list of report suites, identify the report suite you want the data written to. Create a comma-separated list for multiple-suite tagging.
charSet	The character set used on the page (the default is ISO-8859-1). If your site is following a different CharSet, update that here. The code needs to match the report suite settings.
currencyCode	The currency code used to track the revenue. This needs to match your report suite settings.
cookieDomainPeriods	The number of periods in your domain. This impacts the VisitorID cookie settings.
fpCookieDomainPeriods	The same data as the cookieDomainPeriods variable above but, this overrides the value of cookieDomainPeriods for JavaScript cookies.
cookieLifetime	Sets the lifetime of the SiteCatalyst visitor cookie.
doPlugins	The plug-ins are ready-made JavaScript functions that you can leverage. Joe Christopher has added a section on plug-ins later in the appendix.
dynamicAccountSelection	Set to true if you plan to select the report suite ID based on domain, host, or directory name.
dynamicAccountList	It will be a name-value pair that maps the domain to the report suite IDs.
dynamicAccountMatch	Describe the filters that will apply.

(continues on next page)

Table A.2 Configuration variables (continued)

VARIABLE	DESCRIPTION
trackDownloadLinks	Set to true in order to track clicks on links that have extension names listed in s.linkDownloadFileTypes.
	If set to false, the download links will not be captured.
trackExternalLinks	Set to true in order to track clicks on links that are external. External links are domains not listed in s.linkInternalFilters.
	If set to false, the external links will not be captured.
trackInlineStats	Set to true to capture data for ClickMap reporting.
linkDownloadFileTypes	The list of download files types (based on extensions). This list will need to be exhaustive for the files types to be captured. If any file type is missed, that data will not be tracked.
linkInternalFilters	Internal URL filters are used to determine which referrers, or referring pages, are internal to your site. Once you list the internal referrers, your referrer and exit reports will be more accurate to reflect only external domains.
linkExternalFilters	This is used to limit the number of external links that will be used, not to specify specific links as external. The list of all domains that should be considered external.
linkLeaveQueryString	Set to true to keep querystring of exit links and download links.
	Set to false to remove querystring from exit links and download links.
	Must be set outside of the s.doPlugins() function.
linkTrackVars	The variables that should be sent on custom links, download links, and external links. By default, this variable is set to none so that variables set on the page are not recounted by link clicks.
linkTrackEvents	The events to be sent on custom links, download links, and external links. By default, this variable is set to none so that variables set on the page are not recounted by link clicks.
usePlugins	If set to true, s_doPlugins() will be called by the .JS code prior to creating the image request.

Automatic variables

Automatic variables are obtained by the JavaScript code by accessing the HTTP header information or the control variables. The names of these variables are defined only within the querystring of the image request. Automatic variables are based on the data that Adobe shares in its Knowledge Base and are presented in **Table A.3**.

Table A.3 Automatic variables

AUTOMATIC VARIABLE	DESCRIPTION
r (Referring URL)	The referring URL as defined by the browser. This information is lost if there is a redirect on the page.
g (Current URL)	The current page's URL.
ClickMap data (various)	ClickMap data is sent with the page ID, link clicked, the destination URL, link number, objectId, etc.
t	Local time of the event request.
v	If Java is enabled (Y/N).
j	Version of JavaScript supported by the browser.
bw, bh	The width and height of the browser window.
s	The width and height of the monitor.
c	The number of available monitor colors.
ct	The connection type.
p	Deprecated in Version 15. List of plug-ins installed on Netscape browser if Netscape is being used to access your site.
k	If cookies are enabled in the browser.
hp	Determines if your site is the browser's home page.

Direct variables

Direct variables are set by the browser after accessing the HTTP header of the image request sent to SiteCatalyst. This visitor information is set in every HTTP request. These variables are primarily used to identify a visitor. Direct variables are based on the data that Adobe shares in its Knowledge Base and are presented in **Table A.4**.

Table A.4 Direct variables

DIRECT VARIABLE	DESCRIPTION
IP address	Identifies the IP address is the Internet protocol address of the visitor's browser or machine. Multiple visitors can have the same IP addresses when they use a proxy server, and a single visitor may have multiple IP addresses. The visitor's IP address is used to determine his geolocation.
domain	Identifies the domain from which the visitor is requesting data.
user-agent string	Uniquely identifies the browser and version, and the operating system used.
language	Identifies the language setting of the browser.
cookies	Identifies the names and values of all cookies set by SiteCatalyst.

Custom traffic variables

Deciding on the right set of custom traffic variables depends on your implementation. A good recommendation would be to reserve variables each for acquisition, engagement, persuasion, conversion, and retention. However, this is largely dependent on your organization requirements. **Table A.5** presents commonly used traffic variables.

Table A.5 Custom traffic variables

CUSTOM TRAFFIC VARIABLE	ON WHAT PAGES IT IS SET	VARIABLE NAME	WHAT IT DOES	PATHING ENABLED	SUBRELATION
prop1	All pages	Page URL without querystring parameters	Captures the URL in addition to the page name variable	No	
prop2	All pages	Business unit	Captures the name of the business for comparison	Yes	
prop3	All pages	Visitor type	Set as "customer" only when the visitor authenticates as a customer and as a "conversion" when the visitors buys without authenticating	No	
prop11	All pages	Internal campaigns	Tracks all the internal campaigns that the visitor clicked on	No	
prop12	All pages	Internal search term	Captures any internal search done during a visit	No	Internal search number of results
prop13	All pages	Internal search number of results	Captures the number of search results	No	
prop14	All pages	Video name	Captures the name of the video	Yes	
prop15	Pages with forms	Form analysis	Captures the form fallout		
prop16	All pages	Custom links	Captures any custom links that the visitor clicks on	Yes	

(continues on next page)

Table A.5 Custom traffic variables (continued)

CUSTOM TRAFFIC VARIABLE	ON WHAT PAGES IT IS SET	VARIABLE NAME	WHAT IT DOES	PATHING ENABLED	SUBRELATION
prop17	All pages	Menu navigation	Captures any menu navigation that the visitor clicks on	Yes	
prop1	All pages	Page URL without querystring parameters	Captures the URL in addition to the page name variable	No	
prop2	All pages	Business unit	Captures the name of the business for comparison	Yes	
prop3	All pages	Visitor type	Set as "customer" only when the visitor authenticates as a customer and as a "conversion" when the visitors buys without authenticating	No	
prop11	All pages	Internal campaigns	Tracks all the internal campaigns that the visitor clicked on	No	
prop12	All pages	Internal search term	Captures any internal search done during a visit	No	Internal search number of results
prop13	All pages	Internal search number of results	Captures the number of search results	No	
prop14	All pages	Video name	Captures the name of the video	Yes	
prop15	Pages with forms	Form analysis	Captures the form fallout		
prop16	All pages	Custom links	Captures any custom links that the visitor clicks on	Yes	
prop17	All pages	Menu navigation	Captures any menu navigation that the visitor clicks on	Yes	

Custom conversion variables

Deciding on the right set of custom conversion variables is dependent on your implementation. All third-party integration that was noted in Chapter 9, "External Data Analytics," requires custom conversion variables to be reserved. These are outlined in **Table A.6**.

Table A.6 Custom converion variables

CUSTOM CONVERSION VARIABLE	VARIABLE NAME	WHAT IT DOES?	ALLOCATION	EXPIRATION
eVar1	Page URL without querystring parameters	Full URL	Most recent (last)	Page view
eVar2	Business group	Identifies the business group	Most recent (last)	Page view
eVar3	Visitor type	Identifies prospects and customers	Most recent (last)	Visit
eVar4	Internal campaigns	Identifies Internal campaigns	Most recent (last)	Visit
eVar11	Internal search term	Identifies the search term	Most recent (last)	Visit
eVar12	Custom links	Identifies the custom link	Most recent (last)	Page view
eVar13	Menu navigation	Any menu navigation—header or footer	Most recent (last)	Page view
eVar14	Video name	Video integration	Most recent (last)	Page view
eVar15	Segment name	Video integration	Most recent (last)	Page view
eVar16	Content type	Video integration	Most recent (last)	Page view
eVar41	Email vendor—Email creative ID	Email integration	Most recent (last)	Visit
eVar42	Email vendor—Email subscriber ID	Email integration	Most recent (last)	Visit
eVar43	VOC vendor—Survey ID	VOC integration	Most recent (last)	Visit
eVar44	VOC vendor—Respondent ID	VOC integration	Most recent (last)	Visit
eVar45	SEO vendor—Search term	SEO integration	Most recent (last)	Visit
eVar46	SEO vendor—Landing page URL	SEO integration	Most recent (last)	Visit

Custom events

The events are based on the macro- and microconversions that your site has. All third-party integration that was noted in Chapter 9 requires custom events to be reserved. An effort is made to outline those for you in **Table A.7**.

Table A.7 Custom events

CUSTOM EVENT	ON WHAT PAGES IT IS SET	WHAT IT DOES	EVENT SERIALIZATION
event1	Page A	Newsletter registration	No
event2	Page B	Lead generation—step 1	No
event3	Page C	Lead generation—step 2	No
event4	Page D	Lead generation—step 3	No
event5	Page E	Order ID	Yes
event11	Page F	Video time—counter event that counts the number of seconds spent watching video since last request	No
event12	Page G	Video views—counter event that tracks the number of video views	No
event13	Page E	Video completes—counter event that tracks video ends	No
event14		Video segment views—counts the number of video segment views. Determine milestone events to track	No
event41		Email integration: Email sent	No
event42		Email integration: Email delivered	No
event43		Email integration: Email opened	No
event44		Email integration: Email clicked	No
event45		Email integration: Email unsubscribed	No
event46		Email integration: Email total bounces	No
event47		SEO integration: SEO keyword rank	
event48		SEO integration: SEO search volume	
event49		SEO integration: SEO denominator	
event50		SEO integration: SEO competitor 1	
event51		SEO integration: SEO competitor 2	
event52		SEO integration: SEO competitor 3	

Select plug-ins

The text below is provided by Joe Christopher, Director of Analytics at Blast Analytics & Marketing

SiteCatalyst plug-ins are widely used in implementations to easily accomplish specific data collection requirements. These plug-ins are JavaScript code snippets that you add to your `s_code.js` file. You can find the majority of the plug-ins listed below in the SiteCatalyst Knowledge Base. There are other plug-ins that you might need to request from ClientCare or get from other websites.

getQueryParam

This plug-in is the most popular of all. It does a very simple job of being able to grab the value of a querystring parameter. If you have a URL of http://mysite.com/?cid=123, and you execute `s.getQueryParam('cid')` on this page, it will return 123 as the value. You can then store this in the s.campaign variable or elsewhere as needed for your implementation.

getValOnce

This plug-in is used to prevent a variable from being set to the previous value that is stored in a cookie. The cookie and logic is automatically handled for you by this plug-in. It is most commonly used when you don't want the instance metric to be inflated for a conversion variable. Instead of sending the same data on every page hit, you use this plug-in to only send the value if it actually changes.

getTimeParting

This plug-in has logic to return the day of the week, time of day, and whether it is a weekday or weekend. You can use these values in traffic variables (`sProps`) or conversion variables (`eVars`). This simplifies the reporting if you wanted to see how a specific day of week performs over a large date range. In the plug-in configuration, you should set your time zone as well as daylight saving time rules.

getPreviousValue

By using this plug-in, you can easily grab the variable value that was set on the previous page view. An example of leveraging this would be for the `getPercentPageViewed` plug-in noted below.

getPercentPageViewed

This plug-in (which requires the `getPreviousValue` plug-in) captures the percentage of the previous page that the visitor viewed and lets you store this data into a variable for reporting. If a visitor scrolls to the bottom of the page (or the entire page is already viewable), this plug-in will return 100 percent as the value. You can then leverage this data to optimize the length of pages based on this value. If you take this a step further, you can leverage a SAINT classification to group the percentages into buckets such as less than 25 percent and more than 50 percent.

getVisitNum

This plug-in returns the visit number for the visitor, and it can then be stored in a conversion variable. You may recall that there is already a Visit Number report in SiteCatalyst and might be asking yourself why you would use this. The answer is that you may want to classify (via SAINT) the visit number, and you can only do that from the conversion variable and not the standard Visit Number report.

getDaysSinceLastVisit

This plug-in returns a value based on the visitor's return frequency. Values returned will include first visit, less than 1 day, less than 7 days, and more. You can then leverage this data for reporting on the return frequency as it relates to conversions.

getNewRepeat

This plug-in determines whether a visitor is new or returning, and then lets you store this value into a variable. You could use this plug-in to easily breakdown another conversion variable by this getNewRepeat variable to determine how each visitor segment is performing.

getAndPersistValue

This plug-in will store a specific value in a cookie for a specified number of days to allow you to set it as often as you want. An example of this would be to grab the campaign code from s.campaign and set it in a traffic variable (sProp) on all pageviews throughout the visit and for the lifespan that you've defined.

getTimeToComplete

By using this plug-in, you can trigger a start command to initiate a timer, and then a stop command to grab the total amount of time before an action is completed. This value can then be stored in a conversion variable. A popular usage would be to track the amount of time it takes to complete an online application (even across multiple sessions if you like).

I've listed just ten of the most common plug-ins used in SiteCatalyst implementations and provided example use cases for many of them. Do keep in mind that most of the plug-ins above have optional parameters and settings that control behavior. As such, it is important to have a qualified implementation specialist ensure correct configuration for your implementation. Plug-ins will minimize your development time for complex tracking needs, expand your own horizons on what is possible in SiteCatalyst, and deliver reports that better answer your business questions.

Thanks to Joe Christopher for his permission to share his thoughts on the popular plug-ins.

Set and share calculated metrics

Decide on the calculated metrics that need to be set up for your organization. A calculated metric can be set up for any formula using the basic algebraic calculations. If you see a calculated formula resulting in a zero, odds are there is an issue with the syntax of the calculated metric formula or one or more of the variables used does not contain data. If you attempt to divide by a metric that contains a zero, the resultant value in the calculated metric will be '#DIV/0!'. However, if the parenthesis is not set correctly in the formula, no data will be visible.

You cannot combine traffic with conversion in a calculated metric. If conversion visitors and visits have been enabled on the report suite, then you can use unique visitors and visits with conversion metrics in the formula. For example, orders/unique visitors will work if conversion visitors were enabled. Orders/weekly unique visitors will not be supported since "orders" is a conversion metric and weekly unique visitors is specific to traffic reports only.

To share calculated metrics with other users, create a report with a calculated metric and add it to the dashboard. If the dashboard contains the full report option (not available with KPI gauge), the other SiteCatalyst users will be notified and allowed to download the calculated metric.

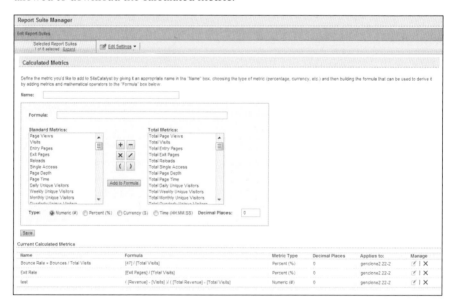

Implementation decisions

You've done the groundwork and decided what variables and metrics you need in place, so now you need to architect the solution. You have a few steps in place for that.

First-party or third-party cookies

Depending on your organization policy, you'll need to choose between using first- or third-party cookies for SiteCatalyst. First-party cookies will give you more accurate data, since most visitors configure their browsers to trust and accept first-party cookies, but disable third-party cookies.

Decide on the visitor cookie lifetime

Depending on your sales cycle, you can determine the optimal length of the visitor cookie.

Architect report suite structure or multisuite architecture

Much of the implementation is deciding how to structure the data so that you can minimize the number of server calls (and hence the cost of SiteCatalyst) and how you can support multiple reporting needs. The good news is that SiteCatalyst 15 has an amazing array of segments you can create to segment data in a single report suite. The drawback in Version 14 was that the lack of that segmentation required more of the multisuite tagging.

As a recommendation, structure the report suites similar to how your balance sheet is structured in combination with your organizational structure.

A few things to remember before you say—"I get it!"

- If you are statically defining the report suites to write to, the report suite IDs need to match the report suite ID and not the report suite name. The report suite ID is populated in s_account variable. If you are doing multisuite tagging, you can list the report suites ids as a comma separated list.

- If you are planning to provide the report suites dynamically, based on the domain, set the s.dynamicAccountSelection to true, the s.dynamicAccountList to be a name value pair of the domain and report suite ids. Use the s.dynamicAccountMatch to apply any filters.

- Also, most importantly, if you are doing multisuite tagging, only the same value can be set in both the report suites. For example, you cannot set eVar1 as page URL in report suite A and eVar1 as date of purchase in report suite B.

Processing rules

The main objective with SiteCatalyst data is to ensure data quality and data integrity with multiple engineers having to know and understand the custom traffic and conversion variables, their structure, and mapping in your report suite. You can do simple things that you may have previously used a VISTA rule for or had to do via code The processing rules can optionally leverage the creation of a semantic layer or a context data that creates a common object that engineers can populate. The mapping from that semantic layer to SiteCatalyst can be done in the processing rules.

For example, you can set the product name, product family as:

```
s.contextData['productName']="product a";

s.contextData['productFamily']="family a";
```

These variables can be mapped to both a custom conversion variable and a custom traffic variable using a processing rule.

Processing rules can be used even without the use of context data variables. For example, if the purchaseID is set, then you can set a custom conversion variable to the value of the purchase ID. You can add multiple conditions and actions.

More importantly, you can use this to preserve the data quality by running any data quality rules and fixing errors. Processing rules are run before the VISTA rules.

Now the catch! In order to add or edit processing rules, you must pass a test and have ClientCare expose this feature for you.

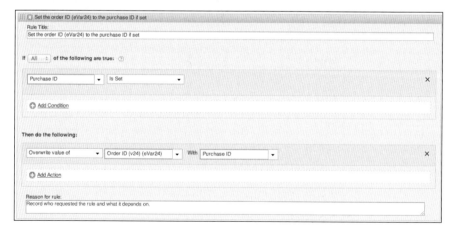

VISTA rule

After the processing rules are complete, the Visitor Identification, Segmentation, and Transformation Architecture (VISTA) rule allows you a server-side approach to transform data at collection and assign it to custom traffic and custom conversion variables. Common uses of a VISTA rule are to take a value from the URL and assign it to a variable, then concatenate variables and segregate them based on delimiters and filtering data. You can also consider the database lookup or the DB VISTA rule, as it is commonly called to do a secure lookup on proprietary and confidential information such as product pricing.

While you don't have to pass a test here, you still need to work with the Adobe engineering team to add or edit these rules.

Cross this off your list if you don't think you need a VISTA rule.

General account settings

Set some of the account settings like the report suite title, base URL, and so forth. The time zone settings impact the time-related metrics like daily and weekly reports. All the date and time recorded for the report suite are in relation to this setting. You can also set the currency that you want your revenue to be tracked in.

When to call Adobe ClientCare

A number of features require intervention by ClientCare. Here's a laundry list of all of them, so you can take care of them in one phone call (aren't you happy you got this book?):

- Identifying supported users who can call ClientCare

- Enabling pathing on custom traffic variables (the number of variables that can have pathing enabled is determined by your contract)

- Enabling hierarchy variables

- Enabling conversion visitors and visits

- Enabling processing rules

- Enabling s.transactionID for data integrations

- Enabling s.tnt variable for Test & Target integration

- Changing the currency variable in report suite setting after creation

- Disabling a report suite (deletion is not possible)

- Enabling event serialization

- Enabling marketing channel reports
- Enabling participation metrics
- Decreasing visit expiration to less than 30 minutes (if applicable)
- Modifying exit links as page views to appear in pathing reports
- Enabling your report suite to allow four pages of depth in a path finder report

Update internal URL Filters

Next, you can update the internal URL filters. So often you see that your source code has been plagiarized by other websites. When that happens, your SiteCatalyst tags fire as well. To guard against that, set the internal URL filters. If a page view comes into SiteCatalyst from a URL that is not considered "internal" to your site for any reason, and does not have an `s.pageName` value, it will be grouped into this "Other" category in the Pages report. Filters can be set in the Admin > General > Internal URL Filters. Remember the domains you researched in the groundwork section? You can use it here.

Exclude traffic by cookies and IP

This functionality is different from the internal URL filter, since this excludes the traffic from being counted in any report suite, while the internal URL filters indicate which traffic is included. The intent of this setting is to exclude certain computers or range of computers from being included in your traffic.

One advisable practice is to exclude your own browser visits from being included in the report suite by clicking on the opt-out page that Adobe provides at http://collection_domain/optout.html for first-party cookies or at https://intuitinc.122.2o7.net/optout.html?locale=en_US&popup=true if you're using third-party cookies. Since cookies are browser specific, you would need to opt out for every browser you use. A specific IP address can also be excluded from your data collection. These settings are report-suite specific.

Create traffic variables

Traffic variables or `s.props` are variables that need to be set on every page. For example, when you set a page name, it is different on every page and does not persist across pages. You can assign either a single value to an `s.props` variable or a list value with a comma-separated list of values.

Navigate to Edit Settings > Traffic > Traffic Variables, and set up the variables based on the ones decided in the previous section. This part is easy since it has limited settings—just the name and whether it is enabled or disabled.

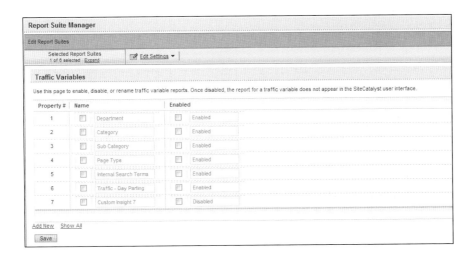

Create conversion variables

Conversion variables or s.eVars are session-based variables that persist across pages.

Navigate to Edit Settings > Conversion > Conversion Variables, and set up the variables based on the ones decided in the previous section.

Create success events

Navigate to Edit Settings > Conversion > Success Events, and set up the variables based on the ones decided in the previous section.

Create segments

We covered segments in Chapter 2, "Establish Business Strategy and KPIs." To avoid repetition, refresh your memory, if you need to. Based on the personas we discussed earlier, you can create the segments that can be used across your organization.

Note: You can also use these segments in conjunction with each other and not in isolation. Some suggestions are listed below.

For the visitor container, you could create segments by:

- Geographical locations you are interested in
- Visitors from a specific channel
- Customer loyalty

For the visits container, you could create segments that have:

- Visits from mobile devices, specific browsers
- Visits that included at least one video view
- Visits that included visits to one page of influence
- Visits with no orders
- Visits with orders
- Visits with revenue higher than $x
- Visits with cart abandonment
- Visits with funnel drop-off

For the page view container, you could create segments that have:

- Page views where time spent on page is greater than x
- Bounce rate is greater than x percent
- Single access is greater than x percent

Set up calendar

The calendar needs to be synchronized with the calendar in your balance sheet or the calendar year considered by your company. The default is the Gregorian calendar that runs from January to December. The modified Gregorian calendar will allow you to modify the first month of the year and the first day of the week.

The retail calendar allows you to use the 4-5-4 week distribution of a quarter. Finally, if your business has a custom calendar, you can define that with a pattern and the first day of the year. These can done in Edit Settings > General > Customize Calendar.

Set up overall admin tasks

Now on to some of the administrative aspects, like setting up users and groups.

Enforce security

In the Admin > Admin Console > Company > Security, you can set password requirements, password expiration, IP login restrictions, and email domain restrictions. You can add a password recovery notification as well. Should you decide to enable single sign-on, you can do that in the single sign-on tab.

Set up users, groups, and publishing lists

Navigate to Admin > Admin Console > User Management > Users to create users. Apart from setting the credentials, you can assign access to specific report suites and features. You can also restrict the date range for which their login is valid.

Set bot rules

The bot rules were covered extensively in Chapter 6, "Persuasion Analytics." This is a placeholder to ensure you have checked it off your list! Navigate to Edit Settings > General > Bot Rules to add your changes.

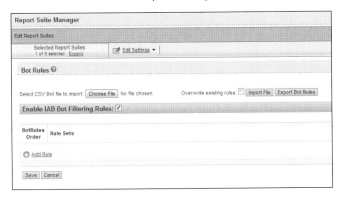

Marketing channel tracking decisions

These are some of the tasks associated with categorizing the marketing channels that require decisions in advance to avoid potential issues.

Add paid search detection

Organic traffic will not have a campaign ID. SiteCatalyst deduces organic traffic by taking the total traffic from paid search and isolating the traffic from paid search. This rule indicates to SiteCatalyst what traffic should be considered as paid search traffic. Set the rules for "Paid Search Detection" by navigating to Edit Settings > General > Paid Search Detection.

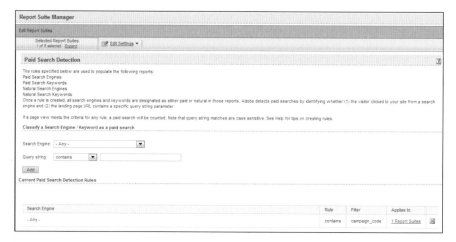

For the paid search detection tool, it is important to have a common regex pattern that identifies all paid search campaigns. An example could be "cpc_."

Paid search detection rules are used to populate the following reports:

Note: The querystring parameter is case sensitive.

- Paid search engines

- Paid search keywords

- Natural search engines

- Natural search keywords

Add finding methods

Navigate to Edit Settings > Conversion > Finding Methods to add finding methods for deducting the reports in traffic sources such as search engines, search keywords, natural search engines, paid search engines, natural search keywords, and paid search keywords.

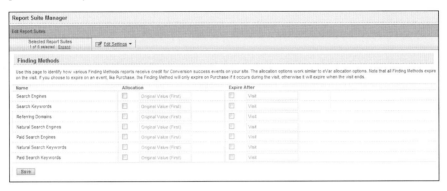

Marketing channels

Marketing channel processing rules run after processing rules and VISTA rules and determine the channel attribution. Marketing channel data is collected in real time. Marketing channel data is processed upon data collection, and thus is 100 percent permanent. Data cannot be changed retroactively. For example, if you set up a marketing rule to classify a campaign as an email campaign, it cannot be changed to paid traffic later.

First, you can set the list of channels you use by navigating to Edit Settings > Marketing Channel > Marketing Channel Manager.

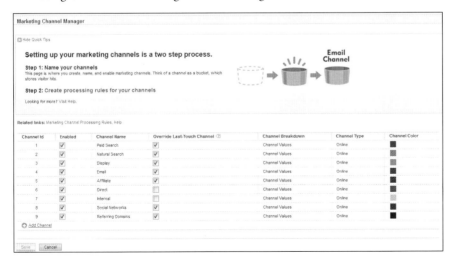

Next, you can set the list of channels you use by navigating to Edit Settings > Marketing Channel > Marketing Channel Processing Rules.

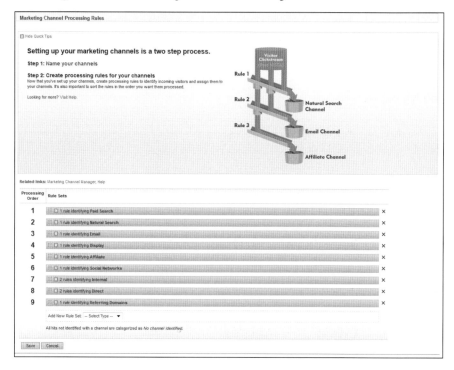

If you have cost information on your channels to see the ROI, enter that data in Edit Settings > Marketing Channel > Marketing Channel Costs.

You can also set visitor campaign cookie expiry by navigating to Edit Settings > Marketing Channel > Visitor Engagement Expiration.

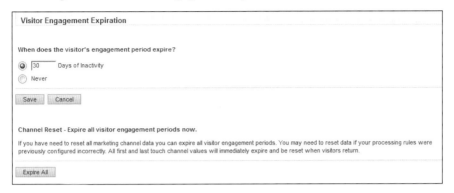

Data classification tasks

The SiteCatalyst Attribute Importing and Naming Tool (SAINT) lets you aggregate data based on a key value. Most importantly, data can be classified retroactively and reclassified at any time.

Before using SAINT, you'll need to set up the column you intend to classify a variable by.

Set up data traffic classifications

Navigate to Edit Settings > Traffic > Traffic Classifications. Traffic classifications can be set up on custom traffic variables and some default variables from SiteCatalyst. This allows you to aggregate data by your custom variables too.

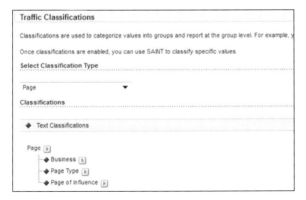

Set up data conversion classifications

Navigate to Edit Settings > Conversion > Conversion Classifications. Conversion classifications can be set up on custom conversion variables and some default variables from SiteCatalyst.

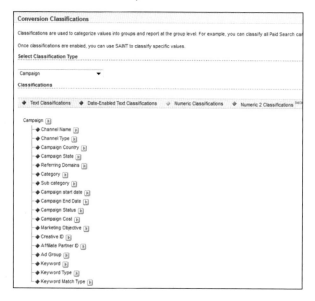

Set up data conversion hierarchies

Conversion hierarchies can be set up on custom conversion variables and some default variables from SiteCatalyst.

Automate SAINT classification

Manually classifying SAINT files is very tedious and not a great use of your time. With automated report downloads, you can export the variable data to a secure FTP location. Then use any popular scripting language to automatically classify the variable based on some rules. And finally, upload the file again to the FTP location for automatic import. Note here that each variable you enable SAINT classification for will need a separate automation file.

Enable video integrations

Before video analytics can be use, it needs to be enabled by navigating to Edit Settings > Video Management > Video Reporting.

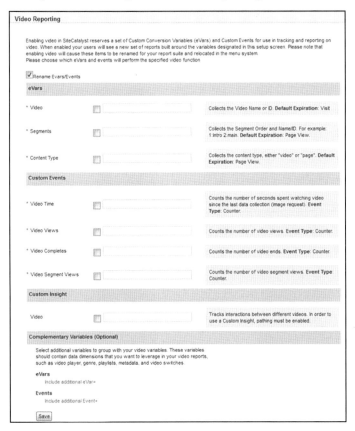

Final touch-ups

Finally, you must set up default metrics, customize menus, set support information, and set up your company announcements.

Set up default metrics

Based on the metrics your users use the most, you can set up the top three default metrics. Navigate to Edit Settings > Individual Report Suite Settings > Default Metrics.

Customize menus

Reduce the number of frantic calls you receive by customizing the menus and hiding functionality that is not used in your organization. You may also choose to create custom reports by navigating to Edit Settings > General > Customize Menus and save them by department.

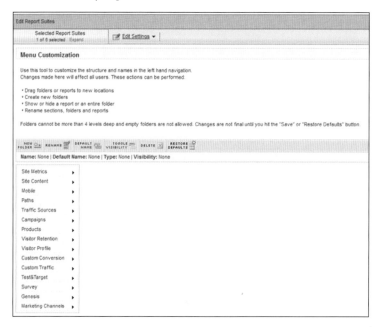

Set support information

Overwrite the support information with internal contact information in Admin > Admin Console > Company > Support Information. Each company lists some supported users who are authorized to call ClientCare on behalf of their company after gathering questions internally. Unsupported users (or those who are not in that list) can view the contact details of their supported users in the footer of SiteCatalyst. Set that information here.

Make company announcements

Click on Notices > Add Announcement to make any company-wide announcements that other users can see in the Notices screen.

Conclusion

Well, that's that! You are all set in terms of setting up SiteCatalyst. Now, not only do you know how to set up Adobe SiteCatalyst, but you also know how to apply it to any business problem.

Go ahead and conquer Mount Everest next!!

INDEX

inbound marketing, 18

instances, explained, 37

Integrating Customer Support Report, 243

Integrating Lead-Generation Data Report, 244

Internal Banner and Links Performance Report
clicks, 82
code implementation, 82
console settings, 82
conversions, 82
key insights, 82

internal online campaigns.
See also online campaigns
analyzing, 81–82
banners, 25
cross-selling, 26
links, 25
metrics, 81
reports, 81
searches, 26

internal URL filters, updating, 292.
See also URLs

J

Java Report, accessing, 167

JavaScript Version Report, accessing, 167

K

KPI examples, 35
Custom Events Funnel, 33–34
numeric measure, 32
Purchase Conversion Funnel, 31–32
quantifying goals, 30–34

KPI targets
establishing thresholds for, 44–45
setting, 44–45
setting alerts for, 45

KPIs (key performance indicators)
acquisition analytics, 92–93, 261, 263–264
arriving at, 35
awareness analytics, 54–56
conversion analytics, 178–183, 260–263, 265
engagement analytics, 116–118, 261, 263–264
establishing, 272
explained, 30
external data analytics, 226–228
persuasion analytics, 160–161, 265
quantifying goals, 30–34
retention analytics, 210–213

L

landing pages preferences.
See also page views
entry pages, 149
exit pages, 151
original entry pages, 150

lifetime metrics, 41

links, custom, 152

LiveChat, 12

M

macroconversion. *See also* conversion analytics
affiliate agency, 17
blog, 17
branded site, 17
educational website, 17
explained, 16
search engine, 17
social networking website, 17

macroconversions (carts). *See also* cart conversion metrics
adding items to carts, 193
average dollar value, 193
cart additions, 196–197
Cart Conversion Funnel, 192–193
cart removals, 197–198
cart views, 195–196
checkouts, 198–199
code implementation, 193
console settings, 193
interpretation of report data, 193
key insights, 192–193
number of carts, 194–195

macroconversions (custom events).
See also events
console settings, 205
conversion funnel, 204–205
form abandonment, 205
form fulfillment, 205

macroconversions (products)
product categories, 202–203
product conversion funnel, 199–200
product cross-sell, 201–202
products, 200–201

macroconversions (purchases)
conversion rate, 184
example, 186
number of orders, 184
number of purchases, 184
Purchase Conversion Funnel, 184–187
revenue, 186–187
revenue report, 187–189
serialized events, 187
units report, 190–191
visits resulting in orders, 184

Marketing Channel Overview Report, 84–87
"closing" channels, 85
code implementation, 86–87
common usage, 85
console settings, 86–87
interpretation of report data, 85
key insights, 85
visits to "opening" channels, 85

marketing channel tracking, 296
finding methods, 297
marketing channels, 297–299
paid search detection, 296

marketing channels. *See also* channel analytics
determining, 22
gauging success of, 19

marketing content, distributing, 18

marketing efforts effectiveness
analyzing, 57–62
channel analytics, 57
channel performance report, 58–59
online vs. offline campaign report, 57–58
referrers and referrer types report, 61–62
referring domains report, 60–61
`s.campaign` parameter, 58

marketing efforts, focusing, 104–108

marketing strategies
acquisition, 20
advocacy, 21
awareness, 19
conversion, 21
engagement, 20
funnel, 19
inbound, 18
outbound, 18
persuasion, 20
retention, 21

menus, customizing, 302

messages, personalizing, 18

metrics. *See also* calculated metrics
calculated, 40
establishing, 272
explained, 36
fluctuations, 43
lifetime, 41
mobile, 40
participation, 39
setting defaults, 302
standard, 36–39
video, 39

microconversion
affiliate agency, 17
blog, 17
branded site, 17
educational website, 17

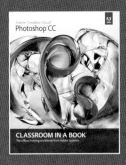

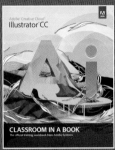

The fastest, easiest, most comprehensive way to learn

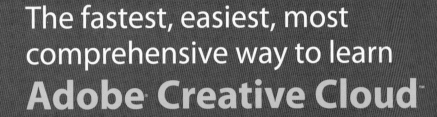

Classroom in a Book®, the best-selling series of hands-on software training books, helps you learn the features of Adobe software quickly and easily.

The **Classroom in a Book** series offers what no other book or training program does—an official training series from Adobe Systems, developed with the support of Adobe product experts.

To see a complete list of our Adobe Creative Cloud titles go to: www.adobepress.com/adobecc

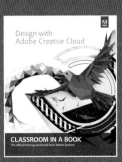

Adobe Photoshop CC Classroom in a Book
ISBN: 9780321928078

Adobe Illustrator CC Classroom in a Book
ISBN: 9780321929495

Adobe InDesign CC Classroom in a Book
ISBN: 9780321926975

Adobe Dreamweaver CC Classroom in a Book
ISBN: 9780321919410

Adobe Flash Professional CC Classroom in a Book
ISBN: 9780321927859

Adobe Premiere Pro CC Classroom in a Book
ISBN: 9780321919380

Adobe After Effects CC Classroom in a Book
ISBN: 9780321929600

Adobe Audition CC Classroom in a Book
ISBN: 9780321929532

Adobe SpeedGrade CC Classroom in a Book
ISBN: 9780321927002

Digital Video with Adobe Creative Cloud Classroom in a Book
ISBN: 9780321934024

Design with the Adobe Creative Cloud Classroom in a Book
ISBN: 9780321940513

AdobePress

WATCH READ CREATE

Unlimited online access to all Peachpit, Adobe Press, Apple Training and New Riders videos and books, as well as content from other leading publishers including: O'Reilly Media, Focal Press, Sams, Que, Total Training, John Wiley & Sons, Course Technology PTR, Class on Demand, VTC and more.

No time commitment or contract required! Sign up for one month or a year. **All for $19.99 a month**

SIGN UP TODAY
peachpit.com/creativeedge

creative edge